William Henry Hurlbert

Ireland under coercion

William Henry Hurlbert
Ireland under coercion
ISBN/EAN: 9783743341814
Manufactured in Europe, USA, Canada, Australia, Japa
Cover: Foto ©ninafisch / pixelio.de

Manufactured and distributed by brebook publishing software (www.brebook.com)

William Henry Hurlbert

Ireland under coercion

MAP TO ILLUSTRATE DIARY OF AN AMERICAN.

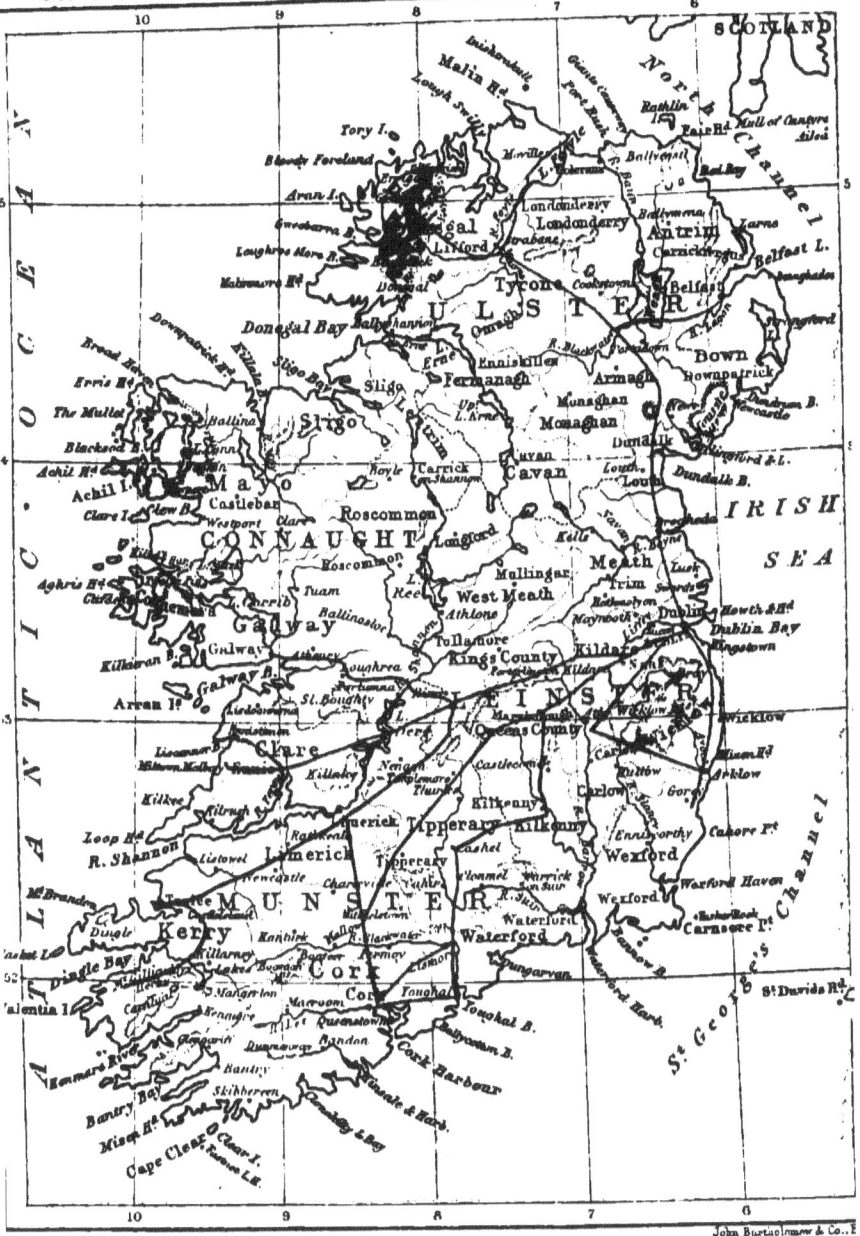

Most Disorderly Districts ☐   Most Distressful Districts ▨

IRELAND UNDER COERCION

THE DIARY OF AN AMERICAN

BY

WILLIAM HENRY HURLBERT

"Upon the future of Ireland hangs the future of the British Empire."
CARDINAL MANNING TO EARL GREY, 1868

VOL. I.

SECOND EDITION.

EDINBURGH: DAVID DOUGLAS
1888

[All rights reserved.]

PREFACE TO THE SECOND EDITION.

ALTHOUGH barely a month has elapsed since the publication of these volumes, events of more or less general notoriety have so far confirmed the views taken in them of the actual state and outlook of affairs in Ireland, that I gladly comply with the request of my publisher for a Preface to this Second Edition.

Upon one most important point—the progressive demoralisation of the Irish people by the methods of the so-called political combinations, which are doing the work of the Agrarian and Anti-Social Revolution in Ireland, some passages, from a remarkable sermon delivered in August in the Cathedral of Waterford by the Catholic bishop of that diocese, will be found to echo almost to the letter the statement given to me in June by a strong Protestant Home Ruler, that "the Nationalists are stripping Irishmen as bare of moral sense as the bushmen of South Africa."

Speaking of what he had personally witnessed in one of the lanes of Waterford, the Bishop says, in the report which I have seen of his sermon, "the "most barbarous tribes of Africa would justly feel "ashamed if they were guilty of what I saw, or "approached to the guilt I witnessed, on that occa-"sion." As a faithful shepherd of his people, he is not content with general denunciations of their misconduct, but goes on to analyse the influences which are thus reducing a Christian people to a level below that of the savages whom Cardinal Lavigerie is now organising a great missionary crusade to rescue from their degradation.

He agrees with Archbishop Croke in attributing much of this demoralisation to the excessive and increasing use of strong drink, striking evidences of which came under my own observation at more than one point of my Irish journeys. But I fear Archbishop Croke would scarcely agree with the Bishop of Waterford in his diagnosis of the effects upon the popular character of what has now come to pass current in many parts of Ireland as "patriotism."

The Bishop says, "The women as well as the men "were fighting, and when we sought to bring them "to order, one man threatened to take up a weapon "and drive bishop, priests, and police from the "place! On the Quay, I understand, it was one scene "of riot and disorder, and what made matters worse "was that when the police went to discharge their "duty for the protection of the people, the moment "they interfered the people turned on them and mal-"treated them in a shocking way. I understand that "some police who were in coloured clothes were "picked out for the worst treatment—knocked down "and kicked brutally. One police officer, I learn, "had his fingers broken. This is a state of things "that nothing at all would justify. It is not to be "justified or excused on any principle of reason or "religion. What is still worse, sympathy was shown "for those who had obstructed and attacked the "police. The only excuse I could find that was "urged for this shameful misconduct was that it "was dignified with the name of 'patriotism'! All "I can say is, that if rowdyism like this be an "indication of the patriotism of the people, as far "as I am concerned, I say, better our poor country "were for ever in political slavery than attain to "liberty by such means."

This is the language of a good Catholic, of a good Irishman, and of a faithful Bishop. Were it more often heard from the lips of the Irish Episcopate the true friends of Ireland might look forward to her future with more hope and confidence than many of the best and ablest of them are now able to feel. As things actually are, not even the Papal Decree has yet sufficed to restrain ecclesiastics, not always of the lowest degree, from encouraging by their words and their conduct "patriotism" of the type commemorated by the late Colonel Prentiss of Louisville, in a story which he used to tell of a tipsy giant in butternut garments, armed with a long rifle, who came upon him in his office on a certain Fourth of July demanding the loan of a dollar on the ground that he felt "so confoundedly patriotic!"

The Colonel judiciously handed the man a dollar, and then asked, "Pray, how do you feel when you feel confoundedly patriotic?"

"I feel," responded the man gravely, "as if I should like to kill somebody or steal something."

It is "patriotism" of this sort which the Papal Decree was issued to expel from within the pale of the Catholic Church. And it is really, in the last analysis of the facts of the case, to the suppression of "patriotism" of this sort that many well-intentioned, but certainly not well-informed, "sympathisers" with what they suppose to be the cause of Ireland, object, in my own country and in Great Britain, when they denounce as "Coercion" the imprisonment of members of Parliament and other rhetorical persons who go about encouraging or compelling ignorant people to support "boycotting" and the "Plan of Campaign."

Yet it would seem to be sufficiently obvious that "patriotism" of this sort, once full-blown and flourishing on the soil of Ireland, must tend to propagate itself far beyond the confines of that island, and to diversify with its blood-red flowers and its explosive fruits the social order of countries in which it has not yet been found necessary for the Head of the Catholic Church to reaffirm the fundamental principles of Law and of Liberty.

Since these volumes were published, too, the Agrarian Revolution in Ireland has been brought into open and defiant collision with the Catholic Church by its leader, Mr. Davitt, the founder of the Land League. In the face of Mr. Davitt's contemptuous and angry repudiation of any binding force in the Papal Decree, it will be difficult even for the Cardinal-Archbishop of Sydney to devise an understanding between the Church and any organisation fashioned or led by him. It may be inferred from Mr. Davitt's contemporaneous and not less angry intimation, that the methods of the Parnellite party are inadequate to the liberation of Ireland from the curse of landlordism, that he is prepared to go further than Mr. George, who still clings in America to the shadowy countenance given him by the Cardinal-Archbishop of Baltimore, and that the Nationalisation of the Land will ere long be urged both in Ireland and in Great Britain by organisations frankly Anti-Catholic as well as Anti-Social.

This is to be desired on many accounts. It will bring the clergy in Ireland face to face with the situation, which will be a good thing both for them and for the people; and it should result in making an end of the pernicious influence upon the popular mind of such extraordinary theological outgivings; for example, as the circular issued in 1881 to the clergy and laity of Meath by the Bishop of that diocese, in which it was laid down that "the land of every country is the common property of the people of that country, because its real owner, the Creator who made it, has transferred it as a voluntary gift to them."

Language of this sort addressed to ignorant multitudes must do harm of course whenever and by whomsoever used. It must tend to evil if addressed by demagogues to the Congress of a Trade Union. But it must do much more harm when uttered with the seeming sanction of the Church by a mitred bishop to congregations already solicited to greed, cunning, and dishonesty, by an unscrupulous and well-organised "agitation."

Not less instructive than Mr. Davitt's outburst from the Church is his almost furious denunciation of the Irish tenants who obeyed an instinct, thought honourable to mankind in most ages and countries, by agreeing together to present to their landlord, Earl Fitzwilliam, a token of their respect and regard on the celebration of his golden wedding day.

These tenants are denounced, not because they

were paying homage to a tyrannical or an unworthy landlord, though Mr. Davitt was so transported beyond his ordinary and cooler self with rage at their action that he actually stooped to something like an insinuation of disbelief in the excellence of Lord Fitzwilliam's character. The true and avowed burden of his diatribe was that no landlord could possibly deserve well of his tenants. The better he is as a man, the more they ought to hate him as a landlord.

The ownership of land, in other words, is of itself in the eyes of Mr. Davitt what the ownership of a slave was in the eyes of the earlier Abolitionists— a crime so monstrous as to be beyond pardon or endurance. If this be true of Great Britain and Ireland, where no allodial tenure exists, how much more true must it be of New York? And if true of the man who owns a thousand acres, it must be equally true of the man who owns an acre. There could not be a better illustration than Mr. Davitt has given in his attack on the Fitzwilliam tenants of the precise accuracy of what I have had occasion to say in these volumes of the "irrepressible conflict" between his schemes and the establishment of a peasant proprietorship in Ireland. It is more than this. It is a distinct warning served upon the smallest tenants as well as upon the greatest landlords in the United Kingdom that fixity of any form of individual tenure is irreconcilable with the Agrarian agitations.

I anticipated this demonstration, but I did not anticipate that it would come so fully or so soon.

I anticipated also abundant proof from my own side of the water of the accuracy of my impressions as to the drift of the American-Irish towards Protection and Republicanism in American politics. This, too, has come earlier and not less fully than I had expected. Mr. Patrick Ford, the most influential leader of the American-Irish, issued early in August a statement of his views as to the impending Presidential election. "The issue to-day," he says, "is the Tariff. It is the American system *versus* the British Colonial system. The Irish are instinctively Protectionists." And why? Mr. Ford goes on to explain. "The fact," he observes, "that the Lion and the Unicorn have taken the stump for Cleveland and Thurman is not calculated to hurt Harrison and Morton in the estimation of the Irish, who will, I promise, give a good account of themselves in the coming Presidential election." Hatred of England, in other words, is an axiom in their Political Economy !

Mr. Davitt's menacing allusion to Parnell as a landlord, and Mr. O'Leary's scornful treatment in a letter to me of the small-fry English Radicals,[1]

---
[1] Vol. ii. p. 376.

when taken together, distinctly prefigure an imminent rupture between the Parnellite party and the two wings—Agrarian and Fenian—of the real revolutionary movement in Ireland. It is clear that clerical agitators, high and low, must soon elect between following Mr. George, Dr. M'Glynn, and Mr. Davitt, and obeying fully the Papal Decree.

It is a most curious feature of the situation in Ireland that much more discontent with the actual conditions of life in that country seems to be felt by people who do not than by people who do live in Ireland. It is the Irish in America and Australia, who neither sow nor reap in Ireland, pay no taxes there, and bear no burdens, who find the alien oppression most intolerable. This explains the extreme bitterness with which Mr. Davitt in some recent speeches and letters denounces the tameness of the Irish people, and rather amusingly berates the British allies of his Parnellite associates for their failure to develop any striking and sensational resistance to the administration of law in Ireland. I have printed in this edition[1] an instructive account, furnished to me by Mr. Tener, of some recent evictions on the Clanricarde property in Galway, which shows how hard it is for the most determined "agitators" to keep the Irish tenants up to that high concert pitch of resistance

[1] Vol. ii. p. 364-370.

to the law which alone would meet the wishes of the true agrarian leaders; and how comparatively easy it is for a just and resolute man, armed with the power of the law resolutely enforced, to break up an illegal combination even in some of the most disturbed regions of Ireland.[1] While this is encouraging to the friends of law and order in Ireland, it must not be forgotten that it involves also a certain peril for them. The more successfully the law is enforced in Ireland, the greater perhaps is the danger that the British constituencies, upon which, of course, the administrators of the law depend for their authority, may lose

[1] The exasperation of the local agitators under the cool and determined treatment of Mr. Tener may be measured by the facts stated in the following communication received by me from Mr. Tener on the 20th of September. I leave them to speak for themselves :—

"POLICE BARRACKS, WOODFORD,
17th Sept. 1888.

"DEAR MR. HURLBERT,—I enclose you *a printed* placard found posted up in Woodford district on Sunday morning the 9th inst. It alludes to *tenants* who had paid me their rent, —and broken the 'unwritten law of the League.' All the men named are now in great danger. The police force of the district has been increased—for their protection; but the police are very anxious about their safety!

"I send you also a *pencil* copy taken from a more *perfect* placard which the police preserve. John White or Whyte is the tenant whose name I already have given you. He is the tall dark man whom you saw (with an ex-bailiff) at Portumna. He was then an "Evicted Tenant." He has since been, on payment of his rent, restored to his farm by me. And now,

PREFACE

sight and sense of the Revolutionary forces at work there. History shows that this has more than once happened in the past. Englishmen and Scotchmen will be better able than I am to judge how far it is unlikely that it should happen again in the future.

As to one matter of great moment—the effect of Lord Ashbourne's Act—a correspondent sends me a statement, which I reproduce here, as it gives a very satisfactory account of the automatic financial machinery upon which that Act must depend for success:—

as you see in the placard, he is held up to the vengeance of the "League of Hell," as P. J. Smyth called it.—Yours, etc.

"ED. TENER.

"*P.S.*—The evictions were finished on the 1st of September, and on the 9th (*after* it became known that the men whose names are in the placard had paid) the placard was issued."

(*Placard.*)

"IRISHMEN!—Need we say in the face of the desperate Battle the People are making for their Hearths and Homes that the time has come for every HONEST MAN, trader and otherwise, to extend a helping hand to the MEN in the GAP. You may ask, How will that be done? The answer is plain.

"Let those who have become traitors to their neighbours and their Country be shunned as if they were possessed by a devil. Let no man buy from them or sell to them, let no man work for them. Leave them to Tener and his Emergency gang. The following are a few of the greatest traitors and meanest creatures that ever walked—John Whyte, of Dooras; Fahey (of the hill) of Dooras; big Anthony Hackett, of Rossmore; Tom Moran, of Rossmore! Your Country calls on you to treat them as they deserve. Bravo Woodford! Remember Tom Larkin!—'GOD SAVE IRELAND!'"

"Out of £90,630 of instalments due last May, less than £4000 is unpaid at the present moment, on transactions extending over three years with all classes of tenants. The total amount which accrued, due to the Land Commission in respect of instalments since the passing of the Act to the 1st November 1887, was £50,910. Of this there is only now unpaid £731, 17s. 9d. There accrued a further amount to the 1st May 1888 of £39,720, in respect of which only £4071, 16s. 11d. is now unpaid, making in all only £4803, 14s. 8d. unpaid, out of a total sum of £90,630 due up to last gale day, some of which by this time has been paid off."

This would seem to be worth considering in connection with the objection made to any serious extension of Lord Ashbourne's Act by Mr. Chamberlain in his extremely clear and able preface to a programme of "Unionist Policy for Ireland" just issued by the "National Radical Union."

LONDON, 21st *Sept.* 1888.

CONTENTS OF VOL. I.

CLUE MAP,	*Frontispiece*
PREFACE TO SECOND EDITION,	p. v
PROLOGUE,	xxi-lxvii

I.

London to Dublin, Jan. 20, 1888,	p. 1
Irish Jacobite,	1
Proposed Mass in memory of Charles Edward,	2
Cardinal Manning,	3
President Cleveland's Jubilee Gift to Leo XIII.,	4
Arrival at Kingstown,	5
Admirable Mail Service,	5
"Davy," the newsvendor,	6
Mr. Davitt,	7
Coercion in America and Ireland,	8
Montgomery Blair's maxim,	8
Irish cars,	9
Maple's Hotel,	9
Father Burke of Tallaght,	10, 11
Peculiarities of Post-offices,	12, 13
National League Office,	13
The Dublin National Reception,	14
Mr. T. D. Sullivan, M.P.,	14
Dublin Castle,	15
Mr. O'Brien, Attorney-General,	16
The Chief-Secretary, Mr. Balfour,	17-24
Fathers M'Fadden and M'Glynn,	18
Come-outers of New England,	18
Mr. Wilfrid Blunt,	19, 20
Sir West Ridgway,	24
Divisional Magistrates,	24
Colonel Turner,	25
The Castle Service,	p. 25-29
Visit of the Prince of Wales,	27
Lord Chief-Justice Morris,	29-37
An Irish Catholic on Mr. Parnell,	31-33
Mr. Justice Murphy,	36
Lord Ashbourne,	37, 38
Unionist meeting,	39
Old Middle State type of American-Irish Protestant,	39
Protestantism and Roman Catholicism in America,	41
Difficulties of the Roman Catholic Church in Ireland,	43
Dr. Jellett,	43
Dinner at the Attorney-General's,	43-46
Sir Bernard Burke,	46-49
Irish Landlords at Kildare Street Club,	49-52
The people and the procession,	53-55
Ripon and Morley,	54, 55

II.

Dublin to Sion, Feb. 3,	56
Poor of the city,	57
Strabane,	58-60
Sion flax-mills,	60-62
Dr. Webb,	63-65
Gweedore, Feb. 4,	65
A good day's work,	65
Strabane,	66
Names of the people,	66
Bad weather judges,	67

VOL. I.

CONTENTS

Letterkenny,	p. 67, 68
Picturesque cottages,	67
Communicative gentleman,	68
Donegal Highlands,	68-70
Glen Veagh,	71
Errigal,	72
Dunlewy and the Clady,	72
Gweedore, Feb. 5,	73
Lord George Hill,	74
Gweedore 1838 to 1879,	75-81
Do. 1879 to 1888,	81-91
Father M'Fadden,	83-104
A Galway man's opinions,	84-89
Value of tenant-right,	83
Condition of tenantry,	84
Woollen stuffs,	87, 88
Distress in Gweedore,	88, 89
Do. Connemara,	88
Mr. Burke,	90
Plan of Campaign,	93
Emigration,	94, 95
Settlement with Captain Hill,	94
Landlord and tenant,	96-98
Land Nationalisation,	98
Father M'Fadden's plan,	98
Gweedore, Feb. 6,	104
On the Bunbeg road,	104-110
Falcarragh,	111-123
Ballyconnell House,	112-123
Townland and Rundale,	118
Use and abuse of tea,	119
Lord Leitrim,	121
A "Queen of France,"	121
The Rosses,	123

III.

Dungloe, Feb. 7,	124
From Gweedore,	124
Irish "jaunting car,"	125
"It will fatten four, feed five, and starve six,"	125
Natural wealth of the country,	125
Isle of Arran and Anticosti,	p. 12
The Gombeen man,	126-130
Dungloe,	126-131
Burtonport,	129
Lough Meela,	128
Attractions of the Donegal coast,	128
Compared with Isles of Shoals and Appledore,	129
Wonderful granite formations,	129
Material for a new industry,	129
Father Walker,	131
Migratory labourers,	133
Granite quarries,	133
Stipends of the Roman Catholic clergy,	134-137
Herring Fisheries,	137
Arranmore,	137
Dungloe woollen work,	138
Baron's Court, Feb. 8,	139
Dungloe to Letterkenny,	139-141
Doocharry Red Granite,	140
Fair at Letterkenny,	142
Feb. 9,	143
On Clare and Kerry,	143
A Priest's opinion on Moonlighters,	143
The Lixnaw murder,	143
Baron's Court,	144
James I.'s three castles,	145
Ulster Settlement,	146
Descendants of the old Celtic stock,	146
The park at Baron's Court,	146
A nonogenarian O'Kane,	148
Irish "Covenanters,"	150
Shenandoah Valley people,	151
The murderers of Munterlony,	151
A relic of 1689,	152
Woollen industry,	152-155
Londonderry Orange symposium,	156
February 11,	157
Sergeant Mahony on Father M'Fadden,	157-163

IV.

Abbeyleix, Feb. 12,	p. 164
Newtown-Stewart,	164
An absentee landlord,	164
"The hill of the seven murders,"	165
Newry, Dublin, Maple's Hotel, Maryborough,	165
"Hurrah for Gilhooly,"	166
Abbeyleix town, chapel, and church,	168
Embroidery and lace work,	169
Wood-carving,	170
General Grant,	171
Kilkenny,	172
Kilkenny Castle,	173
Muniment-room,	174
Table and Expense Books,	176
Dublin once the most noted wine-mart of Britain,	177, 178
Cathedral of St. Canice,	178
The Waterford cloak,	179
The College,	180
Irish and Scotch whisky,	180
Duke of Ormonde's grants,	181
The Plan of Campaign,	182–186
Ulster tenant-right,	186, 187

V.

Dublin, Feb. 14,	188
The Irish National Gallery,	188–191
Feb. 15,	192
London: Mr. Davitt,	192
Irish Woollen Company,	193
Mr. Davitt and Mr. Blunt,	193
Mr. Davitt's character and position,	192-199

VI.

Ennis, Feb. 18,	200
Return to Ireland,	200
Irish Nationalists,	200, 201
Home Rule and Protection,	p. 202
Luggacurren and Mr. O'Brien,	204
Dublin to Limerick and Ennis,	204, 205
Colonel Turner,	205
Architecture of Ennis Courthouse—Resemblance to White House, Washington,	206
Number of public-houses in Ennis, and in Ireland,	207, 208
Innkeepers of Milltown Malbay,	208, 209
Father White (see Note E),	209
Sir Francis Head,	210, 211
Different opinions in Ennis,	212, 213
State of trade in Ennis,	213, 214
Edenvale, Heronry,	215 seq.
Feb. 19,	215
The men of Ennis at Edenvale,	216
Killone Abbey,	218-221
Stephen J. Meany,	220
"Holy Well" of St. John,	221
Superstition as to rabbits,	222
Religious practices under Penal Laws,	222
Experiences under National League,	223, 224
Case of George Pilkington,	224-226
Trees at Edenvale,	227
Moonlighters, a reproduction of Whiteboys,	227, 228
Difficulty in getting men to work,	228
A testimonial to Mr. Austen Mackay,	229-232
Effect of testimonials,	232
Feb. 20,	232
The case of Mrs. Connell at Milltown Malbay,	232 seq.
Estate accounts and prices,	240
A rent-warner,	245
Mr. Redmond, M.P.,	245
Father White's Sermon,	246
A photograph,	246

APPENDIX.

NOTES—
   A. Mr. Gladstone and the American War (Prologue xxix), . p. 249
   B. Mr. Parnell and the Dynamiters (Prologue xxxiii), . . 251
   C. The American "Suspects" of 1881 (Prologue xlvii), . . 255
   D. The Parnellites and the English Parties (Prologue l.), . . 262
   E. The "Boycott" at Miltown-Malbay (p. 209), . . . 264

PROLOGUE.

I.

THIS book is a record of things seen, and of conversations had, during a series of visits to Ireland between January and June 1888.

These visits were made in quest of light, not so much upon the proceedings and the purposes of the Irish "Nationalists,"—with which, on both sides of the Atlantic, I have been tolerably familiar for many years past—as upon the social and economical results in Ireland of the processes of political vivisection to which that country has been so long subjected.

As these results primarily concern Great Britain and British subjects, and as a well-founded and reasonable jealousy exists in Great Britain of American intromission in the affairs of Ireland, it is proper for me to say at the outset, that the condition of Ireland interests me not because I believe, with Cardinal Manning, that upon the future of Ireland hangs the future of the British Empire, but because I know that America is largely responsible for the actual condition of Ireland, and because the future condition of Ireland, and of the British

Empire, must gravely influence the future of my own country.

In common with the vast majority of my countrymen, who come with me of what may now not improperly be called the old American stock—by which I mean the three millions of English-speaking dwellers in the New World, who righteously resented, and successfully resisted, a hundred years ago, the attempt—not of the Crown under which the Colonies held their lands, but of the British Parliament in which they were unrepresented—to take their property without their consent, and apply it to purposes not passed upon by them, I have always felt that the claim of the Irish people to a proper control of matters exclusively Irish was essentially just and reasonable. The measure of that proper control is now, as it always has been, a question not for Americans, but for the people of Great Britain and of Ireland. If Lord Edward Fitzgerald and his associates had succeeded in expelling British authority from Ireland, and in founding an Irish Republic, we should probably have recognised that Republic. Yet an American minister at the Court of St. James's saw no impropriety in advising our Government to refuse a refuge in the United States to the defeated Irish exiles of '98.

It is undoubtedly the opinion of every Irish

American who possesses any real influence with the people of his own race in my country, that the rights and liberties of Ireland can only be effectually secured by a complete political separation from Great Britain. Nor can the right of Irish American citizens, holding this opinion, to express their sympathy with Irishmen striving in Ireland to bring about such a result, and with Englishmen or Scotchmen contributing to it in Great Britain, be questioned, any more than the right of Polish citizens of the French Republic to express their sympathy with Poles labouring in Poland for the restoration of Polish nationality. It is perhaps even less open to question than the right of Americans not of Irish race, and of Frenchmen not of Polish race, to express such sympathies; and certainly less open to question than the right of Englishmen or Americans to express their sympathy with Cubans bent on sundering the last link which binds Cuba to Spain, or with Greeks bent on overthrowing the authority of the Sultan in Crete.

But for all American citizens of whatever race, the expression of such sympathies ceases to be legitimate when it assumes the shape of action transcending the limits set by local or by international law. It is of the essence of American constitutionalism that one community shall not lay hands upon the domestic affairs of another; and it is an undeniable fact that the sympathy of the great body of the American people with Irish efforts for self-government has been diminished, not increased, since 1848, by the gradual transfer of the head-quarters and machinery of those efforts from Ireland to the United States. The recent refusal of the Mayor of New York, Mr. Hewitt, to allow what is called the "Irish National flag" to be raised over the City Hall of New York is vastly more significant of the true drift of American feeling on this subject than any number of sympathetic resolutions adopted at party conventions or in State legislatures by party managers, bent on harpooning Irish voters. If Ireland had really made herself a "nation," with or without the consent of Great Britain, a refusal to hoist the Irish flag on the occasion of an Irish holiday would be not only churlish but foolish. But thousands of Americans, who might view with equanimity the disruption of the British Empire and the establishment of an Irish republic, regard, not only with disapprobation, but with resentment, the growing disposition of Irish agitators in and out of the British Parliament to thrash out on American soil their schemes for bringing about these results with the help of Irishmen who have assumed the duties by acquiring the rights of American citizenship. It is not in accordance with the American doctrine of "Home Rule" that "Home Rule" of any sort for

Ireland should be organised in New York or in Chicago by expatriated Irishmen.

No man had a keener or more accurate sense of this than the most eloquent and illustrious Irishman whose voice was ever heard in America.

In the autumn of 1871 Father Burke of Tallaght and San Clemente, with whom I had formed at Rome in early manhood a friendship which ended only with his life, came to America as the commissioned Visitor of the Dominican Order. His mission there will live for ever in the Catholic annals of the New World. But of one episode of that mission no man living perhaps knows so much as I, and I make no excuse for this allusion to it here, as it illustrates perfectly the limits between the lawful and the unlawful in the agitation of Irish questions upon American soil.

While Father Burke was in New York Mr. Froude came there, having been invited to deliver before a Protestant Literary Association a series of lectures upon the history of Ireland. My personal relations with Mr. Froude, I should say here, and my esteem for his rare abilities, go back to the days of the *Nemesis of Faith*, and I did not affect to disguise from him the regret with which I learned his errand to the New World. That his lectures would be brilliant, impressive, and interesting, was quite certain; but it was equally certain, I thought, that they would do a world of mischief, by stirring up ancient issues of strife between the Protestant and the Catholic populations of the United States.

That they would be answered angrily, indiscreetly, and in a fashion to aggravate prejudices which ought to be appeased on both sides of the questions involved, was much more than probable. All this accordingly I urged upon Father Burke, begging him to find or make time in the midst of his engrossing duties for a systematic course of lectures in reply. What other men would surely say in heat and with virulence would be said by him, I knew, temperately, loftily, and wisely. Three strenuous objections he made. One was that his work as a Catholic missionary demanded all his thought and all his time; another that he was not historically equipped to deal with so formidable an antagonist; and a third that America ought not to be a battle-ground of Irish contentions. It was upon the last that he dwelt most tenaciously; nor did he give way until he had satisfied himself, after consulting with the highest authorities of his Church, and with two or three of the coolest and most judicious Irish citizens of New York, that I was right in believing that his appearance in the arena as the champion of Ireland, would lift an inevitable controversy high above the atmosphere of unworthy passion, and put it beyond the reach of political mischief-makers.

How nobly he did his work when he had become convinced that he ought to do it, is now matter of history. But it is a hundredfold more needful now than it was in 1871 and 1872, that the spirit in which he did it should be known and published abroad. In the interval between the delivery of two of his replies to Mr. Froude, Mr. Froude went to Boston. A letter from Boston informed me that upon Mr. Froude's arrival there, all the Irish servants of the friend with whom he was to stay had suddenly left the house, refusing to their employer the right to invite under his roof a guest not agreeable to them. I handed this letter, without a word, to Father Burke a few hours before he was to speak in the Academy of Music. He read it with a kind of humorous wrath; and when the evening came, he prefaced his lecture with a few strong and stirring words, in which he castigated with equal sense and severity the misconduct of his countrypeople, anticipating thus by many a year the spirit in which the supreme authority of his Church has just now dealt with the social plague of " boycotting," whereof the strike of the servant girls at Boston sixteen years ago was a precursory symptom.

Father Burke understood that American citizenship imposes duties where it confers rights. Nobody expects the European emigrant who abjures his foreign allegiance to divest himself of his native sympathies or antipathies. But American law, and the conditions of American liberty, require him to divest himself of the notion that he retains any right actively to interfere in the domestic affairs of the country of his birth. For public and political purposes, the Irishman who becomes an American ceases to be an Irishman. When Mr. Gladstone's Government in 1881 seized and locked up indefinitely, on "suspicion" of what they might be about to do, American citizens of Irish birth, these "suspects" clamoured, and had a right to clamour, for the intervention of the American Government to protect them against being dealt with as if they were Irishmen and British subjects. But by the abjuration of British allegiance which gave them this right to clamour for American protection, they had voluntarily made themselves absolute foreigners to Ireland, with no more legal or moral right to interfere in the affairs of that country than so many Chinamen or Peruvians.

Having said this, I ought, in justice to my fellow-citizens of Irish birth, to say that these elementary truths have too often been obscured for them by the conduct of public bodies in America, and of American public men.

No American public man of reputation, holding an executive office in the Federal Government, has ever thrust himself, it is true, so inexcusably into the domestic affairs of Great Britain and Ireland as did Mr. Gladstone into the domestic affairs of the United States when, speaking at Newcastle in the very crisis of our great civil war, he gave all the weight of his position as a Cabinet Minister to the assertion that Mr. Jefferson Davis had created not only an army and a navy, but a nation, and thereby compelled the Prime Minister of Great Britain to break the effect of this declaration by insisting that another Cabinet Minister, Sir George Cornewall Lewis, should instantly make a speech countering it, and covering the neutrality of the British Government.[1]

Nor has either House of the Congress of the United States ever been guilty of the impertinence of adopting resolutions of sympathy with the Home Rule, or any other movement affecting directly the domestic affairs of the British Empire, though, within my own knowledge, very strong pressure has been more than once put upon the Foreign Affairs Committees of both Houses to bring this about.

But such resolutions have been repeatedly adopted by State Legislatures, and individual members, both of the Federal Senate and of the Federal Lower House, have discredited themselves, and brought such discredit as they could upon the Congress, by effusions of the same sort. The bad citizenship of

[1] Appendix, Note A.

Irish-American citizens, however, is not the less bad citizenship because they may have been led into it by the recklessness of State Legislatures—which have no responsibility for our foreign relations—or the sycophancy of public men. If it were proved to demonstration that Home Rule would be the salvation of Ireland, no American citizen would have any more right to take an active part in furthering it than to take an active part in dethroning the Czar of all the Russias. The lesson which Washington administered to Citizen Genet, when that meddlesome minister of the French Republic undertook to "boom" the rights of men by issuing letters of marque at Charleston, has governed the foreign relations of the United States ever since, and it is as binding upon every private citizen as upon every public servant of the Republic.

I must ask my readers, therefore, to bear it constantly in mind that all my observations and comments have been made from an American, not from a British or an Irish point of view. How or by whom Ireland shall be governed concerns me only in so far as the government of Ireland may affect the character and the tendencies of the Irish people, and thereby, through the close, intimate, and increasing connection between the Irish people and the people of the United States, may tend to affect the future of my country. This being my point of view, it will be apparent, I think, that I have at least laboured under no temptation to see things otherwise than as they were, or to state things otherwise than as I saw them.

With Arthur Young, who more clearly than any other man of his time saw the end from the beginning of the fatuous and featherheaded French Revolution of 1789, I have always been inclined to think "the application of theory to methods of government a surprising imbecility in the human mind:" and it will be found that in this book I have done little more than set down, as fully and clearly as I could, what I actually saw and heard in Ireland. My method has been as simple as my object. During each day as occasion served, and always at night, I made stenographic notes of whatever had attracted my attention or engaged my interest. As I had no case to make for or against any political party or any theory of government in Ireland, I took things great and small, and people high and low, as they came, putting myself in contact by preference, wherever I could, with those classes of the Irish people of whom we see least in America, and concerning myself, as to my notes, only that they should be made under the vivid immediate impress of whatever they were to record. These notes I have subsequently written out in the spirit in which I made them, in all cases taking what pains

I could to verify statements of facts, and in many cases, where it seemed desirable or necessary, submitting the proofs of the pages as finally printed to the persons whom, after myself, they most concerned.

I have been more annoyed by the delay than by the trouble thus entailed upon me; but I shall be satisfied if those who may take the pains to read the book shall as nearly as possible see what I saw, and hear what I heard.

I have no wish to impress my own conclusions upon others who may be better able than I am accurately to interpret the facts from which these conclusions have been drawn. Such as they are, I have put them into a few pages at the end of the book.

It will be found that I have touched only incidentally upon the subject of Home Rule for Ireland. Until it shall be ascertained what "Home Rule for Ireland" means, that subject seems to me to lie quite outside the domain of my inquiries. "Home Rule for Ireland" is not now a plan—nor so much as a proposition. It is merely a polemical phrase, of little importance to persons really interested in the condition of Ireland, however invaluable it may be to the makers of party platforms in my own country, or to Parliamentary candidates on this side of the Atlantic. It may mean anything or nothing, from Mr. Chamberlain's imperialist scheme of four Provincial Councils — which recalls the outlines of a system once established with success in New Zealand—to that absolute and complete separation in all particulars of the government of Ireland from the government of Great Britain, which has unquestionably been the aim of every active Irish organisation in the United States for the last twenty years, and which the accredited leader of the "Home Rule" party in the British Parliament, Mr. Parnell, is understood in America to have pledged himself that he will do anything to further and nothing to impede. On this point, what I took to be conclusive documentary evidence was submitted to me in New York several years ago by Mr. Sheridan, at a time when the fever-heat of British indignation excited by those murders in the Phœnix Park, for which I believe it is now admitted by the best informed authorities that Mr. Sheridan had no responsibility, was driving Mr. Parnell and his Parliamentary associates into disavowals of the extreme men of their connection, which, but for Mr. Sheridan's coolness and consciousness of his well-assured domination over them, might have led to extremely inconvenient consequences to all concerned.[1] But whatever "Home Rule" may or may not mean, I went to Ireland, not to find some achromatic meaning for a prismatic phrase, which is flashed at you fifty times

[1] Appendix, Note B.

in England or America where you encounter it once in Ireland, but to learn what I could of the social and economical condition of the Irish people as affected by the revolutionary forces which are now at work in that country.

I have watched the development of these forces too long and too closely to be under any illusion as to the real importance relatively with them of the so-called "Parliamentary" action of the Irish Nationalists.

II.

The visits to Ireland, of which this book is a record, were made on my return from a sojourn in Rome during the celebration of the Jubilee of His Holiness Leo XIII. What I then and there learned convinced me that the Vatican was on the eve of grappling in Ireland with issues substantially identical with those which were forced, in my own country, two years ago, upon a most courageous and gifted member of the American Catholic hierarchy, the Archbishop of New York, by the open adhesion of an eminent Irish American ecclesiastic, the Rev. Dr. M'Glynn, to the social revolution of which Mr. Henry George is the best-equipped and most indefatigable apostle. Entertaining this conviction (which events have since shown to have been well-founded), I was anxious to survey on the

To get at the origin and the meaning of this agitation we must be content, I believe, to go no further back than ten years, and to look for them, not in Ireland, but in America, not to Mr. Parnell and Mr. Gladstone primarily, but to Mr. Davitt and Mr. Henry George.

III.

In a very remarkable letter written to Earl Grey in 1868, after the Clerkenwell explosions had brought the disestablishment of the Irish Protestant Church into Mr. Gladstone's scheme of "practical politics," the Archbishop of Westminster, not then a Cardinal, called the attention of Englishmen to the fact, not yet I fear adequately apprehended by them, that "the assimilating power of America upon the Irish people, if seven days slower than that of England in reaching Ireland, is sevenfold more penetrating and powerful upon the whole population." By this the Archbishop meant, what was unquestionably true, that even in 1868, only twenty years after the great Irish exodus to America began, the social and political ideas of America were exerting a seven-fold stronger influence upon the character and the tendencies of the Irish people than the social and political ideas of England. Thanks to the development of the cables and the telegraph since 1868, and to the enormous progress of America since that time in wealth and population, this "assimilating power" reaches Ireland much more rapidly, and exerts upon the Irish people a very much more drastic influence than in 1868. This establishes, of course, a return current westward, which is as necessary to be watched, and is as much neglected by American as the original eastward current is by British public men.

In this letter of 1868 to Earl Grey, the Archbishop of Westminster desiring, as an Englishman, to counteract, if possible, this influence which was drawing Ireland away from the British monarchy, and towards the American Republic, maintained that by two things the "heart of Ireland" might be won, and her affections enlisted with her interests in the support of the unity, solidity, and prosperity of the British Empire. One of these two things was "perfect religious equality between the Catholics and the Protestants of Ireland." The other was that the Imperial Legislature should by statute make it impossible for any landlord in Ireland to commit three wrongs,—"first, the wrong of abusing his rights by arbitrary eviction; secondly, by exacting an exorbitant rent; thirdly, by appropriating to his own use the improvements effected by the industry of his tenants."

Perfect religious equality has since been estab-

PROLOGUE   xxxix

lished between the Catholics and the Protestants of Ireland. The three wrongs which the Archbishop called upon the Imperial Legislature to make impossible to Irish landlords have since been made impossible by Statute.

Yet it is on all hands admitted that the "unity, solidity, and prosperity" of the British Empire have never been so seriously threatened in Ireland as during the last ten years. Was the Archbishop wrong, therefore, in his estimate of the situation in 1868? Or has the centripetal influence of remedial British legislation since 1868 failed to check a centrifugal advance "by leaps and bounds," in the "assimilating power" of America upon Ireland?

IV.

Just ten years ago, in 1878, Mr. Michael Davitt and Mr. John Devoy (the latter of whom had been commissioned in 1865 by the Fenian leader Stephens, as "chief organiser of the Irish Republican Brotherhood in the British army"), being then together in America, promulgated, Mr. Davitt in a speech at Boston, and Mr. Devoy in a letter sent to the *Freeman's Journal* in Dublin, the outlines of a scheme for overthrowing British rule in Ireland by revolutionising the ownership of land in that country.

The basis of this scheme had been laid thirty years before, in 1848, by Finton Lalor, John Mitchel, and the present Archbishop of Cashel, then a simple curate.

It was thus stated by Lalor in his paper, the *Irish Felon* :—

"The entire ownership of Ireland, moral and material, up to the sun and down to the centre of the earth, is vested, as of right, in the people of Ireland. The soil of the country belongs as of right to the entire people of the country, not to any one class, but to the nation."

This was a distinct denial of the right of private property in land. If true of Ireland and the Irish people this proposition was true of all lands and of all peoples. Lalor, though more of a patriot than of a philosopher, saw this plainly ; and in one of the three numbers of his paper which appeared before it was suppressed by the British Government, he said "the principle I propose goes to the foundations of Europe, and sooner or later will cause Europe to uprise." Michael Davitt saw this as clearly in 1878 as Finton Lalor thirty years before. He had matured his plans in connection with this principle during the weary but not wasted years of his imprisonment as a Fenian at Dartmoor, a place, the name of which is connected in America with many odious memories of the second war between England and the United States ; and going out to America almost immediately after his release on a ticket of leave, he there found the ideas of Finton Lalor and his associates of 1848, ripened and harvested in the mind of an American student of sociology, Henry George. Nowhere in the world has what a shrewd English traveller calls "the illegitimate development of private wealth" attained such proportions in modern times as in America, and especially in California. Nowhere, too, in the world is the ostentatious waste of the results of labour upon the antics of a frivolous plutocracy a more crying peril of our times than in America. Henry George, an American of the Eastern States, who went to the Pacific coast as a lad, had grown up with and watched the progress of this social disease in California; and when Davitt reached America in 1878, Henry George was preparing to publish his revolutionary book on *Progress and Poverty*, which appeared in 1879. Dates are important from this point, as they will trace for the reader the formation of the strongest forces which, as I believe, are to-day at work to shape the future of Ireland, and, if Cardinal Manning is right, with the future of Ireland, the future of the British Empire.

The year 1878 saw the "Home Rule" movement in Irish politics brought to an almost ludicrous halt by the success of Mr. Parnell, then a young member of Parliament for Meath, in unhorsing the leader of that movement, Mr. Butt. As the Irish members then had no coherent purpose or policy, Mr. Parnell had, without much trouble, dominated and brigaded them to follow him blindly into a system of parliamentary obstruction, which there is reason to suppose was suggested to him by a friend who had studied the Congressional proceedings of the United States, the native country of his mother, and especially the tactics which had enabled Mr. Randall of Pennsylvania, the leader of the Democratic minority in the House of Representatives, to check the so-called "Civil Rights Bill," sent down by the Senate to that House, during a continuous session of forty-six hours and a half, with no fewer than seventy-seven calls of the house, in the month of January 1875, some time before Mr. Parnell first took his seat in the House of Commons.

When Mr. Parnell, early in 1878, thanks to this system, had ousted Mr. Butt, and got himself elected as President of the Irish "Home Rule Confederation," he found himself, as an Irish friend of mine wrote to me at the time, in an awkward position. He had command of the "Home Rule" members at Westminster, but he had no notion what to do with them, and neither they nor he could see any way open to securing a permanent hold upon the Irish voters. Three bad harvests in succession had thrown the Irish tenants judicious quarrel into which he drifted with a portion of the American press, and which was distinctly deepened by his inexcusable misrepresentations of the conduct of Queen Victoria during the famine of 1847, and by his foolish attacks upon the management and objects of the Duchess of Marlborough's fund for the relief of Irish distress. The friends of Mr. Davitt in America, however, and the leaders of the most active Irish organisations there, came to the rescue, and as the two American parties were preparing their lines of battle for the Presidential conflict of 1880, Mr. Parnell was not only " put through " the usual course of " receptions " by Mayors and State legislatures, but invited on an " off-day " to address the House of Representatives at Washington. His tour, however, on the whole, harmed more than it helped the new Irish movement on my side of the Atlantic, and when he was called back to take his part in the electoral contest precipitated by Lord Beaconsfield's dissolution of Parliament at Easter 1880, Mr. Davitt went out to America himself to do what his Parliamentary associate had not succeeded in doing. During this visit of Mr. Davitt to the United States, Mr. Henry George finally transferred his residence from San Francisco to New York, and made his arrangements to visit England and Ireland, and bring about a practical combination between the advocates of "the land for the people" on both sides of the ocean. These arrangements he carried out in 1881-82, publishing in 1881, in America, his treatise on the Irish Land question, while Mr. Davitt, who had been arrested after his return to Europe by Mr. Gladstone's Government in February 1881, on a revocation of his ticket-of-leave, lay a prisoner at Portland. Mr. George himself, while travelling in Ireland with an academical English friend, came under "suspicion" in the eyes of one of Mr. Forster's officers, and was arrested, but at once released. During the protracted confinement of Mr. Davitt at Portland, the utter incapacity of Mr. Parnell and his Parliamentary associates to manage the social revolution initiated by the founder of the Land League became fully apparent, not only to impartial, but even to sympathetic observers in America, long before it was demonstrated by the incarceration of Mr. Parnell in Kilmainham, the disavowal, under pressure, of the no-rent manifesto by Archbishop Croke, and the suppression of the Land League. In sequestrating Mr. Davitt, Mr. Forster, as was shown by the extraordinary scenes which in the House of Commons followed his arrest, had struck at the core of the revolution, and had the Irish Secretary not been deserted by Mr. Gladstone, under influences which originated at Kilmainham, and were reinforced by the pressure of the United States Government in the spring of 1882, history might have had a very different tale to tell of the last six years in Ireland and in Great Britain.[1]

V.

It was after the return of Mr. George from Ireland to New York in 1882 that the first black point appeared on the horizon, of the conflict, inevitable in the nature of things, between the social revolution and the Catholic Church, which assumed such serious proportions two years ago in America, and which is now developing itself in Ireland. Among the ablest and the most earnest converts in America to the doctrine of the new social revolution was the Rev. Dr. M'Glynn, a Catholic priest, standing in the front rank of his order in New York, in point alike of eloquence in the pulpit, and of influence in private life. Finding, like Michael Davitt, in the doctrine of Henry George an outcome and a confirmation of the principle laid down in 1848 for the liberation of Ireland by Finton Lalor, Dr. M'Glynn threw himself ardently into the advocacy of that doctrine,—so ardently that in August 1882 the Prefect of the Propaganda, Cardinal Simeoni, found it necessary to invite the attention of Car-

[1] Appendix, Note C.

dinal M'Closkey, then Archbishop of New York, to speeches of Dr. M'Glynn, reported in the *Irish World* of New York, as " containing propositions openly opposed to the teachings of the Catholic Church."

It did not concern the Propaganda that these propositions ran on all-fours with the policy of the Irish Land League established by Mr. Davitt, and accepted by Mr. Parnell. What concerned the Propaganda in the propositions of Dr. M'Glynn at New York in 1882 was precisely what concerns the Propaganda in the programme of Mr. Davitt as mismanaged by Mr. Dillon in Ireland in 1888—the incompatibility of these propositions, and of that programme, with the teachings of the Church.

Upon receiving the instructions of the Propaganda in August 1882, Cardinal M'Closkey sent for Dr. M'Glynn, and set the matter plainly before him. Dr. M'Glynn professed regret for his errors, promised to abstain in future from political meetings, and begged the Cardinal to inform the authorities at Rome of his intention to walk more circumspectly. The submission of Dr. M'Glynn was approved at Rome, but it was gently intimated to him that it needed to be crowned by public reparation for the scandal he had caused. He disregarded this pastoral hint, and when the Archbishop Coadjutor of New York, Dr. Corrigan, went to Rome in 1883 to represent the Cardinal, who was unequal to the journey, he found the Propaganda by no means satisfied with the attitude of Dr. M'Glynn. Two years after this, in October 1885, Cardinal M'Closkey died, and Dr. Corrigan succeeded him as Archbishop of New York.

Between the first admonition given to the sacerdotal ally of Mr. George in 1882 and this event much had come to pass in Ireland. The Land League suppressed by Mr. Forster had been suffered to reappear as the National League by Earl Spencer and Mr. Trevelyan. Sir William Harcourt's stringent and sweeping "Coercion Act" of July 11th, 1882, passed under the stress of the murders in the Phœnix Park, expiring by its own terms in July 1885, Mr. Gladstone found himself forced either to alienate a number of his Radical supporters by proposing a renewal of that Act, or to invite a catastrophe in Ireland by attempting to rule that country under "the ordinary law."

He elected to escape from the dilemma by inviting a defeat in Parliament on a secondary question of the Budget. He went out of power on the 9th of June 1885, leaving Lord Salisbury to send the Earl of Carnarvon as Viceroy to Ireland, and the Irish party in Parliament to darken the air on both sides of the Atlantic with portentous intimations of a mysterious compact, under which they were to secure Home Rule for Ireland by establishing the Conservatives in their places at the general election in November.¹

What came of all this I may briefly rehearse. Going out to America in November 1885, and returning to England in January 1886, I remained in London long enough to assure myself, and to publish in America my conviction of the utter hopelessness of Mr. Gladstone's " Home Rule " measure, the success of which would have made his government the ally and the instrument of Mr. Parnell in carrying out the plans of Mr. Davitt, Mr. Henry George, and the active Irish organisations of the United States. All this is matter of history.

The effect of Mr. Gladstone's speech of April 8, 1886, introducing his Home Rule Bill, upon the Irish in America was simply intoxicating. They saw him, as in a vision, repeating for the benefit of Ireland at Dublin, on a grander scale, the impressive scene of his surrender in 1858 at Corfu of the Protectorate of the Ionian Islands to Greece.

Upon thousands also of Americans, interested more or less intelligently in British affairs, but neither familiar, nor caring to be, with the details of the political situation in Great Britain, this appearance of the British Premier, as the champion of Home Rule for Ireland, denouncing the " base-

¹ Appendix, Note D.

ness and blackguardism" of Pitt and his accomplices, the framers of the Union of 1800, naturally produced a very profound impression. What might be almost called a "tidal wave" of sympathy with the Irish National League, and with him as its ally, made itself felt throughout the United States. Had I witnessed the drama from the far-off auditorium in New York, I might doubtless have shared the conviction of so many of my countrymen that we were about to behold the consummation tunefully anticipated so many years ago by John Quincy Adams, and—

> "Proud of herself, victorious over fate,
> See Erin rise, an independent state."

The moment seemed propitious for a resolute forward move in America of Mr. Henry George, and the other American believers in the doctrine of "the land for the people." It would have been more propitious had not the political managers of the Irish party, misapprehending to the last moment the drift of things in the British Parliament, and counting firmly upon a victory for Mr. Gladstone, either at Westminster or at the polls, insisted upon holding a great convention of the Irish in America at Chicago in August 1886. A proposition to do this had been made in the spring of 1885, and put off, in judicious deference to the disgust which many independent Americans of both parties then felt at the course pursued by Mr. Parnell's friends, Mr. Egan and Mr. Sullivan in 1884, when these leaders openly led the Irish with drums beating and green flags flying out of the Democratic into the Republican camp.

As it was, however, Mr. Gladstone having gone out of power a second time, on the second day of June in 1886, the non-parliamentary and real leader in Ireland of the Irish revolutionary movement, Mr. Davitt, came overtly to the front, and crossed the Atlantic to ride the whirlwind and direct the storm at the Convention appointed to be held in Chicago on the 18th of August.

In New York he found Mr. Henry George quietly preparing to put the emotions of the moment to profit at the municipal election which was to occur in that city in November, and Dr. M'Glynn more enamoured than ever of the doctrine of "the land for the people," and more defiant than ever of the Propaganda and of his ecclesiastical superiors. It was resolved that Mr. George should come forward as a candidate for the mayoralty in November, and Dr. M'Glynn determined to take the field in support of him.

VI.

We now come to close quarters.

Dr. Corrigan, as I have said, had become the Archbishop of New York in October 1885. The Irish-American Convention met at Chicago, Mr. Davitt dominating its proceedings by his courageous and outspoken support of his defeated Parliamentary allies in England. The candidacy of Mr. Henry George had not yet been announced in New York. But Dr. M'Glynn resumed his practice of addressing public meetings in support of the doctrines of Mr. Davitt and of Henry George. The Archbishop's duty was plain. It was not pleasant. A Catholic prelate of Irish blood living in New York might have been pardoned for avoiding, if he could, an open intervention at such a moment, to prevent an able and popular priest from disobeying his ecclesiastical superiors in his zeal for a doctrine hostile to "landlordism," and cordially approved by the most influential of the Irish leaders.

But on the 21st August 1886, while all the Irishmen in New York were wild with excitement over the proceedings at Chicago, Archbishop Corrigan did his duty, and admonished Dr. M'Glynn to restrain his political ardour. The admonition was thrown away. A month later, the canvass of Mr. Henry George being then fully opened, Dr. M'Glynn sent Mr. George himself to wait upon the Archbishop with a note of introduction as his "very dear and valued friend," in the hope of inducing the Archbishop to withdraw his inhibition and allow him to speak at a great meeting, then about to be held, of the supporters of Mr. George.

The Archbishop replied in a firm but friendly note, forbidding Dr. M'Glynn "in the most positive manner" to attend the meeting referred to, or "any other political meeting whatever."

Dr. M'Glynn deliberately disobeyed this order, attended the meeting, and threw himself with ever increasing heat into the war against landlordism. On the 2d of October 1886, therefore, he was formally "suspended" from his priestly functions —nor has he ever since been permitted to resume them. Another priest presides over the great church of St. Stephen, of which he was the rector. More than once the door of repentance and return has been opened to him; but, I believe, he is still waging war in his own way, and beyond the precincts of the priesthood, both upon the right of private property in land and upon the Pope.

He is a man of vigorous intellect; and he has defined the issue between himself and the Church in language so terse and clear that I reproduce it here. It defines also the real issue of to-day between the Church speaking through the Papal Decree of

April 20, 1888, and the National League of Ireland acting through the " Plan of Campaign."

No heed having been paid by Dr. M'Glynn to several successive intimations summoning him to go to Rome and explain his attitude, he finally, on the 20th of December 1886, wrote a letter in which, with a single skilful turn of his wrist, he took out the core of Henry George's doctrine as to land, which really is the core also of the Irish Plan of Campaign, and thus laid it before the Archbishop of New York:—

" My doctrine about land has been made clear in speeches, in reports of interviews, and in published articles, and I repeat it here. I have taught, and I shall continue to teach in speeches and writings, as long as I live, that land is rightfully the property of the people in common, and that private ownership of land is against natural justice, no matter by what civil or ecclesiastical laws it may be sanctioned; and I would bring about instantly, if I could, such change of laws all over the world as would confiscate private property in land without one penny of compensation to the miscalled owners."

There is no shuffling here. With logical precision Dr. M'Glynn strips Mr. George's doctrine of its technical disguise as a form of taxation, and presents it to the world as a simple Confiscation of Rents. Many acute critics of *Progress and Poverty* have failed to see that when Mr. George calls upon the State to take over to itself, and to its own uses, the whole annual rental value of the bare land of a country, the land, that is, irrespectively of improvements put upon it by man, he proposes not "a single tax upon land" at all, but an actual confiscation of the rental of the land—which for practical purposes is the land—to the uses of the State, without a levy, and without compensation to "the miscalled owners."

When a tax is levied, the need by the State levying it of a certain sum of money must first be ascertained by competent authority, legislative or executive, as the case may be, and the law-making power must then, according to a prescribed form, enact that to raise such a sum a certain tax shall be levied on designated property or occupations. If the exigencies of the State are held to require it, a tax may be levied upon property of more than its value, as in the case, for example, of the customs duty which was imposed in one of our "tariff revisions" upon plate glass imported into the United States by way of "protecting" a single plate-glass factory then existing in the United States. This was an abominable abuse of a constitutional power, but it was not "confiscation." What Henry George proposes is confiscation, as Dr. M'Glynn plainly sees and courageously says. What he proposes is that the State shall compel the annual rental value of all land to be paid into the public treasury, without regard to the question whether the State does or does not need such a sum of money. That is confiscation pure and simple, the State, in the assumed interest of the State, proceeding against the private owners of land, or the "miscalled owners," to use Dr. M'Glynn's significant phrase, precisely as under the feudal system the State proceeded against the private property of rebels and traitors. No good reason can be shown why the process should not be applied to personalty and to debts as well as to land.

This was the doctrine indorsed at the polls in New York in November 1886 by 68,000 voters. Nor can there be much doubt that it would have been indorsed by the few thousand more votes needed to defeat Mr. Hewitt, the actual Mayor of New York, and to put Mr. Henry George into the Chief Magistracy of the first city of the New World, had not its teachers and preachers been confronted by the quiet, cool, and determined prelate who met it as plainly as it was put. "Your letter," said the Archbishop, "has brought the painful intelligence that you decline to go to Rome, and that you have taught, and will continue to teach, the injustice of private ownership of land, no matter by what laws of Church or State it may be sanctioned. In view of such declarations, to permit you to exercise the holy ministry would be manifestly wrong."

In these few words of the Archbishop of New York, we have plainly affirmed in 1886 the principle underlying the Papal Decree of 1888 against the Plan of Campaign and Boycotting in Ireland. There is no question of parties or of politics in the one case or in the other. When Dr. M'Glynn talked about the private ownership of land in New York as "against natural justice," he flung himself not only against the Eighth Commandment and the teachings of the Catholic Church, touching the rights of property, but against the constitutions of the State of New York and of the United States. That "private property shall not be taken for public uses without just compensation" is a fundamental provision of the Constitution of the United States, which is itself a part of the Constitution of every State of the Union; and the right of private ownership in land is defined and protected beyond doubt or cavil in New York under the State Constitution. An Act passed in 1830 provides and declares that all lands within the State "are allodial, so that, subject only to the liability to escheat, the entire and absolute property is vested in the owners according to the nature of their respective estates."

By this Act "all feudal tenures of every description, with all their incidents," were "abolished."

Most of the "feudal incidents" of the socage tenure had been previously abolished by an Act passed in 1787, under the first Constitution of the State, adopted at Kingston in 1777, a year after the Declaration of American Independence; and socage tenure by fixed and determinate service, not military or variable by the lord at his will, had been adopted long before by an Act of the first Assembly of the Province of New York held in 1691 under the first Royal Governor, after the reconquest of the province from Holland, and in the reign of William and Mary. This Act provided that all lands should "be held in free and common socage according to the tenure of East Greenwich in England." It is an interesting circumstance that the right of private ownership in land, thus rooted in our history, should have been defended against a threatening revolutionary movement in New York by the courage and loyalty to the Constitution of his country as well as to his Church of a Catholic Archbishop. For this same Assembly of the Province of New York in 1693, in an Act "to maintain Protestant ministers and churches," enacted that "every Jesuit and popish priest" found in the Province after a certain day named, should be put into "perpetual imprisonment," with the proviso that if he escaped and was retaken he should suffer death. And even in the Constitution of 1777 the

Protestantism of New York expressed its hostility to the Catholic Church by exacting subjection "in all matters ecclesiastical as well as civil."

The position of the Archbishop, both as a churchman and as a citizen, was impregnable. When Dr. M'Glynn advocated the plan of Henry George, he advocated at one and the same time the immoral seizure and confiscation of the whole income of many persons within the protection of the Constitution of New York, and the overthrow of the Constitution of that State and of the United States. It may be within the competency of the British Parliament to enact such a confiscation of rent without a revolution, there being not only no allodial tenure of land in Great Britain, but, it would appear, no limit to the power of a British Parliament over the lives, liberties, and property of British subjects, but the will of its members. But it is not within the competency of the Congress of the United States, or of the Assembly of New York, to do such a thing, the powers of these bodies being controlled and defined by written Constitutions, which can only be altered or amended in a prescribed manner and through prescribed and elaborate forms.

VII.

By the middle of October 1886 it became clear that Mr. George, whose candidacy had at first been regarded with indifference by the party managers, both Democratic and Republican, in New York, would command a vote certainly larger than that of one of these parties, and possibly larger than that of either of them. To put him at the head of a poll of three parties would elect him. This was so apparent that he and his friends, including Dr. M'Glynn and Mr. Davitt, were warranted in expecting a victory.

It was hardly therefore by a mere coincidence that this precise time was selected for opening the war in Ireland against Rent. It is quite possible that if Mr. Dillon and his Parliamentary friends had been in less of a hurry to open this war before the return of Mr. Davitt from America, it might have been opened in a manner less "politically stupid," if not less "morally wrong." But, of course, if Mr. Henry George had been elected Mayor of New York, as he came so near to being in November 1886, and Mr. Davitt had returned to Ireland with the prestige of contributing to place him in the municipal chair of the most important city in the New World, Mr. Dillon and his Parliamentary friends would probably have found it necessary to accept a much less conspicuous part in the conduct of the campaign.

It was on the 17th of October 1886 that Mr. John Dillon, M.P., first promulgated the "Plan of Campaign" at Portumna, in a speech which was promptly flashed under the Atlantic to New York, there to feed the flame, already fanned by the eloquence of Dr. M'Glynn, into a blaze of enthusiasm for the apostle of the New Gospel of Confiscation.

Had the "Plan of Campaign" then been met by the highest local authority of the Catholic Church in Ireland, as Henry George's doctrine of Confiscation was met in New York by Archbishop Corrigan, it might never have been necessary to issue the Papal Decree of April 1888. But while the Bishop of Limerick unhesitatingly denounced the "Plan of Campaign" as "politically stupid and morally wrong," the Archbishop of Dublin bestowed upon it what may be called a left-handed benediction. Admitting that it empowered one of the parties to a contract to "fix the terms on which that contract should continue in force," the Archbishop actually condoned the claim of this immoral power by the tenant, on the ground that the same immoral power had been theretofore exercised by the landlord! Peter having robbed Paul from January to July, that is, Paul should be encouraged by his spiritual guides to rob Peter from July to January!

PROLOGUE   lxiii

That the Catholic Church should even seem for a time to speak with two voices on such a point as the moral quality of political machinery, or that speaking with one voice upon such a point in America, it should even seem to speak with another voice in Ireland, would clearly be a disaster to the Church and to civilisation. From the moment therefore, in 1886, when the issue between Dr. M'Glynn and the Archbishop of New York was defined, as I have shown, and the Irish National League, with a quasi-indorsement from the Archbishop of Dublin, had arrayed itself practically and openly on the side of Dr. M'Glynn and against the Archbishop of New York, interests far transcending those of any political party in Ireland, in Great Britain, or in the United States, were involved. Unfortunately for the immediate and decisive settlement by Rome of the issue between Dr. M'Glynn and the Archbishop of New York, a certain vague but therefore more vexatious measure of countenance had been given, before that issue was raised, to the theories of Mr. Henry George by another American prelate, the Cardinal Archbishop of Baltimore, and by more than one eminent ecclesiastic in Europe. Of course this would have been impossible had these ecclesiastics penetrated, like Dr. M'Glynn, to the heart of Mr. George's contention, or discerned with the acumen of the

Archbishop of New York the fundamental difference between any imaginable exercise of the power of taxation by a Constitutional Government, and Mr. George's doctrine of the Confiscation of Rent. But this having occurred, it was inevitable that Rome, which has to deal with a world-wide and complex system of the most varied and delicate human affairs, should proceed in the matter with infinite patience and care. In January 1887 the Propaganda accordingly cabled thus to the Archbishop of New York,—Dr. M'Glynn persisting in his refusal to go to Rome—" for prudential reasons Propaganda has heretofore postponed action in the case of Dr. M'Glynn. The Sovereign Pontiff has now taken the matter into his own hands."

In the hands of his Holiness the matter was safe; and in the Papal Decree of April 20, 1888, we have at once the most conclusive vindication of the wisdom and courage shown by the Archbishop of New York in 1886, and the most emphatic condemnation of the attitude assumed in 1886 by the Archbishop of Dublin.

VIII.

It must not be assumed that Mr. George has been finally defeated in America. On the contrary, he was never more active. A legacy left to him by an Irish-American for the propagation of his doctrines has just been declared by the Vice-Chancellor of New Jersey, to be invalid on the ground that George's doctrines are "in opposition to the laws"; and this decision has bred an uproar in the press which is reviving popular attention all over the country to the doctrines and to their author. He is astute, persevering, as much in earnest as Mr. Davitt, and as familiar with the weak points in the political machinery of the United States as is Mr. Davitt with the weak points in the political machinery of Great Britain. This is a Presidential year. The election of 1888 will be decided, as was the election of 1884, in New York. The Democratic party go into the contest with a New York candidate, President Cleveland, who was presented to the Convention at St. Louis for nomination, not by an Irishman from New York, but by an Irishman from the hopelessly Republican State of Pennsylvania, and whose renomination, distasteful to the Democratic Governor of the State, was also openly opposed by the Democratic Mayor of the city of New York, Mr. Hewitt, Mr. George's successful competitor in the Municipal election of 1886. Leaving Dr. M'Glynn to uphold the Confiscation of Land against the Pope in New York, as Mr. Davitt, Mr. Dillon, and a certain number of Irish priests uphold the Plan of Campaign and Boycotting against the

Pope in Ireland, Mr. George supports President Cleveland, and in so doing cleverly makes a flank movement towards his "exclusive taxation of land," by promoting, under the cover of "Revenue Reform," an attack on the indirect taxation from which the Federal Revenues are now mainly derived. Meanwhile the Cardinal Archbishop of Baltimore, who is also a political supporter of President Cleveland, has not yet been confronted by the supreme authority at Rome with such a final sentence upon the true nature of Mr. George's "exclusive taxation of land," as the clear-sighted Archbishop of New York is said to be seeking to obtain from the Holy Office. What the end will be I have little doubt. But for the moment, it will be seen, the situation in America is only less confused and troublesome than the situation in Ireland. It is confused and troubled too, as I have tried in this prologue to show, by forces identical in character with those which confuse and trouble the situation in Ireland.

Of the social conditions amid and against which those forces are working in America, I believe myself to have some knowledge.

To get an actual touch and living sense of the social conditions amid and against which they are working in Ireland was my object, I repeat, in making the visits, of which this book is a record. More than this I could not hope, in the time at my disposal, to do. With very much less than this, it appears to me, many persons, whose views of Irish affairs I had been inclined, before making these visits, to regard with respect, must have found it possible to rest content.

CHAPTER I.

DUBLIN, *Monday, Jan.* 30, 1888.—I left London last night. The train was full of people going to attend levees and drawing-rooms about to be held at Dublin Castle.

Near Watford we lost half an hour by the breaking of a connecting-rod; but the London and North-Western is a model railway, and we ran alongside the pier at Holyhead exactly "on time." There is no such railway travelling in America, excepting on the Pennsylvania Central; and the North-Western sleeping-carriages, if less monumental and elaborate than ours, are better ventilated, and certainly not less comfortable.

I had expected to come upon unusual things and people in Ireland, but I had not expected to travel thither in company with an Irish Jacobite. Two of my fellow-passengers, chatting as they smoked their cigarettes in the little vestibule between the cabins of the carriage, had much to say about Lord Ashburnham, and the "Order of the White Rose," and the Grand Mass to be celebrated to-morrow morning at the Church of the Carmelites in London, in memory of Charles Edward Stuart, who died at Rome in 1788, and now lies buried as Charles III., King of Great Britain and Ireland, in the vaults of the Vatican, together with his father "James III.," and his brother "Henry IX." One of the two was as hot and earnest about the "Divine Right of Kings" as the parson who, less than forty years ago, preached a sermon to prove that the great cholera visitation of 1849 was a direct chastisement of the impiety of the Royal Mint in dropping the letters D. G. from the first florins of Queen Victoria issued in that year. He bewailed his sad fate in being called over to Ireland by family affairs at such a moment, and evidently did not know that the Mass in question had been countermanded by the Cardinal Archbishop.

The incident, odd enough in itself, interested me the more that yesterday, as it happens, the Cardinal had spoken with me of this curious affair.

He heard of it for the first time on Saturday, and, sending at once for the priest in charge of the

Carmelite Church, forbade the celebration. Later on in the evening, two strangers came to the Archbishop's house, and in great agitation besought him to allow the arrangements for the Mass to go on. He declined to do this, and sent them away impaled on a dilemma. "What you propose," said the Cardinal, "is either a piece of theatrical tomfoolery, in which case it is unfit to be performed in a church, or it is flat treason, in which case you should be sent to the Tower!"

They went away, like the Senatus of Augsburg from the presence of Napoleon—"*très mortifiés et peu contents.*" After they had gone, the Cardinal remembered that for some time past queer documents had reached him through the post-office, setting forth the doctrine of Divine Right, and the story of the Stuarts. One of these, which with the rest he had thrown into the fire, was an elaborate genealogical chart, designed to show that the crowns of Great Britain and Ireland ought rightfully to be worn by a certain princess in Bavaria!

If there is anything more in all this than a new variety of the "blue China craze," may it not be taken as a symptom of that vague but clearly growing dissatisfaction with the nineteenth century doctrine of government by mere majorities, which is by no means confined to Europe? This feeling underlies the "National Association" for getting a preamble put into the Constitution of the United States, "recognising Almighty God as the source of all authority and power in Civil Government." There was such a recognition in the Articles of Confederation of 1781. Archbishop Ryan of Philadelphia should have mentioned to His Holiness the existence of this Association, when he presented to Leo XIII., the other day at Rome, President Cleveland's curious Jubilee gift of an emblazoned copy of what a Monsignore of my acquaintance calls "the godless American Constitution."[1]

We made a quick quiet passage to Kingstown. These boats—certainly the best appointed of their sort afloat—are owned, I find, in Dublin, and managed exclusively by their Irish owners, to whom the credit therefore belongs of making the mail service between Holyhead and Kingstown as admirable, in

[1] Since this was written fifteen Catholic bishops in England, headed by the Cardinal Archbishop of Westminster, have united (April 12, 1888) in a public protest against the Optional Oaths Bill, in which they say: "To efface the recognition of God in our public legislature is an act which will surely bring evil consequences." Yet how can the recognition of God be more effectually "effaced" than by the unqualified assertion that the will of the people, or of a majority, is the one legitimate source of political authority?

all respects, as the mail services between Dover and the Continental ports are not.

I landed at Kingstown with Lord Ernest Hamilton, M.P. for North Tyrone, with whom I have arranged an expedition to Gweedore in Donegal, one of the most ill-famed of the "congested districts" of Ireland, and just now made a point of special interest by the arrest of Father M'Fadden, the parish priest of the place, for "criminally conspiring to compel and induce certain tenants not to fulfil their legal obligations."

I could understand such a prosecution as this in America, where the Constitution makes it impossible even for Congress to pass laws "impairing the validity of contracts." But as the British Parliament has been passing such laws for Ireland ever since Mr. Butt in 1870 raised the standard of Irish Land Reform under the name of Home Rule, it seems a little absurd, not to say Hibernian, of the British authorities to prosecute Father M'Fadden merely for bettering their own instruction in his own way. I could better understand a prosecution of Father M'Fadden on such grounds by the authorities of his own Church.

A step from the boat at Kingstown puts you into the train for Dublin. Before we got into motion, a weird shape as of one just escaped from the Wild West show of Buffalo Bill peered in at the window, inviting us to buy the morning papers, or a copy of "the greatest book ever published, 'Paddy at Home!'" This proved to be a translation of M. de Mandat Grancey's lively volume, *Chez Paddy*. The vendor, "Davy," is one of the "chartered libertines" of Dublin. He is supposed to be, and I dare say is, a warm Nationalist, but he has a keen eye to business, and alertly suits his cries to his customers. Recognising the Conservative member for North Tyrone, he promptly recommended us to buy the *Irish Times* and the *Express* as "the two best papers in all Ireland." But he smiled approval when I asked for the *Freeman's Journal* also, in which I found a report of a speech delivered yesterday by Mr. Davitt at Rathkeale, chiefly remarkable for a sensible protest against the ridiculous and rantipole abuse lavished upon Mr. Balfour by the Nationalist orators and newspapers. I am not surprised to see this. Mr. Davitt has the stuff in him of a serious revolutionary leader, and no such man can stomach the frothy and foolish vituperation to which parliamentary agitators are addicted, not in Ireland only. Unlike Mr. Parnell, who is forced to have seriously than Englishmen do. Certainly we stand by it more sternly in bad weather. Even so good a Constitutionalist as Professor Parsons at Harvard, I remember, when a student asked him if he would not suspend the *Habeas Corpus* in the case of a man caught hauling down the American flag, promptly replied, " I would not suspend the *Habeas Corpus*; I would suspend the *Corpus*."

We found no " hansoms " at the Dublin Station, only " outside cars," and cabs much neater than the London four-wheelers. One of these brought us at a good pace to Maple's Hotel in Kildare Street, a large, old-fashioned but clean and comfortable house. My windows look down upon a stately edifice of stone erecting on Kildare Street for all sorts of educational and " exhibitional " purposes, with the help of an Imperial grant, I am told, and to be called the Leinster Hall. The style is decidedly composite, with colonnades and loggie and domes and porticos, and recalls the ancient Roman buildings depicted in that fresco of a belated slave-girl knocking at her mistress's door which with its companion pieces is fast fading away upon the walls of the " House of Livia " on the Palatine.

At one end of this street is the fashionable and hospitable Kildare Street Club; at the other the Shelburne Hotel, known to all Americans. This seems to have been "furbished-up" since I last saw it. There, for the last time as it proved, I saw and had speech of my friend of many years, the prince of all preachers in our time, Father Burke of Tallaght and of San Clemente.

I had telegraphed to him from London that I should halt in Dublin for a day, on my way to America, to see him. He came betimes, to find me almost as badly-off as St. Lawrence upon his gridiron. The surgeon whom the hotel people had hastily summoned to relieve me from a sudden attack of that endemic Irish ecstasy, the lumbago, had applied what he called the "heroic treatment" on my telling him that I had no time to be ill, but must spend that day with Father Burke, dine that night with Mr. Irving and Mr. Toole, and go on the next day to America.

"What has this Inquisitor done to you?" queried Father Tom.

"Cauterised me with chloroform."

"Oh! that's a modern improvement! Let me see—" and, scrutinising the results, he said, with a merry twinkle in his deep, dark eyes—"I see how it is! They brought you a veterinary!"

This was in 1878. On that too brief, delightful morning, we talked of all things—supralunar, lunar, and sublunary. Much of Wales, I remember, where he had been making a visit. "A glorious country," he said, "and the Welsh would have been Irish, only they lost the faith." Full of love for Ireland as he was, he was beginning then to be troubled by symptoms in the Nationalist movement, which could not be regarded with composure by one who, in his youth at Rome, had seen, with me, the devil of extremes drive Italy down a steep place into the sea.

Five years afterwards I landed at Queenstown, in July 1883, intending to visit him at Tallaght. But when the letter which I sent to announce my coming reached the monastery, the staunchest soldier of the Church in Ireland lay there literally "dead on the field of honour." Chatham, in the House of Lords, John Quincy Adams, in the House of Representatives, fell in harness, but neither death so speaks to the heart as the simple and sublime self-sacrifice of the great Dominican, dragging himself from his dying bed into Dublin to spend the last splendour of his genius and his life for the starving children of the poor in Donegal.

What would I not give for an hour with him now!

After breakfast I went out to find Mr. Davitt, hoping he might suggest some way of seeing the Nationalist meeting on Wednesday night without undergoing the dismal penance of sitting out all the speeches. I wished also to ask him why at Rathkeale he talked about the Dunravens as "absentees." He was born in Lord Lucan's country, and may know little of Limerick, but he surely ought to know that Adare Manor was built of Irish materials, and by Irish workmen, under the eye of Lord Dunraven, all the finest ornamental work, both in wood and in stone, of the mansion, being done by local mechanics; and also that the present owners of Adare spend a large part of every year in the country, and are deservedly popular. He was not to be found at the National League headquarters, nor yet at the Imperial Hotel, which is his usual resort, as Morrison's is the resort of Mr. Parnell. So I sent him a note through the Post-Office.

"You had better seal it with wax," said a friend, in whose chambers I wrote it.

"Pray, why?"

"Oh! all the letters to well-known people that are not opened by the police are opened by the Nationalist clerks in the Post-Offices. 'Tis a way we've always had with us in Ireland!"

I had some difficulty in finding the local habitation of the "National League." I had been told it was in O'Connell Street, and sharing the usual and foolish aversion of my sex to asking questions on the highway, I perambulated a good many streets and squares before I discovered that it has pleased the local authorities to unbaptize Sackville Street, "the finest thoroughfare in Europe," and convert it into "O'Connell Street." But they have failed so ignominiously that the National League finds itself obliged to put up a huge sign over its doorways, notifying all the world that the offices are not where they appear to be in Upper Sackville Street at all, but in "O'Connell Street." The effect is as ludicrous as it is instructive. Oddly enough, they have not attempted to change the name of another thoroughfare which keeps green the "pious and immortal memory" of William III., dear to all who in England or America go in fear and horror of the scarlet woman that sitteth upon the seven hills! There is a fashion, too, in Dublin of putting images of little white horses into the fanlights over the doorways, which seems to smack of an undue reverence for the Protestant Succession and the House of Hanover.

What you expect is the thing you never find in Ireland. I had rather thoughtlessly taken it for granted the city would be agog with the great Morley reception which is to come off on Wednesday night. There is a good deal about it in the *Freeman's Journal* to-day, but chiefly touching a sixpenny quarrel which has sprung up between the Reception Committee and the Trades Council over the alleged making of contracts by the Committee with "houses not employing members of the regular trades."

. For this the typos and others propose to "boycott" the Committee and the Reception and the Liberators from over the sea. From casual conversations I gather that there is much more popular interest in the release, on Wednesday, of Mr. T. D. Sullivan, ex-Lord Mayor, champion swimmer, M.P., poet, and patriot. A Nationalist acquaintance of mine tells me that in Tullamore Mr. Sullivan has been most prolific of poetry. He has composed a song which I am afraid will hardly please my Irish Nationalist friends in America:

> "We are sons of Sister Isles,
> Englishmen and Irishmen,
> On our friendship Heaven smiles;
> Tyrant's schemes and Tory wiles
> Ne'er shall make us foes again."

There is to be a Drawing-Room, too, at the Castle on Wednesday night. One would not unnaturally gather from the "tall talk" in Parliament and the press that this conjuncture of a great popular demonstration in favour of Irish nationality, with a display of Dublin fashion doing homage to the alien despot, might be ominous of "bloody noses and cracked crowns." Not a bit of it! I asked my jarvey, for instance, on an outside car this afternoon, whether he expected a row to result from these counter currents of the classes and the masses. "A row!" he replied, looking around at me in amazement. "A row is it? and what for would there be? Shure they'll be through with the procession in time to see the carriages!"

Obviously he saw nothing in either show to offend anybody; though he could clearly understand that an intelligent citizen might be vexed if he found himself obliged to sacrifice one of them in order to fully enjoy the other.

Lady Londonderry, it seems, is not yet well enough to cross the Channel; but the Duchess of Marlborough, who is staying here with her nephew the Lord-Lieutenant, has volunteered to assist him in holding the Drawing-Room, whereupon a grave question has arisen in Court circles as to whether the full meed of honours due to a Vice-Queen regnant ought to be paid also to an ex-Vice-Queen. This is debated by the Dublin dames as hotly as official women in Washington fight over the eternal question of the relative precedence due to the wives of Senators and "Cabinet Ministers." It will be a dark day for the democracy when women get the suffrage—and use it.

At luncheon to-day I met the Attorney-General, Mr. O'Brien, who, with prompt Irish hospitality, asked me to dine with him to-morrow night, and Mr. Wilson of the London *Times*, an able writer on Irish questions from the English point of view. Mr. Balfour, who was expected, did not appear, being detained by guests at his own residence in the Park.

I went to see him in the afternoon at the Castle,

and found him in excellent spirits; certainly the mildest-mannered and most sensible despot who ever trampled in the dust the liberties of a free people. He was quite delightful about the abuse which is now daily heaped upon him in speeches and in the press, and talked about it in a casual dreamy way which reminded me irresistibly of President Lincoln, whom, if in nothing else, he resembles alike in longanimity and in length of limb. He had seen Davitt's *caveat*, filed at Rathkeale, against the foolishness of trying to frighten him out of his line of country by calling him bad names. "Davitt is quite right," he said, "the thing must be getting to be a bore to the people, who are not such fools as the speakers take them to be. One of the stenographers told me the other day that they had to invent a special sign for the phrase 'bloody and brutal Balfour,' it is used so often in the speeches." About the prosecution of Father M'Fadden of Gweedore, he knew nothing beyond the evidence on which it had been ordered. This he showed me. If the first duty of a government is to govern, which is the American if not the English way of looking at it, Father M'Fadden must have meant to get himself into trouble when he used such language as this to his people: "I am the law in Gweedore; I despise the recent Coercion Act; if I got a summons to-morrow, I would not obey it." From language like this to the attitude of Father M'Glynn in New York, openly flouting the authority of the Holy See itself, is but an easy and an inevitable step.

Neither "Home Rule" nor any other "Rule" can exist in a country in which men whose words carry any weight are suffered to take up such an attitude. It is just the attitude of the "Comeouters" in New England during my college days at Harvard, when Parker Pillsbury and Stephen Foster used to saw wood and blow horns on the steps of the meeting-houses during service, in order to free their consciences "and protest against the Sabbatarian laws."

To see a Catholic priest assume this attitude is almost as amazing as to see an educated Englishman like Mr. Wilfrid Blunt trying to persuade Irishmen that Mr. Balfour made him the confidant of a grisly scheme for doing sundry Irish leaders to death by maltreating them in prison.

I see with pleasure that the masculine instincts of Mr. Davitt led him to allude to this nonsense yesterday at Rathkeale in a half contemptuous way. Mr. Balfour spoke of it to-day with generosity and good feeling. "When I first heard of it," he said, "I resented it, of course, as an outrageous imputation on Mr. Blunt's character, and denounced it accordingly. What I have since learned leads me to fear that he really may have said something capable of being construed in this absurd sense, but if he did, it must have been under the exasperation produced by finding himself locked up."

I heard the story of Mr. Balfour's meeting with Mr. Blunt very plainly and vigorously told, while I was staying the other day at Knoyle House, in the immediate neighbourhood of Clouds, where the two were guests under conditions which should be at least as sacred in the eyes of Britons as of Bedouins. In Wiltshire nobody seemed for a moment to suppose it possible that Mr. Blunt can have really deceived himself as to the true nature of any conversation he may have had with Mr. Balfour. This is paying a compliment to Mr. Blunt's common sense at the expense of his imagination. In any view of the case, to lie in wait at the lips of a fellow guest in the house of a common friend, for the counts of a political indictment against him, is certainly a proceeding, as Davitt said yesterday of Mr. Blunt's tale of horror, quite "open to question." But, as Mr. Blunt himself has sung, "'Tis conscience makes us sinners, not our sin," and I have no doubt the author of the *Poems of Proteus* really persuaded himself that he was playing lawn tennis and smoking cigarettes in Wiltshire with a modern Alva, cynically vain of his own dark and bloody designs. Now that he finds himself struck down by the iron hand of this remorseless tyrant, why should he not cry aloud and warn, not Ireland alone, but humanity, against the appalling crimes meditated, not this time in the name of "Liberty," but in the name of Order?

What especially struck me in talking with Mr. Balfour to-day was his obviously unaffected interest in Ireland as a country rather than in Ireland as a cock-pit. It is the condition of Ireland, and not the gabble of parties at Westminster about the condition of Ireland, which is uppermost in his thoughts. This, I should say, is the best guarantee of his eventual success.

The weakest point of the modern English system of government by Cabinets surely is the evanescent tenure by which every Minister holds his place. Not only has the Cabinet itself no fixed term of office, being in truth but a Committee of the Legislature clothed with executive authority, but any member of the Cabinet may be forced by events or by intrigues to leave it. In this way Mr. Forster, when he filled the place now held by Mr. Balfour, found himself driven into resigning it by Mr. Gladstone's indisposition or inability to resist the peremptory pressure put upon the British Premier at a critical moment by our own Government in the spring of 1882. Mr. Balfour is in no such peril, perhaps. He is more sure, I take it, of the support of Lord Salisbury and his colleagues than Mr. Forster ever was of the support of Mr. Gladstone; and the "Coercion" law which it is his duty to administer contains no such sweeping and despotic clause as that provision in Mr. Gladstone's "Coercion Act" of 1881, under which persons claiming American citizenship were arrested and indefinitely locked up on "suspicion," until it became necessary for our Government, even at the risk of war, to demand their trial or release.

But if Mr. Balfour were Chief Secretary for Ireland "on the American plan"; if he held his office, that is, for a fixed term of years, and cared nothing for a renewal of the lease, he could not be more pre-occupied than he seems to be with simply getting his executive duty done, or less pre-occupied than he seems to be with what may be thought of his way of getting it done. If all executive officers were of this strain, Parliamentary government might stand in the dock into which Prince Albert put it with more composure, and await the verdict with more confidence. Surely if Ireland is ever to govern herself, she must learn precisely the lesson which Mr. Balfour, I believe, is trying to teach her—that the duty of executive officers to execute the laws is not a thing debateable, like the laws themselves, nor yet determinable, like the enactment of laws, by taking the yeas and the nays. How well this lesson shall be taught must depend, of course, very much upon the quality of the men who make up the machine of Government in Ireland. That the Irish have almost as great a passion for office-holding as the Spanish, we long ago learned in New York, where the percentage of Irish office-holders considerably exceeds the percentage of Irish citizens. And as all the witnesses agree that the Irish Government has for years been to an inordinate degree a Government by patronage, there must doubtless be some reasonable ground for the very general impression that "the Castle" needs overhauling. It is not true, however, I find, although I have often heard it asserted in England, that the Irish Government is officered by Englishmen and Scotchmen exclusively. The murdered Mr. Burke certainly was not an Englishman; and there is an apparent predominance of Irishmen in the places of trust and power. That things at the Castle cannot be nearly so bad, moreover, as we in America are asked to believe, would seem to be demonstrated by the affectionate admiration with which Lord Spencer is now regarded by men like Mr. O'Brien, M.P., who only the other day seemed to regard him as an unfit survival of the Cities of the Plain. If what these men then said of him, and of the Castle generally, was even very partially true—or if being wholly false, these men believed it to be true—every man of them who now touches Lord Spencer's hand is defiled, or defiles him.

But that concerns them. Their present attitude makes Lord Spencer a good witness when he declares that the Civil servants of the Crown in

Ireland, called "the Castle," are "diligent, desire to do their duty with impartiality, and to hold an even balance between opposing interests in Ireland," and maintains that they "will act with impartiality and vigour if led by men who know their own minds, and desire to be firm in the Government of the country." All this being true, Mr. Balfour ought to make his Government a success.

Mr. Balfour introduced me to Sir West Ridgway, the successor of Sir Redvers Buller, who has been rewarded for the great services he did his country in Asia, by being flung into this seething Irish stew. He takes it very composedly, though the climate does not suit him, he says; and has a quiet workmanlike way with him, which impresses one favourably at once.

All the disorderly part of Ireland (for disorder is far from being universal in Ireland) comes under his direct administration, being divided into five divisions on the lines originally laid down in 1881 by Mr. Forster. Over each of these divisions presides a functionary styled a "Divisional Magistrate." The title is not happily chosen, the powers of these officers being rather like those confided to a French Prefect than like those which are associated in

England and America with the title of a "magistrate." They have no judicial power, and nothing to do with the trial of offenders. Their business is to protect life and property, and to detect and bring to justice offenders against the law. They can only be called Magistrates as the Executive of the United States is sometimes called the "Chief Magistrate."

One of the most conspicuous and trusted of these Divisional Magistrates, I find, is Colonel Turner, who was Secretary to the Lord-Lieutenant, under Lord Aberdeen. He is now denounced by the Irish Nationalists as a ruthless tyrant. He was then denounced by the Irish Tories as a sympathiser with Home Rule. It is probable, therefore, that he must be a conscientious and loyal executive officer, who understands and acts upon the plain lines of his executive duty.

I dined to-night at the Castle, not in the great hall or banqueting-room of St. Patrick, which was designed by that connoisseur in magnificence, the famous Lord Chesterfield, during his Viceroyalty, but in a very handsome room of more moderate dimensions. Much of the semi-regal state observed at the Castle in the days of the Georges has been put down with the Battle-Axe Guards of the Lord-

Lieutenant, and with the basset-tables of the "Lady-Lieutenant," as the Vice-queen used to be called. At dinner the Viceroy no longer drinks to the pious and immortal memory of William III., or to the "1st of July 1690." No more does the band play "Lillibullero," and no longer is the pleasant custom maintained, after a dinner to the city authorities of Dublin, of a "loving cup" passed around the table, into which each guest, as it passed, dropped a gold piece for the good of the household. Only so much ceremonial is now observed as suffices to distinguish the residence of the Queen's personal representative from that of a great officer of State, or an opulent subject of high rank.

Dublin Castle indeed is no more of a palace than it is of a castle. Its claim to the latter title rests mainly on the fine old "Bermingham" tower of the time of King John; its claim to the former on the Throne Room, the Council Chamber, and the Hall of St. Patrick already mentioned. This last is a very stately and sumptuous apartment. Just twenty years ago the most brilliant banquet modern Dublin has seen was given in this hall by the late Duke of Abercorn to the Prince and Princess of Wales, to celebrate the installation of the Prince as a Knight of St. Patrick. It is a significant fact, testified to by all the most candid Irishmen I have ever known, that upon the occasion of this visit to Ireland in 1868 the Prince and Princess were received with unbounded enthusiasm by the people of all classes. Yet only the year before, in 1867, the explosion of some gunpowder at Clerkenwell by a band of desperadoes, to the death and wounding of many innocent people, had brought the question of the disestablishment of the Irish Church, in the mind of Mr. Gladstone, within the domain of "practical politics"! By parity of reasoning, one would think, the reception of the heir-apparent and his wife in Ireland ought to have taken that question out of the domain of "practical politics."

The Prince of Wales, it is known, brought away from this visit an impression that the establishment of a prince of the blood in Ireland, or a series of royal visits to Ireland, would go far towards pacifying the relations between the two Islands. Mr. Gladstone thought his Disestablishment would quite do the work. Events have shown that Mr. Gladstone made a sad mistake as to the effect of his measure. The pains which, I am told, were taken by Mr. Deasy, M.P., and others to organise hostile demonstrations at one or two points in the south of Ireland, during a subsequent visit of the Prince and Princess, would seem to show that in the opinion of the Nationalists themselves, the impression of the Prince was more accurate than were the inferences of the Premier.

There is nothing froward or formidable in the aspect of Dublin Castle. It has neither a portcullis nor a drawbridge. People go in and out of it as freely as through the City Hall in New York. There is a show of sentries at the main entrance, and in one of the courts this morning the picturesque band of a Scotch regiment was playing to the delectation of a small but select audience of urchins and little girls. A Dublin mob, never so little in earnest and led by a dozen really determined men, ought to be able to make as short work of it as the hordes of the Faubourgs in Paris made of the Bastille, with its handful of invalids, on that memorable 14th of July, about which so many lies have passed into history, and so much effervescent nonsense is still annually talked and printed.

The greater part of the Castle as it existed when the Irish Parliaments sat there under Elizabeth, and just before the last Catholic Viceroy made Protestantism penal, and planned the transformation of

Ireland into a French province, was burned in the time of James II. The Earl of Arran then reported to his father that "the king had lost nothing but six barrels of gunpowder, and the worst castle in the worst situation in Christendom."

Here, as at Ottawa, a viceregal dinner-table is set off by the neat uniforms and skyblue facings of the aides-de-camp and secretaries. For some mysterious reason Lord Spencer put these officers into chocolate coats with white facings. But the new order soon gave place to the old again.

At the dinner to-night was Lord Ormonde, who is returning to London, but kindly promised to make arrangements for showing me at Kilkenny Castle the muniment room of the Butlers, which contains one of the most valuable private collections of charters and State papers in the realm.

Tuesday, Jan. 31.—I lunched to-day with Sir Michael Morris, the Lord Chief Justice of Ireland, whom I had last seen in Rome at the Jubilee Mass of His Holiness. Sir Michael is one of the recognised lights of social life and of the law in Dublin. While he was in Rome some one highly commended him in the presence of that staunch Nationalist the Archbishop of Dublin, who assented so far as to say,

"Yes, yes, there are worse fellows in Dublin than that Morris!" It would be hard to find a more typical Irishman of the better sort than Sir Michael, a man more sure, in the words of Sheridan, to "carry his honour and his brogue unstained to the grave."

The brogue of Sir Michael, it is said, made his fortune in the House of Commons. It has hardly the glow which made the brogue of Father Burke a memory as of music in the ears of all who heard it, and differs from that miraculous gift of the tongue as a ripe wine of Bordeaux differs from a ripe wine of Burgundy. But to the ordinary brogue of the street and the stage, it is as is a Brane Mouton Rothschild of 1868 to the casual Médoc of a Parisian restaurant. "Do you know Father Healy?" said one of the company to whom I spoke of it; "he was at a wedding with Sir Michael. As the happy pair drove off under the usual shower of rice and old slippers, Sir Michael said to the Father, 'How I wish I had something to throw after her!' 'Ah, throw your brogue after her,' replied the Father."

This brogue comes to Sir Michael lawfully enough. He belongs to one of the fourteen tribes of Galway. His father, Mr. Martin Morris, was High Sheriff of the County of Galway City in 1841, being the first Catholic who had served that office since the time of Tyrconnel. His mother was a Blake of Galway, and the family seat, Spiḍdal, came to them through a Fitzpatrick. "Remember these things," said one of the guests to me, a Catholic from the south of Ireland, "and remember that Sir Michael, like myself, and, so far as I know, like every Irish Catholic in this room to-day, is a thoroughgoing Unionist, who would think it midsummer madness to hand Ireland over to the 'Home Rule' of the 'uncrowned king,' Mr. Parnell, who hasn't a drop, I believe, of Irish blood in his veins, and who, whatever else he may be, is certainly not a Catholic. Didn't Parnell vote at first against religion and in favour of Bradlaugh? and didn't he do this to force the bargain for the clerical franchise at the Parliamentary conventions?"

"But there are some good Catholics, are there not," I answered, "and some good Christians, and of Irish blood too, among the associates of Mr. Parnell?"

"Associates!" he exclaimed; "if you know anything of Mr. Parnell, you must know that he has no associates. He has followers, and he has instruments, but he has no associates. The only Irishmen whom he has really taken counsel with, or treated, I was about to say, with ordinary civility, were Egan and Brennan. His manner with them was always conspicuously different from his cold and almost contemptuous bearing towards the men whom he commands in Parliament, and Egan, who directs his forces in your country, rewards him by calling him 'the great and gifted leader of *our* race!' 'Our race' indeed! Parnell comes of the conquering race in Ireland, and he never forgets it, or lets his subordinates forget it. I was in Galway when he came over there suddenly to quell the revolt organised by Healy. The rebels were at white-heat before he came. But he strode in among them like a huntsman among the hounds—marched Healy off into a little room, and brought him out again in ten minutes, cowed and submissive, but filled, as anybody can see, ever since, with a dull smouldering hate which will break out one of these days, if a good and safe opportunity offers."

"How do you account, then," I asked, "for the support which all these men give Mr. Parnell?"

"For the support which they give him!" exclaimed my new acquaintance, "for the support they give him! Bless your heart, my dear sir, it is he gives them the support! Barring Biggar, who, to do him justice, is as free with his pocket as he is with his tongue—and no man can say more for anybody than that—barring Biggar and M'Kenna and M'Carthy, and perhaps a dozen more, all these men are nominated by Mr. Parnell, and draw salaries from the body he controls; they are paid members, like the working-men members. Support indeed!"

"But the constituencies," I urged, "surely the voters must know and care something about their representatives?

The gentleman from the south of Ireland laughed aloud. "Very clear it is," he said, "that you have made your acquaintance with my dear countrymen in America, or in England perhaps—not in Ireland. Look at Thurles, in January '85! The voters selected O'Ryan; Parnell ordered him off, and made them take O'Connor! The voters take their members to-day from the League—that is, from Mr. Parnell, just as they used to take them from the landlords. What Lord Clanricarde said in Galway, when he made all those fagot votes by cutting up his farms, that he could return his grey mare to Parliament if he liked, Mr. Parnell can say with just as much truth to-day of any Nationalist seat in the country. I tell you, the secret of his power is that he understands the Irish people, and how to ride them. He is a Protestant-ascendency man by blood, and he is fighting the unlucky devils of landlords to-day by the old 'landlord' methods that came to him with his mother's milk—that is rightly speaking, I should say, with his father's," and here he burst out laughing at his own bull—"for his mother, poor lady, she was an American."

"Thank you," I said.

"Oh, no harm at all! But did you ever know her? An odd woman she was, and is."

"Her father," I replied, "was a gallant American sailor of Scottish blood."

"Oh yes, and is it true that he got a great hatred of England from being captured in the *Chesapeake* by the English Captain Broke? I always heard that."

I explained that there were historical difficulties in the way of accepting this legend, and that Commodore Stewart's experiences, during the war of 1812, had been those of a captor, not of a captive.

"Well, a clever woman she is, only very odd. She was a great terror, I remember, to a worthy Protestant parson, near Avondale; she used to come at him quite unexpectedly with such a power of theological discussion, and put him beside himself with questions he couldn't answer."

"Very likely," I replied, "but she has transferred her interest to politics now; and she had the good sense, at the Chicago Convention in 1886, to warn the physical-force men against showing their hand too plainly in support of her son."

A curious conversation, as showing the personal bitterness of politics here. It reminded me of Dr. Duché's description in his famous letter to Washington of the party which carried the Declaration of Independence through the Continental Congress. But it had a special interest for me as confirming the inferences I have often drawn as to Mr. Parnell's relations with his party, from his singular and complete isolation among them. I remember the profound astonishment of my young friend Mr. D——, of New York, who, as the son of, perhaps, the most conspicuous and influential American advocate of Home Rule, had confidently counted upon seeing Mr. Parnell in London, when he found that the most important member of the Irish Parliamentary party, in point of position, was utterly unable to get at Mr. Parnell for him, or even to ascertain where Mr. Parnell could be reached by letter.

Though a staunch Unionist, Sir Michael is no blind admirer of things as they are, nor even a thick-and-thin partisan of English rule in Ireland. "If you will have the Irish difficulty in a nutshell," he is reported to have said to a prosy British politician, "here it is: It is simply a very dull people trying to govern a very bright people."

He has quick and wide intellectual sympathies, or, as he put it to a lawyer who was kindly enlightening him about some matters of scientific notoriety, "I don't live in a cupboard myself." His own terse summing up of the Irish difficulty could hardly be better illustrated than by the current story of the discomfiture of an English Treasury official, who came into his official chambers to complain of the expenditure for fuel in the Court over which he presides. The Lord Chief-Justice looked at him quietly while he set forth his errand, and then, ringing a bell on his table, said to the servant who responded: "Tell Mary the man has come about the coals."

At Sir Michael's I had some conversation also with Mr. Justice Murphy, who won a great reputation in connection with those murders in the Phœnix Park, which went near to breaking the heart and hope of poor Father Burke, and with

Lord and Lady Ashbourne, whom I had not seen since I met them some years ago under the hospitable roof of Lord Houghton. Lord Ashbourne was then Mr. Gibson, Q.C. He is now the Lord Chancellor of Ireland, and the author of the Land Purchase Act of 1885, which many well-informed and sensible men regard as the Magna Charta of peace in Ireland, while others of equal authority assure me that by reversing the principle of the Bright clauses in the Act of 1871 it has encouraged the tenants to expect an eventual concession of the land-ownership to them on merely nominal terms.

Naturally enough, he is carped at and reviled almost as much by his political friends as by his political foes. In the time of Sir Michael Hicks Beach I remember hearing Lord Ashbourne denounced most bitterly by a leading Tory light as "a Home Ruler in disguise, who had bedevilled the Irish Question by undertaking to placate the country if it could be left to be managed by him and by Lord Carnarvon."

The disguise appears to me quite impenetrable, and after my talk with him, I remembered a characteristic remark about him made to me by Lord Houghton after he had gone away: "A very clever man with a very clever wife. He ought to be on our side, but he has everything the Tories lack, so they have stolen him, and will make much of him, and keep him. But one of these days he will do them some great service, and then they'll never forgive him!"

Lord Ashbourne went off early to look up some fine old wooden mantelpieces and wainscotings in the "slums" of Dublin. A brisk trade it seems has for some time been driven in such relics of the departed splendour of the Irish capital. In the last century, when Dublin was further from London than London now is from New York, the Irish landlords were more fond of living in Dublin than a good many of the Irish Nationalists I know now are. In this way the Iron Duke came to be born in Dublin, where his father and mother had a handsome town house, whereas when they went up to London they used to lodge, according to old Lady Cork, "over a pastry-cook's in Oxford Street." In those days there must have been a good many fine solidly built and well decorated mansions in Dublin, of a type not unlike that of the ample rather stately and periwigged houses, all British brick without, and all Santo Domingo mahogany within, which, in my schoolboy days, used to give such a dignified old-world air to Third and Fourth Streets in Philadelphia. It is among such of these as are still standing, and have come to vile uses, that the foragers from London now find their harvest.

From the Chief-Justice's I went with Lord Ernest Hamilton to a meeting of the Irish Unionists. Admission was by tickets, and the meeting evidently "meant business." I suppose Presbyterian Ulster was largely represented: but Mr. Smith Barry of Fota Island, near Cork, one of the kindest and fairest, as well as one of the most determined and resolute, of the southern Irish landlords, was there, and the most interesting speech I heard was made by a Catholic lawyer of Dublin, Mr. Quill, Q.C., who grappled with the question of distress among the Irish tenants, and produced some startling evidence to show that this distress is by no means so great or so general as it is commonly assumed to be.[1] Able speeches were also made by Mr. T. W. Russell, M.P. for Tyrone, and by Colonel Saunderson, the champion of Ulster at Westminster. Both of these members, and especially

---

[1] Mr. Quill stated that the Savings-Banks deposits increased in Ireland during 1887 eight per cent. more than in thrifty Scotland, and *forty per cent.* more than in England and Wales!

Colonel Saunderson, "went for" their Nationalist colleagues with an unparliamentary plainness of speech which commanded the cordial sympathy of their audience. "Is it possible," asked Colonel Saunderson, "that you should ever consent, on any terms, to be governed by such——, well, by such wretches as these?" to which the audience gave back an unanimous "Never," neither thundered nor shouted, but growled, like Browning's "growl at the gates of Ghent,"—a low deep growl like the final notice served by a bull-dog, which I had not heard since the meetings which, at the North, followed the first serious fighting of the Civil War. I was much struck, too, by the prevalence among the audience of what may be called the Old Middle State type of American face and head. A majority of these men might have come straight from those slopes of the Alleghany which, from Pennsylvania down to the Carolinas, were planted so largely by the only considerable Irish emigrations known to our history, before the great year of famine, 1847, the Irish emigrations which followed the wars against the woollen industries in the seventeenth century, and the linen industries in the eighteenth. A staunch, doggedly Protestant people, loving the New England

Puritans and the Anglicans of Eastern Virginia little better than the Maryland Catholics, but contributing more than their full share of traditional antipathy to that extreme dislike and dread of the Roman Church which showed itself half-a-century ago in the burning of convents, and thirty years ago gave life and fire to the Know-Nothing movement. Even so late as at the time of Father Burke's grand and most successful mission to America, I remember how much astonished and impressed he was by the vigour and the virulence of these feelings. One of the bishops, he told me, in a great diocese tried (though of course in vain) to dissuade him on this account from wearing his Dominican dress. These anti-Catholic passions are much stronger in America to-day than it always suits our politicians to remember, though to forget it may some day be found very dangerous. Even now two of the ablest prelates of the most liberal of the Protestant American bodies, Bishop Cleveland Coxe of Western New York, and Bishop Beckwith of Georgia, the latter of whom I met the other day in Rome on his return from Palestine, are promoting what looks very much like a crusade against the plan for establishing a Catholic University at Washington.

Bishop Cleveland Coxe's denunciations of what he calls "the alien Church," point straight to a revival of the "Native American" movement; and I fear that President Cleveland's gift of a copy of the Constitution to Leo XIII. will hardly make American Catholics forget either the hereditary anti-Catholic feeling which led him, when Governor of New York, to imperil the success of the Democratic party by his dogged resistance to the Catholic demand for the endowment of Catholic schools and protectories, or the scandalous persecution (it can be called by no other name) of Catholics in Alaska, which was carried on in the name and under the patronage of his sister, Miss Cleveland, by a local missionary of the Presbyterian Church, to the point of the removal by the President of a Federal judge, who dared to award a Catholic native woman from Vancouver the custody of her own child.

It is hard to imagine a greater misfortune for the Church in Ireland, and for both the Church and the Irish race in America, than the identification of the Home Rule movement with the Church, and its triumph, after being so identified, and with the help of British sympathisers and professional politicians, over the resistance of Protestant Ireland.

This dilemma of the Church in Ireland, plainly seen at Rome, as I know, to-day, was forcibly presented in the speech of Colonel Saunderson.

The chair at this Loyalist meeting was filled by the Provost of Trinity, Dr. Jellett, a man of winning and venerable aspect, a kind of "angelic doctor," indeed, whose musical and slightly tremulous voice gave a singular pathos and interest to his brief but very earnest speech.[1]

To-night I dined with the Attorney-General, Mr. O'Brien. Among the company were the Chief-Baron Palles, whose appointment dates back to Mr. Gladstone's Administration of 1873, but who is now an outspoken opponent of Home Rule; Judge O'Brien, an extremely able man, with the face of an eagle; Mr. Carson, Q.C.; and other notabilities of the bench and bar. My neighbours at table were a charming and agreeable bencher of the King's Inn, Mr. Atkinson, Q.C., a leader of the Irish bar, and Mr. T. W. Russell, M.P., who told me some amusing things of one of his colleagues, an ideal Orangeman, who writes blood-curdling romances in the vein of La Tosca, and goes in fear of the

[1] This was the Provost's last appearance in public. He died rather suddenly a few weeks afterwards.

re-establishment of the Holy Office in Dublin and London. In view of the clamours about the severity of the bench in Ireland, it was edifying to find an Irish Judge astonished by the drastic decisions of our Courts in regard to the anarchists who were hanged at Chicago, after a thorough and protracted review of the law in their cases. He thought no Court in Great Britain or Ireland could have dealt with them thus stringently, it being understood that the charge of murder against them rested on their connection, solely as provocative instigators to violence, with the actual throwing of the bombs among the police.

Some good stories were told by the lawyers; one of a descendant of the Irish Kings, a lawyer more remarkable for his mental gifts than for his physical graces.

A peasant looking him carefully over at Cork whispered to a neighbour, "And is he really of the ould blood of the Irish kings now, indeed?"

"He is indeed!"

"Well, then, I don't wonder the Saxons conquered the Island!"

Of the Home Rule movement one of the lawyers said to me, "The whole thing is a business operation mainly—a business operation with the people who see in it the hope of appeasing their land hunger—and a business operation for the agitators who live by it. Its main strength, outside of the priests, who for one reason or another countenance or foment it, is in the small country solicitors. The five hundred thousand odd Irish tenants are the most litigious creatures alive. They are always after the local lawyer with half-a-crown to fight this, that, or the other question with some neighbour or kinsman, usually a kinsman. So the solicitors know the whole country."

"When the League has chosen a spot in which to work the 'Plan of Campaign,' the local attorney whips up the tenants to join it. The poorer tenants are the most easily pushed into the plan, having least to lose by it. But the lawyer takes the well-to-do tenants in hand, and promises them that if they yield to the patriotic pressure of the League, and come to grief by so doing, the landlord will at all events have to pay the costs of the proceedings. It is this promise which finally brings down most of them. To enjoy the luxury of a litigation without paying for it tempts them almost as strongly as the prospect of getting the land without paying for it. You will find that the League always insists, when things come to a settlement, that the landlord shall pay the costs. If the landlord through poverty of spirit or of purse succumbs to this demand, the League scores a victory. If the landlord resists, it is a bad job for the League. The local lawyer is discredited in the eyes of his clients, and if he is to get any fees he must come down upon his clients for them. Naturally his clients resent this. If Mr. Balfour keys up the landlords to stand out manfully against paying for all the trouble and loss they are continually put to, he will take the life of the League so far as Ireland is concerned. As things now stand, it is almost the only thriving industry in Ireland!"

Wednesday, Feb. 1.—This morning I called with Lord Ernest Hamilton upon Sir Bernard Burke, the Ulster King-at-Arms, and the editor or author of many other well-known publications, and especially of the "Peerage," sometimes irreverently spoken of as the "British Bible."

Sir Bernard's offices are in the picturesque old "Bermingham" tower of the castle. There we found him wearing his years and his lore as lightly as a flower, and busy in an ancient chamber, converted by him into a most cosy modern study. He received us with the most cordial courtesy, and was good enough to conduct us personally through his domain.

Many of the State papers formerly kept here have been removed to the Four Courts building. But Sir Bernard's tower is still filled with documents of the greatest historical interest, all admirably docketed and arranged on the system adopted at the Hôtel Soubise, now the Palace of the Archives in Paris.

These documents, like the tower itself, take us back to the early days when Dublin was the stronghold of the Englishry in Ireland, and its citizens went in constant peril of an attack from the wild and "mere Irish" in the hills. The masonry of the tower is most interesting. The circular stone floors made up of slabs held together without cement, like the courses in the towers of Sillustani, by their exact adjustment, are particularly noteworthy. High up in the tower Sir Bernard showed us a most uncomfortable sort of cupboard fashioned in the huge wall of the tower, and with a loophole for a window. In this cell the Red Hugh O'Donnell of Tyrconnel was kept as a prisoner for several years under Elizabeth. He was young and lithe, however, and after his friends had tried in vain to buy him out, a happy thought one day struck him. He squeezed himself through the loophole, and, dropping unhurt to the ground, escaped to the mountains. There for a long time he made head against the English power. In 1597 he drove Sir Conyers Clifford from before the castle of Ballyshannon, with great loss to the English, and when he could no longer keep the field, he sought refuge in Spain. He was with the Spanish, as Prince of Tyrconnel, at the crushing defeat of Kinsale in 1601. Escaping again, he died, poisoned, at Simancas the next year.

Sir Bernard showed us, among other curious manuscripts, a correspondence between one Higgins, a trained informer, and the Castle authorities in 1798. This correspondence shows that the revolutionary plans of the Nationalists of 1798 were systematically laid before the Government.

When one thinks how very much abler were the leaders of the Irish rebellion in 1798 than are the present heads of the Irish party in Parliament, how much greater the provocations to rebellion given the Irish people then were than they are now even alleged to be—how little the Irish people in general have now to gain by rebellion, and how much to lose, it is hard to resist a suspicion that it must be even easier now than it was in 1798 for the Government to tap the secrets of the organisations opposed to it.

Sir Bernard showed us also a curious letter written by Henry Grattan to the founder of the great Guinness breweries, which have carried the fame of Dublin porter into the uttermost parts of the earth. The Guinnesses are now among the wealthiest people of the kingdom, and Ireland certainly owes a great deal to them as "captains of industry," but they are not Home Rulers.

At the Kildare Street Club in the afternoon I talked with two Irish landlords from the north of Ireland, who had come up to take their womenkind to the Drawing-Room.

I was struck by their indifference to the political excitements of the day. One of them had forgotten that the Ripon and Morley reception was to take place to-night. The other called it "the love-feast of Voltaire and the Vatican." Both were much more fluent about hunting and farming. I asked if the hunting still went on in their part of the island.

"It has never stopped for a moment," he replied.

"No," added the other, "nor ever a dog poisoned.

They were poisoned, whole packs of them, in the papers, but not a dog really. The stories were printed just to keep up the agitation, and the farmers winked at it so as not to be 'bothered.'"

Both averred that they got their rents "fairly well," but both also said that they farmed much of their own land. One, a wiry, energetic, elderly man, of a brisk presence and ruddy complexion, said he constantly went over to the markets in England. "I go to Norwich," he said, "not to Liverpool. Liverpool is only a meat-market, and overdone at that. Norwich is better for meat and for stores." Both agreed this was a great year for the potatoes, and said Ireland was actually exporting potatoes to America. One mentioned a case of two cargoes of potatoes just taken from Dundrum for America, the vessel which took them having brought over six hundred tons of hay from America.

They were breezy, out-of-door men, both of them. One amused us with a tale of espying, the other day, two hounds, a collie dog, a terrier, and eighteen cats all amicably running together across a farmyard, with their tails erect, after a dairymaid who was to feed them. The other capped this with a story of a pig on his own place, which follows one of his farm lads about like a dog,—" the only pig," he said, "I ever saw show any human feeling!" The gentleman who goes to Norwich thought the English landlords were in many cases worse off than the Irish. "Ah, no!" interfered the other, "not quite; for if the English can't get their rents, at least they keep their land, but we can neither get our rents nor keep our land!" They both admitted that there had been much bad management of the land in Ireland, and that the agents had done the owners as well as the tenants a great deal of harm in the past, but they both maintained stoutly that the legislation of late years had been one-sided and short-sighted. "The tenants haven't got real good from it," said one, "because the claims of the landlord no longer check their extravagance, and they run more in debt than ever to the shopkeepers and traders, who show them little mercy." Both also strenuously insisted on the gross injustice of leaving the landlords unrelieved of any of the charges fixed upon their estates, while their means of meeting those charges were cut down by legislation.

"You have no landlords in America," said one, "but if you had, how would you like to be saddled with heavy tithe charges for a Disestablished Church at the same time that your tenants were relieved of their dues to you?"

I explained to him that so far from our having no landlords in America, the tenant-farmer class is increasing rapidly in the United States, while it is decreasing in the Old World, while the land laws, especially in some of our older Western States, give the landlords such absolute control of their tenants that there is a serious battle brewing at this moment in Illinois[1] between a small army of tenants and their absentee landlord, an alien and an Irishman, who holds nearly a hundred thousand acres in the heart of the State, lives in England, and grants no leases, except on the condition that he shall receive from his tenants, in addition to the rent, the full amount of all taxes and levies whatsoever made upon the lands they occupy.

"God bless my soul!" exclaimed the gentleman who goes to Norwich, "if that is the kind of laws your American Irish will give us with Home Rule, I'll go in for it to-morrow with all my heart!"

[1] In the Census of 1880 it appears that of 255,741 farms in Illinois, 59,624 were held on the métayer system, pronounced by Toubeau the worst of systems, and 20,620 on a money rental.

After an early dinner, I set out with Lord Ernest to see the Morley-Ripon procession. It was a good night for a torchlight parade—the weather not too chill, and the night dark. The streets were well filled, but there was no crowding—no misconduct, and not much excitement. The people obviously were out for a holiday, not for a "demonstration." It was Paris swarming out to the Grand Prix, not Paris on the eve of the barricades; very much such a crowd as one sees in the streets and squares of New York on a Fourth of July night, when the city fathers celebrate that auspicious anniversary with fireworks at the City Hall, and not in the least such a crowd as I saw in the streets of New York on the 12th of July 1871, when, thanks to General Shaler and the redoubtable Colonel "Jim Fiske," a great Orange demonstration led to something very like a massacre by chance medley.

Small boys went about making night hideous with tom-toms, extemporised out of empty fig-drums, and tooting terribly upon tin trumpets. There was no general illumination, but here and there houses were bright with garlands of lamps, and rockets ever and anon went up from the house-tops.

We made our way to the front of a mass of people near one of the great bridges, over which the procession was to pass on its long march from Kingstown to the house of Mr. Walker, Q.C., in Rutland Square, where the distinguished visitors were to meet the liberated Lord Mayor, with Mr. Dwyer Gray, and other local celebrities. A friendly citizen let us perch on his outside car.

The procession presently came in sight, and a grand show it made—not of the strictly popular and political sort, for it was made up of guilds and other organised bodies on foot and on horseback, marching in companies—but imposing by reason of its numbers, and of the flaring torches. Of these there were not so many as there should have been to do justice to the procession. The crowd cheered from time to time, with that curious Irish cheer which it is often difficult to distinguish from groaning, but the only explosive and uproarious greeting given to the visitors in our neighbourhood came from a member of " the devout female sex," a young lady who stood up between two friends on the top of a car very near us, and imperilled both her equilibrium and theirs by wildly waving her handkerchief in the air, and crying out at the top of a somewhat husky voice, "Three cheers for Mecklenburg Street! Three cheers for Mecklenburg Street!"

This made the crowd very hilarious, but as Lord Ernest's local knowledge did not enable him to enlighten me as to the connection between Mecklenburg Street and the liberation of Ireland, I must leave the mystery of their mirth unsolved till a more convenient season.

At Rutland Square the crowd was tightly packed, but perfectly well-behaved, and the guests were enthusiastically cheered. But even before they had entered the house of Mr. Walker it began to break up, and long files of people wended their way to see "the carriages" hastening with their lovely freight to the Castle. Thither Lord Ernest has just gone, arrayed in a captivating Court costume of black velvet, with cut-steel buttons, sword, and buckles—just the dress in which Washington used to receive his guests at the White House, and in which Senator Seward, I remember, insisted in 1860 on getting himself presented by Mr. Dallas to Queen Victoria at Buckingham Palace.

CHAPTER II.

Sion House, County Tyrone, *Feb.* 3*d*.—Hearing nothing from Mr. Davitt yesterday, I gave up the idea of attending the Ripon-Morley meeting last night. As I have come to Ireland to hear what people living in Ireland have to say about Irish affairs, I see no particular advantage in listening to imported eloquence on the subject, even from so clever a man as his books prove Mr. Morley to be, and from so conscientious a man as an acquaintance, going back to the days when he sat with Kingsley at the feet of Maurice, makes me believe Lord Ripon to be. How much either of them knows about Ireland is another matter. A sarcastic Nationalist acquaintance of mine, with whom I conversed about the visitors yesterday, assured me it had been arranged that Lord Ripon should wear the Star of the Garter, "so the people might know him from Morley." When I observed that Dublin must have a short memory to forget so soon the face of a Chief Secretary, he replied: "Forget his face? Why, they never saw his face! It's little enough he was here, and indoors he kept when here he was. He shook hands last night with more Irishmen than ever he spoke to while he was Chief Secretary; for he used to say then, I am told, in the Reform Club, that the only way to get along with the Irish was to have nothing to do with them!"

There was a sharp discussion, I was told, in the private councils of the Committee yesterday as to whether the Queen should be "boycotted," and the loyal sentiments usual in connection with her Majesty's name dropped from the proceedings. I believe it was finally settled that this might put the guests into an awkward position, both of them having worn her Majesty's uniform of State as public servants of the Crown.

During the day I walked through many of the worst quarters of Dublin. I met fewer beggars in proportion than one encounters in such parts of London as South Kensington and other residential regions not over-frequented by the perambulating policemen; but I was struck by the number of persons—and particularly of women—who wore that most pathetic of all the liveries of distress, "the look of having seen better days." In the most wretched streets I traversed there was more squalor than suffering—the dirtiest and most ragged people in them showing no signs of starvation, or even of insufficient rations; and certainly in the most dismal alleys and by-streets, I came upon nothing so revolting as the hives of crowded misery which make certain of the tenement house quarters of New York more gruesome than the Cour des Miracles itself used to be.

This morning at 7.25 A.M. I left Dublin with Lord Ernest Hamilton for Strabane. My attention was distracted from the reports of the great meeting by the varied and picturesque beauty of the landscape, through which we ran at a very respectable rate in a very comfortable carriage. We passed Dundalk, where Edward Bruce got himself crowned king of Ireland, after his brother Robert had won a throne in Scotland.

These masterful Normans, all over Europe from Apulia to Britain, worked out the problem of "satisfied nationalities" much more successfully and simply than Napoleon III. in our own day. If

Edward Bruce broke down where Robert succeeded, the causes of his failure may perhaps be worth considering even now by people who have set themselves the task in our times of establishing "an Irish nationality." Leaving out the Cromwellian English of Tipperary and the South, and the Scotch who have done for Ulster, what he aimed at for all Ireland, they have very much the same materials to deal with as those which he dismally failed to fashion.

Drogheda stands beautifully in a deep valley through which flows the Boyne Water, spanned by one of the finest viaducts in Europe. Here, two years after the discovery of America, Poyning's Parliament enacted that all laws passed in Ireland must be subject to approval by the English Privy Council. I wonder nobody has proposed a modification of this form of Home Rule for Ireland now. Earl Grey's recent suggestion that Parliamentary government be suspended for ten years in Ireland, which I heard warmly applauded by some able lawyers and business men in Dublin, involves like this an elimination of the Westminster debates from the problem of government in Ireland. As we passed Drogheda, Father Burke's magnificent presence and thrilling voice came back to me out of the mist of years, describing with an indignant pathos, never to be forgotten, the fearful scenes which followed the surrender of Sir Arthur Ashton's garrison, when "for the glory of God," and "to prevent the further effusion of blood," Oliver ordered all the officers to be knocked on the head, and every tenth man of the soldiers killed, and the rest shipped as slaves to the Barbadoes. But how different was the spirit in which the great Dominican recalled these events from that in which the "popular orators," scattering firebrands and death, delight to dwell upon them!

At Strabane station we found a handsome outside car waiting on us, and drove off briskly for this charming place, the home of one of the most active and prosperous manufacturers in Ireland. A little more than half way between the station and Sion House, Mr. Herdman met us afoot. We jumped off and walked up with him. Sion House, built for him by his brother, an accomplished architect, is a handsome Queen Anne mansion. It stands on a fine knoll, commanding lovely views on all sides. Below it, and beyond a little stream, rise the extensive flax-mills which are the life of the place, under the eye and within touch of the hand of the master. These works were established here by Mr. Herdman's father, after he had made a vain attempt to establish them at Ballyshannon in Donegal, half a century ago. As all salmon fishers know, the water-power is admirable at Ballyshannon, where the Erne pours in torrents down a thirty feet fall. But the ignorance and indolence of the people made Ballyshannon quite impossible, with this result, that while the Erne still flows unvexed to the sea, and the people of Ballyshannon live very much as they lived in 1835, here at Sion the Mourne enables 1100 Irish operatives to work up £90,000 worth of Irish flax every year into yarn for the Continent, and to divide among themselves some £20,000 a year in wages.

After luncheon we walked with Mr. Herdman through the mills and the model village which has grown up around them. Everywhere we found order, neatness, and thrift. The operatives are almost all people of the country, Catholics and Protestants in almost equal numbers. "I find it wise," said Mr. Herdman, "to give neither religion a preponderance, and to hold my people of both religions to a common standard of fidelity and efficiency." The greatest difficulty he has had to contend with is the ineradicable objection of some of the peasantry to continuous industry. He told us of a strapping lass of eighteen who came to the mills, but very soon gave up and went back to the parental shebeen in the mountains rather than get up early in the morning to earn fourteen shillings a week.

Three weeks of her work would have paid the year's rent of the paternal holding.

In the village, which is regularly laid out, is a reading-room for the workpeople. There are cricket clubs, and one of the mill buildings (just now crammed with bales of flax) has been fitted up by Mr. Herdman as a theatre. There is a drop-curtain representing the Lake of Como, and the flies are flanked by life-size copies in plaster of the Apollo Belvidere and the Medicean Venus. This is a development I had hardly looked to see in Ulster.

After we had gone over the works thoroughly, Mr. Herdman took us back, on a transparent pretext of enlightened curiosity touching certain qualities of spun flax, to give us a glimpse of the "beauty of Sion"—a well-grown graceful girl of fifteen or sixteen summers. She concentrated her attention, as soon as we appeared, upon certain mysterious bobbins and spindles, with an exaggerated determination which proved how completely she saw through our futile and frivolous devices. Mr. Herdman told us, as we came away discomfited, a droll story of the ugliest girl ever employed here—a girl so preternaturally ugly that one of his best blacksmiths having been entrapped into offering to marry her, lost heart of grace on the eve of the sacrifice, and, taking ship at Derry for America, fled from Sion for ever.

In the evening came, with other guests, Dr. Webb, Q.C., Regius Professor of Laws and Public Orator of Trinity at Dublin, well known both as a Grecian capable of composing "skits" as clever as the verses yclept Homerstotle—in which the *Saturday Review* served up the Donnelly nonsense about Bacon and Shakespeare—and as a translator of *Faust*. He was abused by the Loyalists at Dublin, in 1884, for his defence of P. N. Fitzgerald, the leader who beat Parnell and Archbishop Croke so badly at Thurles the other day; and he is in a fair way now to be denounced with equal fervour by the Nationalists as a County Court judge in Donegal. He finds this post no sinecure. "I do as much work in five days," he said to-night, "as the Superior Judges do in five weeks."

He is a staunch Unionist, and laughs at the notion that the Irish people care one straw for a Parliament in Dublin. "Why should they?" he said. "What did any Parliament in Dublin ever do to gratify the one real passion of the Irish peasant— his hunger for a bit of land? So far as the Irish people are concerned, Home Rule means simply agrarian reform. Would they get that from a Parliament in Dublin? If the British Parliament evicts the landlords and makes the tenants lords of the land, they will be face to face with Davitt's demand for the nationalising of the land. Do you suppose they will like to see the lawyers and the politicians organising a labour agitation against the 'strong farmers'? The last thing they want is a Parliament in Dublin. Lord Ashbourne's Act carries in its principle the death-warrant of the 'National League.'"

Some excellent stories were told in the picturesque smoking-room after dinner, one of a clever and humorous, sensible and non-political priest, who, being taken to task by some of his brethren for giving the cold shoulder to the Nationalist movement, excused himself by saying, "I should like to be a patriot; but I can't be. It's all along of the rheumatism which prevents me from lying out at nights in a ditch with a rifle." The same priest being reproached by others of the cloth with a fondness for the company of some of the resident landlords in his neighbourhood, replied, "It's in the blood, you see. My poor mother, God rest her soul! she always had a liking for the quality. As for my dear father, he was just a blundering peasant like the rest of ye!"

GWEEDORE, *Saturday, 4th Feb.*—A good day's work to-day!

We left our hospitable friends at Sion House early in the morning. The sun was shining brightly; the air so soft and bland that the thrushes were singing like mad creatures in the trees and the shrubbery; and the sky was more blue than Italy. "A foine day it is, sorr," said our jarvey as we took our seats on the car. There is some point in the old Irish sarcasm that English travellers in Ireland only see one side of the country, because they travel through it on the outside car. But to make this point tell, four people must travel on the car. In that case they must sit two on a side, each pair facing one side only of the landscape. It is a very different business when you travel on an outside car alone, with the driver sitting on one side of it, or with one companion only, when the driver occupies the little perch in front between the sides of the car. When you travel thus, the outside car is the best thing in the world, after a good roadster, for taking you rapidly over a country, and enabling you to command all points of the horizon. Double up one leg on the seat, let the other dangle freely, using the step as a stirrup, and you go rattling along almost as if you were on horseback.

We drove through a long suburb of Strabane into the busiest quarter of the busy little place. The names on the shops were predominantly Scotch — Maxwells, Stewarts, Hamiltons, Elliotts. I saw but one Celtic name, M'Ilhenny, and one German, Straub. I changed gold for enormous Bank of Ireland notes at a neat local bank, and the cheery landlord of the Abercorn Arms gave us a fresh car to take us on to Letterkenny, a drive of some twenty miles.

The car came up like a small blizzard, flying

about at the heels of an uncanny little grey mare. Lord Ernest knew the beast well, and said she was twenty-five years old. She behaved like an unbroken filly at first, but soon striking her pace, turned out a capital goer, and took us on without turning a hair till her work was done. The weather continued to be good, but clouds rolled up around the horizon.

"It'll always be bad weather," said our saturnine jarvey, "when the Judges come to hold court, and never be good again till they rise."

Here is a consequence of alien rule in Ireland, never, so far as I know, brought to the notice of Parliament.

"Why is this?" I asked; "is it because of the time of the year they select?"

"The time of year, sorr?" he replied, glancing compassionately at me. "No, not at all; it's because of the oaths!"

We reached Letterkenny in time for a very good luncheon at "Hegarty's," one of the neatest little inns I have ever found in a place of the size. It stands on the long main street which is really the town. At one end of this street is a very pretty row of picturesque ivy-clad brick cottages, built by a landlord whose property and handsome park bound the town on the west; and the street winds alongside the slope of a hill rising from the bank of the Swilly river. A fair was going on. The little market-place was alive with bustling, chattering, and chaffering country - folk. Smartly-dressed young damsels tripped in and out of the neat well-filled shops, and in front of a row of semi-detached villas, like a suburban London terrace, on the hill opposite "Hegarty's," a German band smote the air with discordant fury. Decidedly a lively, prosperous little town is Letterkenny, nor was I surprised to learn from a communicative gentleman, nursing his cane near the inn-door, that advantage would be taken of the presence of the Hussars sent to keep order at Dunfanaghy, to "give a ball."

"But I thought all the country was in arms about the trials at Dunfanaghy," I said.

"In arms about the trials at Dunfanaghy? Oh no; they'll never be locked up, Father M'Fadden and Mr. Blane. And the people here at Letterkenny, they've more sinse than at Dunfanaghy. Have you heard of the champagne?"

Upon this he proceeded to tell me, as a grand

joke, that Father M'Fadden and Mr. Blane, M.P., having declined to accept the tea offered them by the authorities during their detention, they had been permitted to order what they liked from the local hotel-keeper. After the trial was over, and they were released on bail to prosecute their appeal, the hotel-keeper demanded of the authorities payment of his bill, including two bottles of champagne ordered to refresh the member for Armagh!

A conspicuous, smart, spick-and-span house on the main street, built of brick and wood, with a verandah, and picked out in bright colours, was pointed out to me by this amiable citizen as the residence of a "returned American." This was a man, he said, who had made some money in America, but got tired of living there, and had come back to end his days in his native place He was a good man, my informant added, "only he puts on too many airs."

A remarkably handsome, rosy-faced young groom, a model of manhood in vigour and grace, presently brought us up a wagonette with a pair of stout nags, and a driver in a suit of dark-brown frieze, whose head seemed to have been driven down between his shoulders. He never lifted it up all the way to Gweedore, but he proved to be a capital jarvey notwithstanding, and knew the country as well as his horses.

Not long after leaving the town by a road which passes the huge County Asylum (now literally crammed, I am told, with lunatics), we passed a ruined church on the banks of a stream. Here the country people, it seems, halt and wash their feet before entering Letterkenny, failing which ceremony they may expect a quarrel with somebody before they get back to their homes. This wholesome superstition doubtless was established ages ago by some good priest, when priests thought it their duty to be the preachers and makers of peace.

We soon left the wooded country of the Swilly and began to climb into the grand and melancholy Highlands of Donegal. The road was as fine as any in the Scottish Highlands, and despite the keen chill wind, the glorious and ever-changing panoramas of mountain and strath through which we drove were a constant delight, until, just as we came within full range of Muckish, the giant of Donegal, the weather finally broke down into driving mists and blinding rain.

We pulled up near a picturesque little shebeen, to water the horses and get our Highland wraps well about us. Out came a hardy, cheery old farmer. He swept the heavens with the eye of a mountaineer, and exclaimed :—" Ah ! it 's a coorse day intirely, it is." " A coorse day intirely " from that moment it continued to be.

Happily the curtain had not fallen before we caught a grand passing glimpse of the romantic gorge of Glen Veagh, closed and commanded in the shadowy distance by the modern castle of Glenveagh, the mountain home of my charming countrywoman, Mrs. Adair.

Thanks to its irregular serpentine outline, and to the desolate majesty of the hills which environ it, Lough Veagh, though not a large sheet of water, may well be what it is reputed to be, a rival of the finest lochs in Scotland. No traces are now discernible on its shores of the too celebrated evictions of Glen Veagh. But from the wild and rugged aspect of the surrounding country it is probable enough that these evictions were to the evicted a blessing in disguise, and that their descendants are now enjoying, beyond the Atlantic, a measure of prosperity and of happiness which neither their own labour nor the most liberal legislation could ever have won for them here. We caught sight, as we drove through Mrs. Adair's wide and rocky domain, of wire fences, and I believe it is her intention to create here a small deer forest. This ought to be as good a stalking country as the Scottish Highlands, provided the people can be got to like "stalking" stags better than landlords and agents.

Long before we reached Glen Veagh we had bidden farewell, not only to the hedges and walls of Tyrone and Eastern Donegal, but to the "ditches," which anywhere but in Ireland would be called "embankments," and entered upon great stone-strewn wastes of land seemingly unreclaimed and irreclaimable. Huge boulders lay tossed and tumbled about as if they had been whirled through the air by the cyclones of some prehistoric age, and dropped at random when the wild winds wearied of the fun. The last landmark we made out through the gathering storm was the pinnacled crest of Errigal. Of Dunlewy, esteemed the loveliest of the Donegal lakes, we could see little or nothing as we hurried along the highway, which follows its course down to the Clady, the river of Gweedore; and we blessed the memory of Lord George Hill when suddenly turning from the wind and the rain into what seemed to be a mediæval courtyard flanked by trees, we pulled up in the bright warm light of an open doorway, shook ourselves like Newfoundland dogs, and were welcomed by a frank, good-looking Scottish host to a glowing peat fire in this really comfortable little hotel, the central pivot of a most interesting experiment in civilisation.

GWEEDORE, *Sunday, Feb. 5th.*—A morning as soft and bright almost as April succeeded the stormy night. Errigal lifted his bold irregular outlines royally against an azure sky. The sunshine glinted merrily on the swift waters of the Clady, which flows almost beneath our windows from Dunlewy Lough to the sea. The birds were singing in the trees, which all about our hotel make what in the West would be called an "opening" in the wide and woodless expanse of hill and bog.

This hotel was for many years the home of Lord George Hill, who built it in the hope of making Gweedore, what in England or Scotland it would long ago have become, a prosperous watering-place. Now that a battle-royal is going on between Lord

George's son and heir and the tenants on the estate, organised by Father M'Fadden under the "Plan of Campaign," it is important to know something of the history of the place.

Is this a case of the sons of the soil expropriated by an alien and confiscating Government to enrich a ruthless invader? I was told by a Nationalist acquaintance in Dublin that the owner of Gweedore is a near kinsman of the Marquis of Londonderry, and that the property came to him by inheritance under an ancient confiscation of the estates of the O'Donnels of Tyrconnel. All of this I find is embroidery.

The "Carlisle" room, which our landlord has assigned to us, contains a number of books, the property of the late Lord George, and ample materials are here for making out the annals of Gweedore. Lord George, it seems, was a posthumous son of the fourth Marquis of Downshire, and a nephew of that Marchioness of Salisbury who was burned to death with the west wing of Hatfield House half a century ago. He inherited nothing in Donegal, nor was any provision made for him under his father's will. His elder brothers made up and settled upon him a sum of twenty thousand pounds.

He entered the Army, and being quartered for a time at Letterkenny, shot and fished all about Donegal. He found the people here kindly and friendly, but in a deplorable state of ignorance and of destitution. Their holdings under sundry small proprietors were entirely unimproved, and as their families increased, these holdings were cut up by themselves into even smaller strips under the system known as "rundale,"—each son as he grew up taking off a slice of the paternal holding, putting up a hut with mud, and scratching the soil after his own rude fashion. This custom, necessarily fatal to civilisation, doubtless came down from the traditional times when the lands of a sept were held in common by the sept, before the native chieftains had converted themselves into landlords, and defeated Sir John Davies's attempt to convert their tribal kinsmen into peasant proprietors.

Whatever its origin, it had reduced Gweedore, or "Tullaghobegly," fifty years ago to barbarism. Nearly nine thousand people then dwelt here with never a landlord among them. There was no " Coercion " in Gweedore, neither was there a coach nor a car to be found in the whole district. The nominal owners of the small properties into which the district was divided knew little and cared less about them. The rents were usually "made by the tenants,"—a step in advance, it will be seen, of the system which the collective wisdom of Great Britain has for the last twenty years been trying to establish in Ireland. But they were only paid when it was convenient. An agent of one of these properties who travelled fourteen miles one day to collect some rents gave it up and drove back again, because the "day was too bad" for him to wander about in the mountains on the chance of finding the tenants at home and disposed to give him a trifle on account. On most of the properties there were arrears of eight, ten, and twenty years' standing.

There was one priest in the district, and one National School, the schoolmaster, with a family of nine persons, receiving the munificent stipend of eight pounds a year. These nine thousand people, depending absolutely upon tillage and pasture, owned among them all one cart and one plough, eight saddles, two pillions, eleven bridles, and thirty-two rakes! They had no means of harrowing their lands but with meadow rakes, and the farms were so small that from four to ten farms could be harrowed in a day with one rake.

Their beds were of straw, mountain grass, or green and dried rushes. Among the nine thousand people there were but two feather-beds, and but eight beds stuffed with chaff. There were but two stables and six cow-houses in the whole district. None of the women owned more than one shift, nor was there a single bonnet among them all, nor a looking-glass costing more than threepence.

The climate and the scenery took the fancy of Lord George. He made up his mind to see what could be done with this forgotten corner of the world, and to that end bought up as he could the small and scattered properties, till he had invested the greater part of his small fortune, and acquired about twenty thousand acres of land. Of this, little was fit for cultivation, even with the help of capital and civilised management. There was not a road in the district, nor a drain.

Lord George came and established himself here. He went to work systematically to improve the country, reclaiming bog-lands, building roads, and laying out the property into regular farms. He went about among the people himself, trying to get their confidence, and to let them know what he wanted to do for them, and with their help.

For a long time they wouldn't believe him to be a lord at all, "because he spoke Irish"; and the breaking up of the rundale system, under which they had lived in higgledy-piggledy laziness, exasperated them greatly. Of the first man who took a fenced and well-defined farm from Lord George, and went to work on it, the others observed that he would come to no good by it, because he would "have to keep a maid just to talk to his wife." Men could not be got for any wages to work at draining, or at making the "ditches" or embankments to delineate the new holdings; and when Lord George found adventurous "tramps" willing to earn a few shillings by honest work of the kind, conspiracies were formed to undo by night what was done by day. However, Lord George persevered.

There was not a shop, nor a dispensary, nor a doctor, nor a warehouse, nor a quay for landing goods in this whole populous and sea-washed region. He put up storehouses, built a little harbour at Bunbeg, established a dispensary, got a doctor to settle in the district, and finally put up the hotel in which we are. He advanced money to tenants disposed to improve their holdings. Finding the women, as usual, more thrifty and industrious than the men, and gifted with a natural aptitude for the loom and the spindle, he introduced the weaving of woollen yarn into stout frieze stuffs and foot-gear for both sexes. This was in 1840, and in 1854 Gweedore hand-knit socks and stockings were sold to the amount of £500, being just about the annual estimated rents of all the properties bought by Lord George at the time when he bought them in 1838! But with this difference : The owners from whom Lord George bought the properties got their £500 very irregularly, when they got it at all; whereas the wives and daughters of the tenants, who made the socks and stockings, were paid their £500 in cash.

Clearly in Gweedore I have a case not of the children of the soil despoiled and trampled upon by the stranger, but of the honest investment of alien capital in Irish land, and of the administration by the proprietor himself of the Irish property so acquired for the benefit alike of the owner and of the occupiers of the land.

That the deplorable state in which he found the people was mainly due to their own improvidence and gregarious incapacity is also tolerably clear.

On the west coast of Norway, dear to the heart of the salmon-fisher, you find people living under conditions certainly no more favourable than here exist. North of the Hardanger Fjord, the spring opens only in June. The farmers grow only oats and barley; but they have no market except for the barley, and live chiefly by the pasturage. It is as rocky a region as Donegal. But the Norsemen never try to make the land do more than it is capable of doing. With them the oldest son takes the farm and works it. The juniors are welcome to work on the farm if they like for their brother, but they are not allowed to cut it up. There is no rundale in Norway; and when the cadets see that there is no room for them they quietly "pull up stakes," and go forth to seek a new home, no matter where.

For fourteen years Lord George Hill spent on Gweedore all the rents he received from it, and a great deal more. During that time the relations between the people and their new landlord seem to have been, in the main, most friendly, notwithstanding his constant efforts to break up their old habits, or, to use their own language, to "bother them." But there were no "evictions"; rents were not raised even where the tenants were visibly able to pay better rents; prizes were given annually for the best and neatest cottages, for the best crops of turnips (neither turnips, parsnips, nor carrots were there at Gweedore when Lord George bought the estate), for the best pigs (there was not a pig in Gweedore in 1838!), for calves and colts, for the best fences, the best ordered tillage farms, the best labourers' cottages, the best beds and bedding, the best butter, the best woollen goods made on the estate. The old rundale plan of dividing up the land among the children was put a stop to, and every tenant was encouraged not to make his holding smaller, but to add to and enlarge it. A corn-mill, saw-mill, and flax-mill were established. In 1838 there was not a baker within ten miles. In 1852 the local baker was driving a good business in good bread. The tenant's wife, for whom in 1838 a single shift was a social superiority, in 1852 went shopping at Bunbeg for the latest fashions from Derry or Dublin.

Whatever "landlordism" may mean elsewhere in Ireland, it is plain enough that in the history of Gweedore it has meant the difference between savage squalor and civilisation.

Lord George Hill died in 1879, the year in which

the Land League began its operations. He bequeathed this property to his son, Captain Hill, by whom the management of it has been left to agents. After Lord George's death two tracts of mountain pasture, reserved by him to feed imported sheep, were let to the tenants, who by that time had come to own quite a considerable number, some thousands, of live stock, cattle, horses, and sheep.

Concurrently with this concession to the tenants the provisions made by Lord George against the subdivision of holdings began to give way. Father M'Fadden, combining the position of President of the National League with that of parish priest, seems to have favoured this tendency, and to have encouraged the putting up of new houses on reduced holdings to accommodate an increasing population. A flood which in August 1880 damaged the chapel and caused the death of five persons gave him an opportunity of bringing before the British public the condition of the people in a letter to the London *Times*, which elicited a very generous response, several hundred pounds, it is said, having been sent to him from London alone. Large contributions of relief were also made to Gweedore from the Duchess of Marlborough's Fund, and Gweedore became a standing butt of British benevolence. Two results seem to have followed, naturally enough,—a growing indisposition on the part of the tenants to pay rent, and a rapid rise in the value of tenant rights. With the National League standing between them and the landlord, with the British Parliament legislating year after year in favour of the Irish tenant and against the Irish landlord, and with the philanthropic public ready to respond to any appeal for help made on their behalf, the tenants at Gweedore naturally became a privileged class. In no other way at least can I explain the extraordinary fact that tenant rights at Gweedore have been sold, according to Lord Cowper's Blue-book of 1886, during the period of the greatest alleged distress and congestion in this district, at prices representing from forty to a hundred-and-thirty years' purchase of the landlord's rent!

In this Blue-book the Rev. Father M'Fadden appears as receiving no less than £115 sterling for the tenant-right sold by him of ground, the head rent of which is £1, 2s. 6d. a year. The worst enemy of Father M'Fadden will hardly suspect him, I hope, of taking such a sum as this from a tenant farmer for the right to starve to death by inches.[1]

A shrewd Galway man, now here, who seems to know the region well, and likes both the scenery and the people, tells me that the troubles which have now culminated in the arrest of Father M'Fadden have been aggravated by the vacillation of Captain Hill, and by the foibles of his agent, Colonel Dopping, who not long ago brought down Mr. Gladstone with his unloaded rifle. That the tenants as a body have been, or now are, unable to pay their rent he does not believe. On the contrary, he thinks them, as a body, rather well off. Certainly I have seen and spoken with none of them about the roads to-day who were not hearty-looking men, and in very good case. Colonel Dopping, according to my Galwegian, is not an Englishman, but a Longford Irishman of good family, who got his training in India as an official of the Woods and Forests in Bengal. "He is not a bad-hearted man, nor

[1] I have since learned that Father M'Fadden sold another holding, rental 6s. 8d., for £80. He has three more holdings from Captain Hill, at 15s., 6s. 8d., and 11s. 2d., for which he was in arrears for two years in April 1887, when ejectment decrees were obtained against him. For his house holding he pays 2s. a year! So he was really fighting his own battle as a tenant in the Plan of Campaign.

unkind," said my Galwegian, " but he is too much of a Bengal tiger in his manner. He went into the cottages personally and lectured the people, and that they never will stand. They don't require or expect you to believe what they say—in fact they have little respect for you if you do—but they like to have the agent pretend that he believes them, and then go on and show that he don't. But he must never lose his temper about it. Colonel Dopping, I have heard, argued with an old woman one day who was telling him more yarns than were ever spun into cloth in Gweedore, till she picked up her cup of tea and threw it in his face. He flounced out of the cottage, and ordered the police to arrest her. That did him more harm than if he had shot a dozen boys." "What with the temper of Colonel Dopping and the vacillation of Captain Hill, who is always of the mind of the last man that speaks to him, Father M'Fadden has had it all his own way. Captain Hill's claim was for £1800 of arrears, long arrears too, and £400 of costs. How much the people paid in under the Plan of Campaign nobody knows but Father M'Fadden. But he is a clever *padre*, and he played Captain Hill till he finally gave up the costs, and settled for £1450."

"And this sum represents what?"

"It represents in round numbers about two years' income from an estate in which Captain Hill's father must have invested, first and last, more nearly £40,000 than £20,000 of money that never came out of it."

"That doesn't sound like a very good operation. But isn't the question, Whether the tenants have earned this sum, such as it is, out of the land let to them by Captain Hill?"

"No, not exactly, I think. You must remember there are some twelve hundred families living here on land bought with Lord George's money, and enjoying all the advantages which the place owes to his investment and his management, much more than to any labour or skill of theirs. You must look at their rents as accommodation rents. Suppose they earn the rent in Scotland, or England, or Tyrone, or wherever you like, the question is, What do they get for it from Captain Hill? They get a holding with land enough to grow potatoes on, and with as much free fuel as ever they like, and with free pasture for their beasts, and all this they get on the average, mind you, for no more than ten shillings a year! Why, there was a time, I can assure you, when the women here earned the value of all the Hill rents by knitting stockings and making woollen stuffs. You see the stuffs lying here in this window that they make even now, and good stuffs too. But before the League boycotted the agency here, the agency ten years ago used to pay out £900 in a year, where it pays less than £100 to the women for their work."

"Why did the League do this?"

"Why? Why, because it wanted to control the work itself, and to know just what it brings into the place. You must remember Father M'Fadden is the President of the League, and the people will do anything for him. I have heard of one old woman who sat up of nights last year knitting socks to send up to London, to pay the Christmas dues to the Father,—six shillings' worth."

"And are these stuffs here in the hotel made for the agency you speak of?"

"Oh no; these are just made by women that know the hotel, and Mr. Robinson here, he kindly takes in the stuffs. You see the name of every woman on every one of them that made it, and the price. If a stranger buys some, he pays the money to Mr. Robinson, and so it goes to the women, and no commission charged."

The "stuffs" are certainly excellent, very evenly woven; and the patterns, all devised, I am told, by the women themselves, very simple and tasteful. The only dyes used are got by the women also from the sea-weeds and the kelp, which must be counted among the resources of the place. The browns and ochres thus produced are both soft and vivid; while nothing can be better than a peculiar warm grey, produced by a skilful mingling of the undyed wools.

"What, then, causes the distress for which the name of Gweedore is a synonym?" I asked.

"It doesn't exist," responded my Galwegian; "that is, there is no such distress in Gweedore as you find in Connemara, for instance;[1] but what distress there is in Gweedore is due much more to the habits the people have been getting into of late years, and to the idleness of them, than to any pressure of the rents you hear about, or

[1] Yet of Connemara, Cardinal Manning, in his letter to the Archbishop of Armagh, August 31, 1873, cites the "trustworthy" evidence of "an Englishman who had raised himself from the plough's tail," and who had gone "to see with his own eyes the material condition of the peasantry in Ireland." It was to the effect that in abundance and quality of food, in rate of wages, and even in the comfort of their dwellings, the working men of Connemara were better off than the agricultural labourers of certain English counties.

even to the poverty of the soil. Go down to the store at Bunbeg, and see what they buy and go in debt for! You won't find in any such place as Bunbeg in England such things. And even this don't measure it; for, you see, two-thirds of them are not free to deal at Bunbeg."

"Why not? Is Bunbeg 'boycotted'?"

"No, not at all. But they are on the books of the 'Gombeen man'—Sweeney of Dungloe and Burtonport. They're always in debt to him for the meal; and then he backs the travelling tea-pedlars, and the bakers that carry around cakes, and all these run up the accounts all the time. Tot up what these people lay out for tea at four shillings a pound — and they won't have cheap tea—and what they pay for meal, and what they pay for interest, and the 'testimonials,'—they paid for the monument here to O'Donnell, the Donegal man that murdered Carey,—and the dues to the priest, and you'll find the £700 or so they don't pay the landlord going in other directions three and four times over."

"Then they are falling back into all the old laziness, the men sauntering about, or sitting and smoking, while the women do all the work."

The maid having told us Mass would be performed at noon, I walked with Lord Ernest a mile or so up the road to Derrybeg, to see the people thronging down from the hills; the women in their picturesque fashion wearing their bright shawls drawn over their heads. But the maid had deceived us. The Mass was fixed for eleven, and I suspect her of being a Protestant in disguise.

On the way back we met Mr. Burke, the resident magistrate. He has a neat house here, with a garden, and had come over from Dunfanaghy to see his wife. He meant to return before dark. The country was quiet enough, he said; but there were some troublesome fellows about, keeping up the excitement over the arrest at Father M'Fadden's trial of Father Stephens—a young priest recently from Liverpool, who has become the curate of quite another Father M'Fadden—the parish priest of Falcarragh, and is giving his local superior a great deal of trouble by his activity in connection with the "Plan of Campaign." Mr. Wybrants Olphert of Ballyconnell, the chief landlord of Falcarragh, has been "boycotted," on suspicion of promoting the arrest of the two priests. Five policemen have been put into his house. At

Falcarragh, where six policemen are usually stationed, there are now forty. Mr. Burke evidently thinks, though he did not say so, that Father Stephens has been spoiled of his sleep by the laurels of Father M'Fadden of Gweedore. He is to be tried at Dunfanaghy on Tuesday, and there are now 150 troops quartered there—Rifles and Hussars.

"Are they not boycotted?" I asked.

"No. The people rather enjoy the bustle and the show, not to speak of the money the soldiers spend."

Lord Ernest, who knows Mr. Olphert, sent him over a message by Mr. Burke that we would drive over to-morrow, and pay our respects to him at Ballyconnell. From this Mr. Burke tried to dissuade us, but what he told us naturally increased our wish to go.

After luncheon I ordered a car, and drove to Derrybeg, to call there on Father M'Fadden, Lord Ernest, who has already seen him, agreeing to call there for me on his return from a walk. We passed much reclaimed bogland, mostly now in grass, and looking fairly well; many piles of turf and clusters of cottages, well-built, but not very neatly kept. From each, as we passed, the inevitable cur rushed out and barked himself hoarse. Then came a waste of bog and boulders, and then a long, neat stone wall, well coped with unhewn stone, which announced the vicinity of Father M'Fadden's house, quite the best structure in the place after the chapel and the hotel. It is of stone, with a neat side porch, in which, as I drove up, I descried Father M'Fadden, in his trim well-fitting clerical costume, standing and talking with an elderly lady. I passed through a handsome iron wicket, and introduced myself to him. He received me with much courtesy, and asked me to walk into his well-furnished comfortable study, where a lady, his sister, to whom he presented me, sat reading by the fire.

I told Father M'Fadden I had come to get his view of methods and things at Gweedore, and he gave it to me with great freedom and fluency. He is a typical Celt in appearance, a M'Fadden Roe, sanguine by temperament, with an expression at once shrewd and enthusiastic, a most flexible persuasive voice. All the trouble at Gweedore, he thought, came of the agents. "Agents had been the curse both of Ireland and of the landlord.

The custom being to pay them by commissions on the sums collected, and not a regular salary, the more they can screw either out of the soil, or out of any other resources of the tenants, the better it is for them. At Gweedore the people earn what they can, not out of the soil, but out of their labour exported to Scotland, or England, or America. Only yesterday," he continued, turning to his neat mahogany desk and taking up a letter, " I received this with a remittance from America to pay the rent of one of my people."

" This was in connection," I asked, " with the ' Plan of Campaign ' and your contest here ?"

" Yes," he replied; "and a girl of my parish went over to Scotland herself and got the money due there for another family, and brought it back to me here. You see they make me a kind of savings-bank, and have done so for a long time, long before the ' Plan of Campaign' was talked about as it is now."

This was interesting, as I had heard it said by a Nationalist in Dublin that the " Plan of Campaign" was originally suggested by Father M'Fadden. He made no such claim himself, however, and I made no allusion to this aspect of the matter. " I have been living here for fifteen years, and they listen to me as to nobody else."

In these affairs with the agents, he had always told his people that "whenever a settlement came to be made, cash alone in the hand of the person representing them could make it properly." "Cash I must have," he said, "and hold the cash ready for the moment. When I had worked out a settlement with Captain Hill, I had a good part of the money in my hand ready to pay down. £1450 was the sum total agreed upon, and after the further collection, necessitated by the settlement, there was a deficit of about £200. I wrote to Professor Stuart," he added, after a pause, "that I wanted about £200 of the sum-total. But more has come in since then. This remittance from America yesterday, for example."

"Do they send such remittances without being asked for them?" I inquired.

"Yes; they are now and again sending money, and some of them don't send, but bring it. Some of them go out to America now as they used to go to England—just to work and earn some money, and come back.

"If they get on tolerably well they stay for a

while, but they find America is more expensive than Ireland, and if, for any cause, they get out of work there, they come back to Ireland to spend what they have. Naturally, you see," said Father M'Fadden, "they find a certain pleasure to be seen by their old friends in the old place, after borrowing the four pounds perhaps to take them to America, coming back with the money jingling in their pockets, and in good clothes, and with a watch and a chain—and a high hat. And there is in the heart of the Irishman an eternal longing for his native land constantly luring him back to Ireland. All do not succeed, though, in your country," he said. "We hear of two out of ten perhaps who do very well. They take care we hear of that. The rest disappear, and are never heard of again."

"Then you do not encourage emigration?" I, asked, "even although the people cannot earn their living from the soil?"

Father M'Fadden hesitated a moment, and then replied, "No, for things should be so arranged that they may earn their living, not out of the country, but on the soil at home. It is to that I want to bring the condition of the district."

At this point Lord Ernest Hamilton came up

and knocked at the door. He was most courteously received by Father M'Fadden. To my query why the Courts could not intervene to save the priests from taking all this trouble on themselves between the owners and the occupiers of the land, Father M'Fadden at first replied that the Courts had no power to intervene where, as in many cases in Gweedore, the holdings are subdivided.

"The Courts," he said, "may not be, and I do not think they are, all that could be desired, though they undoubtedly do supply a more or less impartial arbitrator between the landlord and the tenant. It is an improvement on the past when the landlords fixed the rents for themselves."

I did not remind him of what Lord George Hill tells us, that in the olden time at Gweedore the tenants fixed their own rents—and then did not pay them—but I asked him how this could be said when the tenant clearly must have accepted the rent, no matter who fixed it. "Oh!" said Father M'Fadden, "that may be so, but the tenant was not free, he was coerced. With all his life and labour represented in the holding and its improvements, he could not go and give up his holding. It's a stand-and-deliver business with him—the landlord puts a pistol to his head!"

THE DIARY OF AN AMERICAN 97

"But is it not true," I said, "that under the new Land Bill the Land Commissioner's Court has power to fix the rents judicially without regard to landlord or tenant during fifteen years?"

"Yes, that is so," said Father M'Fadden. "Under Mr. Gladstone's Act of '81, and under the later Act of the present Government, the rents so fixed from '81 to '86 inclusive are subject to revision for three years; but the people have no confidence in the constitution of the Courts, and, as a matter of fact, the improvements of the tenants are confiscated under the Act of '81, and the reductions allowed under the Act of '87 are incommensurate with the fall in prices by 100 per cent. And there still remains the burden of arrears. I feel that I must stand between my people and obligations which they are unable to meet. To that end I take their money, and stand ready to use it to relieve them when the occasion offers. That is my idea of my work under the 'Plan of Campaign'; and, furthermore, I think that by doing it I have secured money for the landlord which he couldn't possibly have got in any other way."

This struck me as a very remarkable statement, nor can I see how it can be interpreted otherwise than as an admission that if the people had the money to pay their rents, they couldn't be trusted to use it for that purpose, unless they put it into the control of the priest or of some other trustee.

Reverting to what he had said of the necessity for some change in the conditions of life and labour here, I asked if, in his opinion, the people could live out of the land if they got the ownership of it.

In existing circumstances he thought they could not.

Was he in favour, then, of Mr. Davitt's plan of Land Nationalisation?

"Well, I have not considered the question of Nationalisation of the land."

To my further question, What remedies he would himself propose for a state of things in which it was impossible for the people to live out of the land either as occupiers or as owners—emigration being barred, Father M'Fadden, without looking at Lord Ernest, replied, "Oh, I think abler men who draw up Parliamentary Acts and live in public life ought to devise remedies, and that is a matter which would be best settled by a Home Government."

The glove was well delivered, but Lord Ernest did not lift it.

"But, Father M'Fadden," I said, "I am told you are a practical agriculturist and engineer, and that you have contrived to get excellent work done by the people here, dividing them off into working squads, and assigning so many perches to so many —surely then you must understand better than a dozen members of Parliament what they can be got to do?"

He smiled at this, and finally admitted that he had a plan of his own. It was that the Government should advance sums for reclaiming the land. "The people could live on part of their earnings while thus employed, and invest the surplus in sheep to be fed on the hill pastures. When the reclamation was effected the families could be scattered out, and the holdings increased. In this district alone there are 350 holdings of reclaimable land of 20 acres each, the reclamation of which, according to a competent surveyor, "would pay well." And the district could be improved by creating employment on the spot, establishing factories, developing fisheries, giving technical education, and encouraging cottage industries, which are so vigorously reviving in this district owing to the benevolent efforts of the Donegal Industrial Fund."

Father M'Fadden spoke freely and without undue heat of his trial, and gave us a piquant account of his arrest.

This was effected at Armagh, just as he was getting into an early morning train. A sergeant of police walked up as the train was about to start, and asked—

"Are you not Father M'Fadden of Gweedore?"

"What interest have you in my identity?" responded the priest.

"Only this, sir," said the officer, politely exhibiting a warrant.

"I had been in Armagh the previous day," said Father M'Fadden, "attending the month's memory of the late deceased Primate of All Ireland, Dr. M'Gettigan, and stayed at a private residence, that of Surgeon-Major Lavery, not suspecting that while enjoying the genial hospitality of the Surgeon-Major my steps were dogged by a detective, and that gentleman's house watched by police."

Of the trial Father M'Fadden spoke with more bitterness. His eyes glowed as he exclaimed, " Can you imagine that they refused me bail, when bail had been allowed to such a felon as Arthur Orton? Why should I have been locked up over two Sundays, for ten days, when I offered to pledge my honour to appear?" He made no other complaint of the magistrate, and none of the prosecutor, Mr. Ross. He praised his own lawyer, too, but he strongly denounced the stenographer who took down his speech, or the parts of it which I told him I had seen in Dublin.

"Why, just think of it," he exclaimed; "it took the clerk just eight minutes to read the report given by that stenographer of a speech which it took me an hour and twenty minutes to deliver! I do not speak from the lips, I speak from the heart, and consequently rather rapidly; and a stenographer who can take down 190 words a minute has told me I run ahead of him!"

I suggested that the report, without pretending even to be a full summary of his speech, might be accurate as to phrases and sentences pronounced by him.

"Yes, as to phrases," he answered, "that might be; but the phrases may be taken out of their true connection, and strung together in an untruthful, yet telling way. Even my words were not fully set down," he said, with some heat. "I was made to call a man 'level,' when I said in the American way that he was 'level-headed.'" *A propos* of this, I am told that the American word "spree" has become Hibernian, and is used to describe meetings of the National League and "other political entertainments."

When I told Father M'Fadden I had just come from Rome, where, as I had reason to believe, the Vatican was anxious to get evidence from others than Archbishop Walsh and Monsignore Kirby, of the Irish College, as to the attitude of the priests in Ireland towards the laws of the United Kingdom, he said he knew that "some Italian prelates neither understood nor approved the 'Plan of Campaign,' nor is the Irish Land question understood at Rome;" but this did not seem to disturb him much, as he was quite sure that in the end the "Plan of Campaign" would be legalised by the British Government. "I think I see plainly," he said, "that Lord Ernest's government is fast going to pieces, though I can't expect him to admit it!" Lord Ernest laughed good-naturedly, and said that Father M'Fadden saw more in Donegal than he (Lord Ernest) was able to see in Westminster. Upon my asking him whether the "Plan of Campaign" did not in effect abrogate the moral duty of a man to meet the legal obligations he had voluntarily incurred, Father M'Fadden advanced his own theory of the subject, which was that, "if a man can pay a fair year's rent out of the produce of his holding, he is bound to pay it. But if the rent be a rack-rent, imposed on the tenant against his will, or if the holding does not produce the rent, then I don't think that is a strict obligation in conscience."

In America, the courts, I fear, would make short work of this theory of Father M'Fadden. If a tenant there cannot pay his first quarter's rent (they don't let him darken his soul by a year's liabilities) they promptly and mercilessly put him out.

Interesting as was our conversation with the parish priest of Gweedore, I felt that we might be trespassing too far upon his kindness and his time. So we rose to go. He insisted upon our going into the dining-room, where, as he told us, he had hospitably entertained sundry visiting statesmen from England, and there offered us a glass of the excellent wine of the country. He excused himself from joining us as being "almost a teetotaller."

On our return to the hotel I met the Galwegian strolling about. When I told him of Father M'Fadden's courteous hospitality, he said, "I am very glad you took that glass he offered. I really believe his quarrel with Captain Hill dates back to Hill's declining that same courtesy under Father M'Fadden's roof."

GWEEDORE, *Monday, Feb.* 6.—Another very beautiful morning—as a farmer said with whom I chatted on my morning stroll, "A grand day, sorr!" Errigal, which in this mountain atmosphere seems almost to hang over our hotel, but is in reality three or four miles away, stood out superbly against a clear azure sky, wreaths of soft luminous mist floating like a divine girdle half way up his bare volcanic peak.

I walked up to the Bunbeg road with Lord Ernest to call upon some peasants whom he knows. In one stone cabin, very well built and plastered, standing sidewise to the road, with doors on either side, we found the house apparently in charge of a little girl of nine or ten years, a weird but pretty child with very delicate well-cut features, who lay couchant upon her doubled-up arm on a low bed in a corner of the main room, and peered at us over her elbow with sparkling inquisitive eyes.

By her side sat a man with his cap on, who might have been the " young Pretender," or the " old Kaiser," so far as his looks went towards indicating his age. He never rose or welcomed us, being, as we afterwards found out, only a visitor like ourselves, and a kinsman of Mrs. M'Donnell, the head of the house. " Mrs. M'Donnell," he said, " is gone to the store at Bunbeg."

This main room rose perhaps ten feet in height to the open roof. It had one large and well-glazed window. When Lord George Hill came here there were not ten square feet of window-glass in the whole parish outside of the Church, the national school, and the residence of the chief police-officer.

Windows when there were any were closed with dried sheepskins, through which the cats ran in and out as freely as through the curious tunnel which the kindly Master of Blantyre has constructed at Sheba's Cross for their special benefit.

There were two beds in the main room; rather high than low, one of rushes, on which lay the child of whom I have spoken, and one of greater pretensions vacant in another corner.

The door stood wide open, but the cabin was warm and comfortable, and a peat fire smouldered, sending up, to me, most agreeable odours. An inner room seemed to be a sort of granary, full of hay and straw. There the cow is kept at night. "It's handy if you want a drink of milk," said the visitor. In comparison with the dwellings of small farmers in Eastern France or in Southern Italy this Donegal cabin was not only clean but attractive. It was more squalid perhaps, but less dreary than the extemporised and flimsy dwellings of settlers in the extreme Far West of the United States, and I should say decidedly a more wholesome habitation than the hermetically sealed and dismal wooden houses of hundreds of struggling farmers in the older Eastern States. I am sure my old friend Mr. Frederick Law Olmsted, who made the only thorough surveys of agricultural life in the United States before the Civil War, would have pronounced it in all respects superior, so far as health and comfort go, to the average home of the average "poor buccra," between the Chesapeake and the Sabine. I am afraid a great deal of not wholly innocuous nonsense has been written and spoken about this part of the United Kingdom by well-meaning philanthropists who have gauged the condition of the people here by their own standards of comfort and enjoyment. Most things in this life of ours are relative. I well remember hearing an American millionaire, who began life in New York as the patentee of a mouse-trap, express his profound compassion for a judge of the Supreme Court condemned to live "upon a pittance of eight thousand dollars a year."

These dwellers in the cabins of Donegal are millionaires, so far as those essentials of life are concerned, which we call room and air and freedom to move and breathe, in comparison with hundreds and thousands of their own race in the slums of New York and Chicago and Liverpool and London.

Mrs. M'Donnell's cousin, however, took dark views of things. The times "were no good at all."

The potatoes, I had heard, were doing well this year.

"No! they wouldn't keep the people; indeed, they wouldn't. There would have to be relief."

"Why not manure the land?"

"Manure? oh yes, the sea-stuff was good manure, but the people couldn't get it. They had no boats; and it cost eighteenpence a load to haul it from Bunbeg. No! they couldn't get it off the rocks. At the Rosses they might; the Rosses were not so badly off as Derrybeg or Gweedore, for all they might say."

"But Father M'Fadden had urged me," I said, "to see the Rosses, because the people there were worse off than any of the people."

"Well, Father M'Fadden was a good man; he was a friend of the people; and they were bad indeed at the Rosses, but they could get the sea-stuff there, and hadn't to pay for cartage. And indeed, if you put the sea-stuff on the bogland, the land was better in among the rocks at the Rosses than was the bogland, it was indeed: the stuff did no good at all the first year. The second and the third it gave good crops—but then you must burn it —and by the fourth year and the fifth it was all ashes, and no good at all! This was God's truth, it was; and there must be relief."

"But could the people earn nothing in Scotland or in Tyrone?"

"Oh no, they could earn nothing at all. They could pay no rent."

So he sat there, a Jeremiah among the potsherds, quite contented and miserable—well and hearty in a ragged frieze coat, with his hat over his eyes.

While we talked, a tall lusty young beggar-girl wandered in and out unnoticed. Chickens pecked and fluttered about, and at intervals the inevitable small dog suddenly barked and yelped.

On our way back we met the elder daughter of Mrs. M'Donnell, a girl of sixteen, the "beauty of Gweedore." A beauty she certainly is, and of a type hardly to have been looked for here.

Her lithe graceful figure, her fine, small, chiselled features, her shapely little head rather defiantly set on her sloping shoulders, her fair complexion and clear hazel eyes, her brown golden hair gathered up behind into a kind of tress, all these were Saxon rather than Celtic. Her trim neat ankles were bare, after the mountain fashion, but she was prettily dressed in a well-fitting dark blue gown, wore a smartly trimmed muslin apron, with lace about her throat, and carried over her arm a new woollen shawl, very tasteful and quiet in colour. She greeted us with a self-possessed smile.

"No," she had not been shopping with her

mother. The shawl was a present from one of her cousins. Did we not think it very pretty? She was only out for a walk, and had no notion where her mother might be. A stalwart red-bearded man who lounged and loitered behind her on the road was "only a friend," she said, "not a relation at all!" Nor did she show, I am sorry to say, any compassion for the evident uneasiness with which, from a distance, he regarded her long and affable parley with two strangers.

We asked her whether she expected and wished to live in Gweedore, or would like to follow elsewhere some calling or trade. "Oh yes," she unhesitatingly replied, "I should like to be a dressmaker in Derry; but," she added pensively, "it's no use my thinking about it, for I know I shouldn't be let!"

"Wouldn't you like Dublin as well?" I asked.

"Perhaps; but I shouldn't be let go to Dublin either!"

Would she like to go to America?

"No!" she didn't think much of "the Americans who came back," and America must be "a very hard country for work, and very cold in the winter."

Now this was a widow's daughter, living in such

a cabin as I have described, and upon a small holding in a parish reputed to be the most "distressful" in Donegal![1]

Returning to the hotel we found our car ready for Falcarragh. Our driver was a quiet, sensible fellow, who did not seem to care sixpence about the great Nationality question, though he knew the country very well.

Iron was visible in the rocks as we drove along, and we passed some abandoned mining works, "lead and silver mines;" he said, "they were given up long before his time." We got many fine views of the mountains Errigal, Aghla More, and Muckish. Lough Altan, a wild tarn, lies between Errigal and Aghla More.

The peasants we met stared at us curiously, but were very civil, even at a place bearing the ominous name of Bedlam, against which Mr. Burke had warned us as the most troublesome on the way. All the countryside was there attending a fair, and we drove through throngs of red-shawled, barelegged women, ponies, horses, cattle, and sheep.

[1] For this holding, of 10 Irish acres, I have since learned the widow O'Donnell pays 10s. a year. She is in the receipt of outdoor relief, there being fever in the house (May 1888).

Of Tory Island, with its famous tower, dating back to the fabled "Fomorians," we had some grand glimpses. The white surf, flashing and leaping high in the air on the nearer islets accented and gave life to the landscape.

In one glorious landlocked bay, we saw not a single boat riding. Our driver said, "The fishermen all live on Tory Island, and send their fish to Sligo. The people on the mainland don't like going out in the boats."

Lord Ernest tells me there is a movement to have a telegraph station set up on Tory Island, to announce the Canadian steamers coming into Moville for Derry.

We found Falcarragh, or "Cross-Roads," a large clean-looking village, consisting of one long and broad street, through which horses and cattle were wandering in numbers, apparently at their own sweet will.

Ballyconnell House, the seat of Mr. Wybrants Olphert, is the manor house of the place. As we drew near, no signs appeared of the dreadful "Boycott." The great gates of the park stood hospitably open, and we drove in unchallenged past a pretty ivy-clad lodge, and through low, but thickly planted groves. A huge boulder, ruddy with iron ore, bears the uncanny and unspellable name of the "Clockchinnfhaelaidh," or "Stone of Kinfaele." Upon this stone, tradition tells us, Balor, a giant of Tory Island, chopped off the head of an unreasonable person named Mackinfeale, for complaining that Balor, under some prehistoric "Plan of Campaign," had driven away his favourite cow, Glasgavlan.

Ballyconnell House, a substantial mansion of the Georgian era, stands extremely well. Over a fine sloping lawn in front, you have a glorious view of the sea, and of a very fine headland, known as "the Duke's Head," from the really remarkable resemblance it bears to the profile of Wellington. The winds have such power here that there are but few well-grown trees, and those near the house. About them paraded many game-hens, spirited birds, looking like pheasants. These, as we learned, never sleep save in the trees.

The "boycotted" lord of the manor came out to greet us—a handsome, stalwart man of some seventy years, with a kindly face, and most charming manners. His family, presumably of Dutch origin, has been established here since Charles II.

He himself holds 18,133 acres here, valued at £1802 a year; and he is a resident landlord in the fullest sense of the term. For fifty years he has lived here, during all which time, as he told us to-day, he has "never slept for a week out of the country." His furthest excursions of late years have been to Raphoe, where he has a married daughter. "Absenteeism" clearly has nothing to do with the quarrel between Mr. Olphert and his tenants, or with the "boycotting" of Ballyconnell.

The dragoons from Dunfanaghy had just ridden away as we came up. They had come over in full fig to show themselves, and to encourage the respectable Catholics of Falcarragh, who side with their parish priest, Father M'Fadden of Glena, and object to the vehement measures promoted by his young curate, Father Stephens, recently of Liverpool. The people had received them with much satisfaction. "They had never seen the cavalry before, and were much delighted!"

Before we sat down to luncheon young Mr. Olphert came in. It was curious to see this quiet, well-bred young gentleman throw down his belt and his revolver on the hall table, like his gloves and his umbrella. "Quite like the Far

West," I said. "And we are as far in the West as we can get," he replied laughingly.

Our luncheon was excellent—so good, in fact, that we felt a kind of remorse as if we had selfishly quartered ourselves upon a beleaguered garrison. But Mr. Olphert said he had no fear of being starved out. Personally he was, and always had been, on the best terms with the people of Falcarragh. The older tenants, even now, if he met them walking in the fields when no one was in sight, would come up and salute him, and say how "disgusted" they were with what was going on. It was the younger generation who were troublesome—more troublesome, he added, to their own parish priest than they were to him. Three or four years ago a returned American Irishman, an avowed unbeliever, but an active Nationalist and one of Mr. Forster's "suspects," had come into the neighbourhood and done his worst to break up the parish. He used to come to Falcarragh on a Sunday, and get up on a stone outside the chapel while Father M'Fadden was saying Mass or preaching, and harangue such people as would listen to him, and caricature the priest and the sermon going on within sound of his own voice. "I am myself a Protestant," said Mr. Olphert, "but I have a great respect for priests who do their duty; and the conduct of Father M'Fadden of Gweedore, in countenancing this man, who tried to overthrow the authority of Father M'Fadden of Glena, excited my indignation. As to what is going on now," said Mr. Olphert, "it is to Father M'Fadden of Gweedore, and to Father Stephens here, that the trouble is chiefly to be charged." This tallies with what I heard at Gweedore from my Galwegian acquaintance. He thought Mr. Olphert, and Mr. Hewson, the agent, ought to have made peace on the terms which Father Stephens said he was willing to accept for the tenants, these being a reduction of 3s. 4d. in the pound, if Mr. Olphert would extend the reduction to the whole year. My Galwegian thought this reasonable, because in this region the rent, it appears, is only collected once a year. With this impartial temper, my Galwegian still maintained that but for the two priests—the parish priest of Gweedore and the curate of Falcarragh—there need have been no trouble at Falcarragh. There had been no "evictions." When the tenants first went to Mr. Olphert they asked a reduction of 4s. in the pound on the non-judicial rents, and this Mr.

Olphert at once agreed to give them. The tenants had regularly paid their rents for ten years before. That they are not going down in the world would appear from the fact that the P. O. Savings Banks' deposits at Falcarragh, which stood at £62, 15s. 10d. in 1880, rose in 1887 to £494, 10s. 8d. A small number of them had gone into Court and had judicial rents fixed; and it was on the contention promoted by the two priests, through these judicial tenants, he said, that all the difficulty hinged. Father M'Fadden of Glena, who thought the quarrel unjustifiable and silly, had an interview with Mr. Blane, M.P., and with Father Stephens, and tried to arrange it all. He would have succeeded, my Galwegian thought, had not the agent, Mr. Hewson, obstinately fought with the obstinate curate, Father Stephens, over the suggestion made by the latter, that the terms granted on the fine neighbouring estate of Mr. Stuart of Ards—a man of wealth, who lives mainly at Brighton, though Ards is one of the loveliest places in Ireland— should be extended by Mr. Olphert for a whole year to his own people, who had never asked for anything of the kind!

Mr. Olphert said he knew Gweedore well. He

owns a "townland"[1] there, on which he has thirty-five tenants, none of them on a holding at more more than £4 a year. Father M'Fadden of Gweedore, he said, finding that the people on Mr. Olphert's townland were going back to the "Rundale" practices, 'tried to induce Mr. Olphert to return all these subdivisions as "tenancies." This he refused to do. As to the resources of the peasantry, he thought them greater than they appeared to be. "This comes to light," said Mr. Olphert, "whenever there is a tenant-right for sale. There is never any lack of money to buy it, and at a round good price." The people also, he thinks, spend a great deal on what they regard as luxuries,

[1] This "townland" is a curious use of a Saxon term to describe a Celtic fact. The territory of an Irish sept seems to have been divided up into "townlands," each townland consisting of four, or in some cases six, groups of holdings, occupied by as many families of the "sept." The chief of the "sept" divided up each "townland" periodically among these groups, while the common fields were cut up among the families as they increased and multiplied according to the system—against which Lord George Hill battled at Gweedore—known as "rundale" or "rundeal," from the Celtic, "ruindioll," a "partition" or "man's share." This is quite unlike the Russian "mir" or collective village, and not more like the South Slav "zadruga" which makes each family a community, the land belonging to all, as, according to M. Eugène Simon, it does in China. But it is as inconsistent with Henry George's State ownership of the land or the rents as either of those systems.

and particularly on tea. "A cup of tea could not be got for love or money in Gweedore, when Lord George Hill came there. You might as well have asked for a glass of Tokay."

Now they use and abuse it in the most deleterious way imaginable. They buy the tea at exorbitant rates, often at five shillings a pound, and usually on credit, paying a part of one bill on running up another, put it into a saucepan or an iron pot, and boil, or rather stew, it over the fire, till they brew a kind of hell-broth, which they imbibe at odd moments all day long! Oddly enough, this is the way in which they prepare tea in Cashmere and other parts of India, with this essential difference, though, that the Orientals mitigate the astringency of the herb with milk and almonds and divers ingredients, tending to make a sort of "compote" of it. Taken as it is taken here, it must have a tremendous effect on the nerves. Mr. Olphert thinks it has had much to do with the increase of lunacy in Ireland of late years. From his official connection with the asylum at Letterkenny, he knows that while it used to accommodate the lunatics of three counties, it is now hardly adequate to the needs of Donegal alone.

Everything about Ballyconnell House is out of key with the actual military conditions of life here. It is essentially what Tennyson calls "an ancient home of ordered peace." In the ample hall hang old portraits and trophies of the chase. The large and handsome library, panelled in rich dark wood, is filled full of well-bound books. Prints, busts, the thousand and one things of "bigotry and virtue" which mark the dwelling-place of educated and thoughtful people are to be seen on every side. Mr. Olphert showed us a cabinet full of bronzes, picked up on the strand of the sea. Among these were brooches, pins, clasps, buckles, two very fine bronze swords, and a pair of bronze links engraved with distinctly Masonic emblems, such as the level, the square, and the compasses. When were these things made, and by what people?

So far as I know, Masonry in the British Islands cannot be historically traced back much, if at all, beyond the Revolution of 1688.

Mr. Olphert and his son walked about the place with us. They have no fears of an attack, but think it wise to keep a force of police on the premises. The only demonstration yet made of any kind against the house was the march from

Falcarragh some time ago of a mob of young men, who promptly withdrew on catching sight of half-a-dozen policemen within the park gates. As to getting his work done, some of his people had steadily refused to acknowledge the "boycott," and they were now strengthened by the attitude of those who had surrendered to the pressure, and were now sullen and angry with the League which had given them nothing to do, and no supplies.

At Falcarragh we met a person who knew much about the late Lord Leitrim, who was murdered in this neighbourhood on the highway some years ago. He spoke freely of the murderer by name, as if it were matter of common notoriety. Of the murdered man, he said that he had made himself extremely unpopular and odious, not so much by certain immoralities freely alleged at the time of his death, as by vexatious meddling with the prejudices and whims of his tenants. "He used to go into the houses and pull down cartoons and placards, if he saw them put up on the walls." "No! he had no party feeling in the matter; he used to pull down William III. and the Pope with an equal hand." It seems that in this region, too, a local legend has grown up of the birth at a place called Cashelmore of a "Queen of France." The case is worth noting as throwing light on the genesis and accuracy of local traditions. The " Queen of France " referred to proves, on inquiry, to have been Miss Patterson, who married Jerome Bonaparte, brother of the first Emperor, afterwards created by him King of Westphalia! This was the lady so well known in America as Mrs. Patterson Bonaparte of Baltimore, who died at a great age only a few years ago. I have no reason to suppose that she was born at Cashelmore at all or in Ireland. But her father, reputed in the time of Washington to be the richest man in the United States, who came from the North of Ireland and settled in Baltimore as a merchant, may very well have been born there.

To my great regret Father M‘Fadden of Glena, or Falcarragh, was absent from home. As we drove homeward we met on the way a young lady on a smart jaunting-car, with a servant in livery. This was the daughter, our driver told us, of Mr. Griffiths, the Protestant clergyman, past whose residence our road lay. His church stands high upon a commanding cliff, and is a feature in the landscape. We met the parson himself also, walking with a friend. The road from Bedlam to Derrybeg goes by a region of the " Rosses," reputed the most woe-begone part of the Gweedore district. This is the scene of a curious tale told about Father M'Fadden of Gweedore, by his ill-wishers in these parts, to the effect that he advises English Members of Parliament and other "sympathising" visitors who come here to make a pilgrimage to "the Rosses," where, no matter at what time of day they appear, they invariably find sundry of the people sitting in their huts and eating stewed seaweed out of iron pots. I cannot vouch for this tale, but certainly I have seen no people here of either sex, or of any age, who look as if they lived on stewed seaweed. Another person at Falcarragh told us, as an illustration of the influence exerted by Father M'Fadden of Gweedore, in this parish, over which he has no proper authority, that, in obedience to an intimation from him, the persons whose seats in the chapel had been occupied on two successive Sundays by the policemen now stationed here, yesterday refused to allow the policemen to occupy them, the only exception being in the case of a man who had been arrested at the same time with Father Stephens, and who had been so well treated by the police, that he felt bound to repay their courtesy by offering one of them his seat.

CHAPTER III.

DUNGLOE, *Tuesday, Feb.* 7.—We rose early this morning at Gweedore; the sun shining so brightly that we were forced to drop the window-shades at breakfast, while I read my letter from Rome, telling me of the bitter cold there, and of a slight snow-fall last week. Here the birds were singing, and the air was as soft and exhilarating as that of an April morning in the Highlands of Mexico or Costa Rica.

Our host gave us a capital car, with a staunch nag and a wide-awake jarvey, thanks to all which I found the thirteen miles drive to this place too short. No doubt it will be a great thing for Donegal when "light railways" are laid down here. But I pity the traveller of the future here, if he is never to know the delight of traversing these wild and picturesque wastes in such weather as we have had to-day, on a car, well-balanced by a single pleasant companion, drinking, as he goes, deep draughts of the Atlantic air! Truly on a jaunting-car "two are company and three are none." You have almost the free companionship of a South American journey in the saddle, jumping off to walk, when you like, more freely still.

We drove near the house of the "beauty of Gweedore," but she was not visible, though we met her mother (by no means a *pulchra mater*) as we crossed the Clady at Bryan's Bridge.

We soon passed from the bogland into a wilderness of granite. Our jarvey, however, maintained that there was "better land among the stones than any bogland could be." He was a shrewd fellow, and summed up the economical situation, I thought, better than some of his betters, when he said of the whole region that "it will fatten four, feed five, and starve six."

It may well fatten six, though, I should say, if the natural wealth of this vast granite range can be properly turned to account. On every side of us lay vast blocks of granite of all hues and grades, all absolutely unworked, but surely not unworkable. We stopped and picked up many specimens, some of them almost as rich in colour as porphyry. Of lakes and lakelets supplying water-power the name too, is legion.

Beyond Annagary we caught a glimpse of the Isle of Arran, the scene, a few years ago, of so much suffering, and that of a kind I should think as much beyond the control of legislation as the misery and destruction which have overtaken successive attempts to establish settlements on Anticosti in the Gulf of St. Lawrence.

This town of Dungloe sprawls along the shore of the sea. It is reputed the most ill-favoured town in Donegal, and it certainly is not a dream of beauty. But it blooms all over with evidences of the prosperity of that interesting type of Irish civilisation, the "Gombeen man," of whom I had heard so much at Gweedore. Over the doorways of most of the shops appear the names of various members of the family of Sweeney, all of them, I am told, brought here and established within a few years past by the head of the sept, who is not only the great "Gombeen man" of the region, but a leading local member of the National League, and Her Majesty's Postmaster. The Sweeneys, in fact, commercially speaking, dominate Dungloe, their only visible rivals being a returned Irish

American, who has built himself a neat two-story house and shop just at the entrance of the village, and our own host, Mr. Maurice Boyle, whose extremely neat little inn just faces a large shop, the stronghold of the Chief of the Sweeneys. I am sorry to find that this important citizen of Dungloe is not now here. We went into his chief establishment to make some purchases, and found it full of customers, chiefly women, neatly dressed after the Donegal fashion, and busily chaffering with the shopgirls and shopmen, who had their hands full, exhibiting goods such as certainly would not be found in any New York or New England village of this sort. When we secured the attention of the chief shopman, a nattily dressed, dark-haired young man who would not have discredited the largest "store" in Grand Street or the Bowery of New York, we asked him to show us some of the home-made woollen goods of the country. These, he assured us, had no sale in Dungloe, and he did not keep them. But he showed us piles of handsome Scottish tweeds at much higher prices. Now as this is an exclusively agricultural region, it is evident that the tenants must be able to make it worth a trader's while to keep on hand such goods as we here found, and therefore that they cannot be exactly on "the ragged edge" of things.

Mr. Sweeney is also the proprietor of the chief "hotel" of Dungloe; our host, Mr. Boyle, being in fact supposed to be "boycotted" for entertaining officers of the police. This "boycott," however, has entailed no practical inconvenience upon us; and Mr. Boyle's pretty and plucky daughters, who manage his house for him, laughed scornfully at the notion of being "bothered" by it.

After luncheon we took a car and drove out to Burtonport, on the Roads of Arranmore, to visit the parish priest there, Father Walker, and Mr. Hammond, the agent of the Conyngham estates.

We passed near a large inland lake, Lough Meela, and the seaward views along the coast were very fine. With peace and order this corner of Ireland might easily become the chosen site of the most delightful seaside homes in the United Kingdom. The Recorder of Cork has discovered this, and passes a great part of the year here. This Donegal coast is no further from the great centres of British wealth and population than are Mount Desert and the other summer resorts of Maine and New Hampshire from New York and Philadelphia; and the islands which break the great roll of the Atlantic here cannot well be more nearly in "a state of nature" than were the Isles of Shoals, for example, in my college days, long after Mr. Lowell first wandered there with the transcendental Thaxters to celebrate the thunders of the surf at Appledore.

The wonderful granitic formations we had seen on the way from Gweedore stretch all along the coast to the Roads of Arranmore. At Burtonport they lie on the very water's edge. At a place called Lickeena, masses of beautiful salmon- and rose-coloured granite actually trend into the tide-water, and at Burtonport proper is a promontory of that richly-mottled granite which I had supposed to be the peculiar heritage of Peterhead, and which is now largely exported from Scotland to the United States. Why should not this Irish granite be shipped directly from Donegal to America, there to be built up into cathedrals, and shaped into monuments for the Exiles of Erin? All these formations which we have seen present themselves in great cubical blocks, so jointed that they may be detached without blasting, with great comparative ease, and with little of the waste which results from the squaring of shapeless masses. At the same time, as we saw while coming from Gweedore, the many lakes of this region offer all the water-power necessary for polishing-works, columnar lathes, and the general machinery used in developing such quarries. Without being an expert in granites, I have seen enough of the granite works at home to feel quite sure that a moderate and judiciously managed investment here ought to return a handsome result. If the National League is as well off as it is reputed to be, it might go into this business open a new and remunerative industry to the people of a "congested" district, and earn dividends large enough to enable it to pay the expenses of the war against England at Westminster, without drawing on the savings of the servant-girls in America. The only person likely to suffer would be the "Gombeen man," if the peasantry earned enough to pay off their debts to him, and stop the flow of interest into his coffers.

At Burtonport we found the "Gombeen man," of Dungloe, represented by a very large "store." He runs steamers between this place and various ports on the Scottish and Irish coasts, bringing in goods and taking out the crops which his debtors turn over to him.

This Burtonport "store" towers high above the modest home of the parish priest, Father Walker. To our great regret he was absent on parochial duty, but his niece very kindly welcomed us into his modest study, where we left a note begging him to honour us with his company at dinner in Dungloe.

Mr. Hammond, too, was absent, so after paying our respects to his wife, we drove back to Dungloe, and walked about the village till dark, chatting with the good-natured, civil people. The local sensation here they tell us is not the trial of the priests at Dunfanaghy, but a "row" breeding between the chief of the Sweeneys and one of his brethren over the possession of Her Majesty's Post-office. It seems there is an official regulation or custom that the post-office once established in a particular building shall not be moved thence without positive cause shown. The head of the Sweeneys, having completed his new and grand establishment, wishes to move the post-office thither; but the brother to whom he confided the office in the older building, where he left it while making the change of his own business, now desires to keep the office where it is, and, I suppose, to become postmaster himself!"[1] A trivial matter enough, but not without edification for students of the actual situation in this most curious country.

About seven o'clock Father Walker made his appearance—a fine-looking, dignified, most amiable man. He is a teetotaller, which we esteemed a stroke of good fortune, a bottle of port wine which we obtained, despite the "boycott," from the Gombeen shop, proving to be of such a quality that it might have been concocted in the last century, expressly to discredit the Methuen treaty.

Father Walker is the President of the National League branch.

Like Father M'Fadden at Gweedore, he speaks of the landlords in this part of Donegal as really owning, not so much farms as residential grounds for tenants who export their thews and sinews to Scotland and other countries, and live by that traffic mainly. It is a common practice here, he tells me, for the children, who are very sharp and bright, to be taken by their parents into Tyrone

[1] From a question just asked (July 12) in the House of Commons, and answered by the Postmaster-General, I gather that this "local question" has been further complicated by the removal of Mr. Sweeney, the sub-postmaster, under an official regulation.

and other parts of the North, and put out to live with the people there, who prize them, and pay very good wages. I asked him if he thought the official estimate I had seen of the proportion of these "migratory labourers" to the whole population of Ulster, as about one-tenth of one per cent., an under-statement. He thought it was an under-statement for this part of the county of Donegal, but to be explained, perhaps, by the fact that so much of the migration is merely from one county into another, and not out of the kingdom. He agreed that the practice goes on upon a much more extensive scale in the County Mayo, where more than thirteen per cent. of all the adult male population are said to belong to the category of migratory labourers. The Irish population of England seems to be recruited at regular seasons in this way, very much as is the Albanian population of Constantinople.

Father Walker was full of information about the granite quarries, and much interested in the prospect of their development. He told us that a practical engineer from Liverpool had, not long ago, been here seeking a lease of the quarries—or, in other words, of the quarrying rights over sixty or seventy miles of Donegal—from the agent of Lord Conyngham. This engineer had come to Donegal on a sporting expedition last year, and gone back full of the capabilities of the granite region. Father Walker had been told by him that similar quarries also exist in the County Mayo at Belmullet, where preparations are now making, he thinks, to develop them, though on a smaller scale than would be both practicable and desirable here.

In Mayo, as in Donegal, labour must be plentiful enough, and the comparatively unskilled labour required in such quarries would be particularly abundant here. It would be a great thing, Father Walker thought, to introduce here the custom of a regular pay-day, and with it gradually habits of exactness and economy, not easily developed without it.

He gave me also, at my request, some valuable information as to the stipends of the Catholic clergy, and the sources from which they are derived. This subject has been agitated in the local press of this part of Ireland in connection with estimates of Father M'Fadden's income at Gweedore, which Father M'Fadden declares, I believe, to be greatly exaggerated. Father Walker has been parish priest at Burtonport for about nine years. In all that time the highest sum reached in one year by the stipend has been £560; this sum having to be divided between the parish priest, who received £280, and two curates receiving £140 each. The annual stipend, however, has more than once fallen below £480, and Father Walker thinks £520 a fair average, giving £260 to the parish priest, and £130 each to his curates. Where there are only two priests in a parish, as is the case, for example, in each of the parishes of Gweedore and Falcarragh, the parish priest receives two-thirds, and the curate one-third of the stipend.

The sources of this stipend are various, and in speaking upon this point Father Walker desired me to note that he could only speak positively of the rules of this particular diocese, as they do not cover in their entirety the usages of other provinces, or even of other dioceses in this province of Ireland. One general and invariable rule indeed exists throughout Ireland, which is that every parish priest is bound to offer the Holy Sacrifice, *pro populo*, for the whole people, without fee or reward, on all Sundays and Holy Days, making in all some eighty-seven times a year.

In the diocese of Raphoe, to which Burtonport belongs, there are four recognised methods by which the revenues of the priests are raised. The first is an annual fixed stipend of four shillings for each household or family. "Sometimes," said Father Walker, "but rarely, the better-off families give more than this; and not unfrequently the poorer families fail to give anything under this head." The second is a fixed stipend of one pound upon the occasion of a marriage. "Sometimes, but not often, this sum is exceeded by generous and prosperous parishioners." The third is a standard stipend of two shillings for a baptism. "This also suffers, but on rare occasions," said the good priest, "a favourable exception. I mention the exceptions as well as the rules," said the good Father, "in order to make grateful allusion to the donors."

The fourth and last consists of the offerings at interments. "These vary very much indeed, but they constitute an important, and, I may say, a necessary item in the incomes of the clergy."

Besides these four forms of stipend, the priests derive a revenue from "those who ask them to offer the Holy Sacrifice 'for their special intention.'" In such cases it is customary to offer a sum, usually of two shillings, but sometimes of half-a-crown, which is intended both as a remuneration for the priest, and to cover the cost of altar requisites.

Father Walker estimates the families in his own parish in round numbers at about thirteen hundred, and in Gweedore and Falcarragh at about nine hundred each. We had some conversation about the great fisheries, which one would think ought to exist, but do not exist, on this coast, such fishing as is done here by the natives being on a very limited scale. Father Walker tells me that formerly £80,000 worth of herring were taken on this coast, though he is not sure that Donegal fishermen took them. But of late years he thinks the herring have deserted these waters. He admits, however, that the people have no liking for the sea. "Going over once," he said, "to Arranmore from the mainland in a boat with a priest of the country, the water was a little rough, and the poor man nearly pinched a piece out of my arm holding on to me!" Father Walker himself thought the trip across the "sound" to Tory Island rather a ticklish piece of business. Yet the natives make it sometimes in their little corraghs or canvas boats, which would seem to show that some of them must be capable of seamanship. Most of these islands, notably Arranmore, Father Walker thought quite incapable of supporting the people who dwell on them, without constant help from the mainland. Is it not an open question whether an age which countenances the condemnation of private property in houses declared unfit for human habitation ought to hesitate at dealing in the same spirit with nurseries of chronic penury and intermittent famine? On one of these islands, known as Scull Island, Father Walker tells me great quantities of human bones are found in circular graves or trenches, very shallow, and going all around the island. There are legends of great battles fought on the little island, and of pestilences, to account for these. But it is likely enough that the island was simply used as a cemetery by the dwellers on the shore at some early date. Father Walker when he was last there had brought away some of these relics. One he showed us, the beautifully formed jawbone of a young child, apparently ten or twelve years old, with exquisite pearly teeth. The chin was not in the least prognathous, but very well formed. In this district of Dungloe, too, the women weave and knit as well as at Gweedore; and Father Walker, before he left us for his home, after a most agreeable evening, promised to send me some specimens of their handiwork. He is sure that with a proper organisation this industry might be so developed as to materially relieve the people here from the pressure of their debts to the dealers of all kinds, a pressure much more severe than that of the rent. According to the dealers themselves, no tenant really in debt to them can now expect to work himself free of the burden under four or five years. It is obvious how much power, political as well as social, is thus lodged in the hands of the dealers, and especially of the "Gombeen men."

BARON'S COURT, *Wednesday, Feb.* 8.—Since last night I have travelled from one extreme to the other of Irish life—from the desolation of the Rosses of Donegal to the grandly wooded, picturesque, and beautiful demesne of Baron's Court. We made an early start from Dungloe on a capital car for Letterkenny, where we were to strike the railway for Strabane and Newtown-Stewart. The morning was clear, but cold. On leaving Dungloe we drove directly into a region of reclaimed land, where improvements of various kinds seemed to be going on.

All this our jarvey informed us, with a knowing look, belonged to Mr. Sweeney.

"Was he a squire of this country?" I asked innocently.

"A squire of this country, sorr? He is just Mr. Sweeney, the Gombeen man; he and his brothers, they all came here from where I don't know."

An energetic man, certainly, Mr. Sweeney, and not likely, I should think, to allow the National League, to push matters here to the point of nationalising the land of Donegal, if he can prevent it. In the highway we met, two or three miles out of Dungloe, a very trim dainty little lady, in a long, well-fitting London waterproof ulster, with a natty little umbrella in her hand, walking merrily towards the town. How weatherwise she was soon appeared, the rain coming up suddenly, and coming down sharply, in the whirling way it has among the hills everywhere. The scenery was desolate, but grand. Countless little lochs give sparkle and life to it. Everywhere the granite. About Doocharry, a romantic little spot, where Lord Cloncurry has a fishing-box in the heart of a glorious landscape, masses crop out of a rich red granite, finer in colour than any we had previously seen. In that neighbourhood the wastes of Donegal take on an aspect which recalls, though upon quite a different key in colour, the inimitable beauty of those treeless North-western highlands of Scotland, upon which Nature has lavished all the wealth of her palette. Vast spaces of brown and red and gold shimmer away under the softly luminous mountain atmosphere to the dark blues and purples of the hills. We passed Glen Veagh again, but from quite a different point of view, which gave us a beautiful picture of Lough Veagh in its length, and of the smiling pastoral landscape upon its further shore.

As we drew near the eastern boundary of Donegal, hedges and civilised agriculture reappeared. With these we came upon mud cottages, such as I had not seen in Donegal, being the huts provided for their labourers by the tenant-farmers, whose comfortable stone-houses and out-buildings stood well back under the long ranges of the hills.

We passed through much striking scenery, perhaps the finest point being a magnificent Gap in the hills, guarded and defined by three colossal headlands, one of them a vast long rampart, the other two gigantic counterscarps. The immediate approach to Letterkenny, too, from the west is charming, passing in full view of the extensive and beautiful park and the large mansion of Colonel Stewart of the Guards, and skirting the well-kept estate of Mr. Boyd, the owner of the ivy-clad cottages which so took my fancy the other day.

In the Ulster settlement under King James I. a patent for Letterkenny was issued to one of the Crawfords. Then, as the records tell us, "Sir George Marburie dwelt there, and there were forty houses all inhabited by British tenants. A great market town, and standeth well for the King's service."

Again we found a fair going on—this time attended by swarms of peddlers vending old clothes and all sorts of small wares, bread-cartmen, and tea-vendors. These latter aver that it is easier to sell tea in the "congested" districts at 4s. 6d. than at 2s. 6d. The people have no test of its quality but its price!

The town was gay with soldiers and police— whose advent had created such a demand for bread and meat, a man told us, that all the butchers and bakers in Letterkenny and Dunfanaghy were at their wits' ends to meet it. "But they don't complain of that!" We reached Newtown-Stewart by railway after dark. As we passed Sion the mills were all lighted up, giving it the look of an English or New England town. A New England snow-storm, too, awaited us at our journey's end; and, after a wild drive of several miles through the whirling white mists, it was a delectable thing to find ourselves welcomed in a hall full of light and warmth and flowers by merry children and lively dogs, the guard of honour of the most gracious and charming of hostesses.

BARON'S COURT, *Thursday, Feb.* 9.—Among a batch of letters received this morning I find one from a most estimable and accomplished priest in the West of Ireland, to whom I wrote from Dublin announcing my intention of visiting the counties of Clare and Kerry. "I shall be very glad," he says, "to learn that no evil hath befallen you during your visit to that solitary plague-spot, where dwell the disgraceful and degraded 'Moonlighters.' Would not 'martial law,' if applied to that particular spot, suffice to stamp out these insensate pests of society?" This language, strong, but not too strong in view of the hideous murder last week near Lixnaw of a farmer in the presence of his daughter for the atrocious crime of taking a farm "boycotted" by the National League, shows that the open alliance between this organisation and the criminal classes in certain parts of Ireland is beginning (not a day too soon) to arouse the better order of priests in Ireland to the peril of playing with edged tools. For my correspondent is not only a priest, but a Nationalist. I have sent him in reply a letter received by me, also to-day, touching the conduct in connection with the Lixnaw murder of a priest, a curate, I think, comparatively new to the place, who, standing by the corpse of the murdered man, endeavoured, so my informant states, to make his unfortunate daughter give up the names of the murderers, the effect of which would have been to put them on their guard, and "under the protection of that public conspiracy of silence, which is the shield of all such criminals in these parts!" Baron's Court is a very large, stately mansion, lacking elevation perhaps like Blenheim, but imposing by its mass and the area it covers. It was rebuilt almost entirely by the late Duke of Abercorn, who also made immense plantations here which cover the country for miles around. His grandfather, the handsome Marquis of the days of the Prince Regent, came here a great deal towards the end of his life, but did little towards making the mansion worthy of its site. Two very good portraits of him here show that he deserved his reputation as the finest-looking man of his day, a reputation attested by a diamond ring, the history of which is still preserved in the family. A fine though irregular pearl given by Philip of Spain to his hapless spouse, Mary Tudor, is another of the heirlooms of Baron's Court; but the ring and the note left by Mary Stuart to Claud Hamilton, Lord Paisley, mysteriously disappeared during the long minority of the late Duke under the trusteeship of the fourth Earl of Aberdeen, and have since, it is said, come into the possession of the Duke of Hamilton.

Of the three castles given to Lord Claud Hamilton by James I., to enable him to hold this country, one which stood at Strabane has disappeared, the memory of it surviving only in the name of Castle Street in that town. The ivy-clad ruins of another adorn a height in this beautiful park. They are "bosomed high in tufted trees," and overlook one of three most lovely lakes, stretching in a shining chain through the length of the demesne.

Another ruined tower of the time of King John stands on an island in one of these lakes. When the Ulster settlement was made, these lands with all the countryside were held by the O'Kanes. With the other Celtic and Catholic inhabitants, they were driven by the masterful invaders into the mountains and bogs. There still remain their descendants, still Celtic and still Catholic, and still dreaming of the day when they shall descend into the low country and drive the Protestant Scotch and English from the "fat lands" which they occupy. In this way the racial and religious animosities are kept alive, which have died out in Tipperary and Waterford, for example, where the Cromwellian English have become more Irish and often more Catholic than the Irish themselves.

I took a long drive and walk with Lord Ernest this afternoon through the park, which rivals Curraghmore in extent. It is nowhere divided from the lands of the adjoining tenants, and with great liberality is thrown open to the people, not only of Newtown-Stewart and Strabane, but of all the country. Parties, sometimes of seven hundred people, from Belfast come down to pass the day in these sylvan solitudes, and it is to be recorded to the praise of Ireland that these visitors always behave with perfect good sense and good feeling.

The "terrible trippers" of the English midlands, as I once heard an old verger in a northern Cathedral call them, who chip off relics from monuments, pull up flowers by the roots, and scatter sandwich papers and empty gingerbeer bottles broadcast over well-rolled lawns, are not known, Lord Ernest tells me, in this island. As he neatly puts it, the Irishman, no matter what his station in life may be, or how great a blackguard he may really be, always instinctively knows when he ought to behave like a gentleman, and knows how to do so. In the lakes were hundreds of wild fowl. The sky was a sky of Constable—silvery-white clouds, floating athwart a dome of clear Italian blue. The soil here must be extraordinarily fertile. The woods and groves are dense beyond belief. Cut down what you like, the growth soon overtakes you, as lush almost as in the tropics.

There was a great cyclone here a year or two ago, which prostrated in a night over a hundred thousand trees. You see the dentated gaps left by this disaster in the great circle of firs and birches on the surrounding hills, but they make hardly a serious break in the thoroughly sylvan character of the landscape. We visited the centre of the devastation, where I found myself in what seemed to be a backwoods clearing in America. An enterprising Scot, Kirkpatrick by name, has taken a contract under the Duke, built himself a neat wooden cabin and stables, set up a small saw-mill driven by steam, and is hard at work turning the fallen trees into timber, and making a very good thing of it, both for the Duke and for himself. He has one or two of his own people with him, but employs the labour of the country, and has no fear of disturbance. He thinks, however, that he must get "a good wicked dog" to frighten away the tramps, who sometimes stray into his woodland, and put the enterprise in peril by smoking and drowsing under haystacks.

Near this clearing is a model village, the houses scrupulously neat, with trees and flowers, and here we met the Duchess with her devoted dog walking briskly along to visit one of her people, a wonderful old man, bearing the ancient name of the O'Kanes, and five years older than the Kaiser William. Until six months ago this veteran was an active carpenter, coming and going about his work at ninety-six like a man in middle age. Then he went to bed with a bad cold, and will probably never rise again. In all his life he never has touched meat or soup, and when they are now offered him rejects them angrily. He has lived, and preferred to live, entirely on oatmeal in the form of cakes and porridge, and on potatoes; so I make a present of him as a glorious example to the vegetarians. As in so many other cases, his memory of recent events is dim and clouded—of events long past, clear and photographic: the negatives taken in youth quite perfect, the lenses which now take, dimmed and fractured.

He perfectly recollects, for example, the assembling here of the recruits going out to the Continent before the battle of Waterloo, and can give the names and describe the peculiarities of stalwart lads long since crumbled into dust around Mont St. Jean. With the curious unconcern about death which marks his people, this expectant emigrant into the unknown world chats about his departure as if it were for Dublin, and his kinsfolk chat with him.

"Ye'll be going soon!"

"Oh yes, I shan't trouble ye more than an hour or two more."

In quite another part of the domain we came

upon a Covenanter—a true, authentic Covenanter, who might have walked out of *Old Mortality*; the name of him, Keyes. He greeted Lord Ernest cheerily enough, nodded to me in a not unfriendly way, and at once broke into exhortation: "It's a very short life we live; man that is born of woman is of few days, and full of trouble. Well for them that are the children of light—if seeing the light they sin not against it"; and so on with amazing volubility.

There are eighty-five of these Covenanters here. They touch not nor have touched the accursed thing. To them all parties and all governments are alike evil. The Whigs persecuted the Solemn League and Covenant—so did the Tories. Nationalists and Unionists are to them alike abominable, sold under sin. Withal they are shrewd, canny, successful farmers—and, as I inferred from sundry incidents, before Lord Ernest confided the fact to me, not averse from a "right gude williewaught" now and then.

Mr. Keyes, I thought, was not a blue-ribbon man, nor a ribbon-man of any kind.

The Duchess told me afterwards she had vainly endeavoured more than once to get these people to vote at elections.

We had a sprinkling of such people, and very good people in quiet times they were, in the Shenandoah Valley during the Civil War, to whom Federals and Confederates were alike anathema.

We wound up our drive to-day just beyond "the Duke's seat," a little rustic bench put up by the late Duke on a hill range which commands a magnificent view over the whole domain of hill and forest and lakes, and far away to the mountains of Munterlony. There, in the bogs and woods James Hamilton, "lord baron of Strabane," with "other rebels, unknown, in his company," hid himself till, after the fall of Charlemont in August 1650, he was captured by a party of the Commonwealth's men—whereby, as the record here runs, "all and singular his manors, towns, lands, and so forth were forfeited to the Commonwealth of England." Under this pressure he sought "protection," and got it a fortnight later from Cromwell's General, Sir Charles Coote, whose descendants still flourish in Wicklow. But on the 31st of December 1650 he "broke the said protection, and joined himself with Sir Phelim O'Neill, being then in rebellion."

Troublous times those, and a "lord baron of Strabane" needed almost the alacrity in turning his coat of a harlequin or a modern politician! It is a comfort to know that at last, on the 16th of June 1655, he found rest, dying at Ballyfathen, "a Roman Catholic and a papist recusant." As we came back into the gardens and grounds, Lord Ernest showed me, imbedded in the earth, a huge anchor presented to the present Duke by the Corporation of Waterford, as having belonged to the French 28-gun frigate, on which in 1689 James II. and Lord Abercorn sailed away from Ireland for France. I believe that because of its weight the present First Lord of the Admiralty avers that it is no anchor at all, but a buoy fixture. It might have been ten times as heavy, and yet not have availed to keep James from getting to sea at that particular time.

BARON'S COURT, *Friday, Feb.* 10.—Here also, in County Tyrone, the Irish women show their skill in women's work. Mrs. Dixon, the English wife of the house-steward of Baron's Court, has charge of a woollen industry founded here, after a discourse on thrift, delivered at a temperance meeting of the people by the then Marquis of Hamilton, had stirred the country up to consider whether the peasant women might not possibly find some better and more profitable way of passing their winter evenings than in sitting huddled around a peat fire with their elbows on their knees, gossiping about their neighbours. Lord Hamilton cited the women of Gweedore as proofs that such a way might by searching be found.

The Duke and Duchess found the funds, the stewardess invested them in buying the necessary yarn and knitting-needles, and the Marchioness of Hamilton acted as corresponding clerk and business agent of the new industry. The clothing department of the British army lent a listening ear to the business proposals made to it, and the work began. From that time on it has been the main substantial resource against suffering and starvation of the families of some three hundred labourers in the hill country near Baron's Court.

These labourers work for the small farmers from April to November; and between the autumn and the spring their wives and daughters knit, and by the Baron's Court machinery are enabled to dispose of, nearly twenty thousand pairs of woollen socks. The yarns are brought from Edinburgh to the store-house at Baron's Court. Thither every Wednesday come the knitters. Mrs. Dixon weighs the hanks of yarn, and gives them out.

On the following Wednesday the knitters reappear, each with her bale of stockings or socks. These are again weighed, and the knitters receive their pay according to the weight, quality, and size of the goods. In some families there are four, five, or six knitters. All these people, with four or five exceptions, are small cottars living on wretched little mountain farms, not on the Duke of Abercorn's property; and but for this industry they would be absolutely without employment all the winter through.

Some of them come from a distance of twelve or fourteen miles, and but for this resource would literally starve. They are nearly all of them Catholics, and the Protestants here being Unionists, they are probably Nationalists. About three hundred knitters in all are employed. In the year 1886-87 the orders given for Baron's Court work enabled Mrs. Dixon to pay out regularly about five pounds a week, not including casual private orders. For the current year the orders have been much larger, and the expenditure proportionally greater. Mrs. Dixon's storehouse was full of goods to-day. The long knickerbocker stockings which she showed us were remarkably good, some in " cross-gartered " patterns, handsomer, I thought, than similar goods in the Scottish Highlands—and all of them staunch and well-proportioned.

For socks such as are supplied to the volunteers and the troops the War Office pays 8¾d. a pair.

It was pleasant to learn from Mrs. Dixon that these people thoroughly appreciate the spirit which prompted and still directs this enterprise. Last spring when the Duchess was thought for a time to be hopelessly ill, a young girl came down to Baron's Court weeping bitterly. On her arm was a basket, in which were two young chanticleers crowing lustily. The poor girl said these were all she had, and she had brought them " to make soup for the Duchess, for she heard that was what the great people lived on, and it might save her life."

This afternoon I went over by the railway to Derry with Lord Ernest to attend a meeting there. The "Maiden City" stands picturesquely on the Foyle, and has a fine, though not large, cathedral of St. Colomb, restored only last year, of which it may be noted that the work never was undertaken while the Protestant Church of Ireland was established by law, and has been successfully carried out since the disendowment of that Church.

The streets were white with snow, but the meeting in the old Town Hall was largely attended. It was, in fact, a sort of Orange symposium—tea being served at long tables, and the platform decorated with a pianoforte. The Mayor of the city presided, and between the speeches, songs, mostly in the Pyramus or condoling vein, were sung by a local tenor of renown. It was very like an American tea-fight in the country, and the audience were unquestionably enthusiastic. They quite cheered themselves hoarse when Lord Ernest Hamilton reminded them that he had made his first political speech in that hall on a "memorable occasion," when, being an as yet unfledged Parliamentarian, he had taken a hand in a successful attempt to prevent the Lord Mayor of Dublin, Mr. Dawson, from making a speech in Derry. One of my neighbours, a merchant in the city, told me that a project is afoot for tearing down the old hall in which we met "to enlarge the street," but he added that "the people of Derry were too proud of their history to allow it!"

I understood him to say it is one of the very few buildings in Derry which witnessed the famous siege, and the breaking of the boom.

We left the "revel" early, caught a fast train to Newtown-Stewart, and returned here an hour ago through a driving snowstorm, most dramatically arranged to enhance the glow and genial charm of our welcome.

BARON'S COURT, *Saturday, Feb. 11th.*—All the world was white with snow this morning. Alas! for the deluded birds we have been listening to for days past; thrushes, larks, and as, I believe, blackbirds, though there is a tradition in these parts that no man ever heard the blackbird sing before the 15th of February. I suspect it grew out of the date of St. Valentine's Day. We had some lovely music, however, within doors this morning; and, in spite of the snow and the chill wind, a little fairy of a girl, with her groom, went off like mad across country on her pony, "Guinea Pig," to fetch the mails from Newtown-Stewart.

Not long after breakfast came in from Letterkenny Sergeant Mahony of the constabulary, on whose testimony Father M'Fadden was convicted. We had heard at Letterkenny that he was now on leave at Belfast, and Lord Ernest had kindly arranged matters so that he should come here and tell us his story of Gweedore.

An admirable specimen he is of a most admirable body of men. He is as thoroughly Celtic in aspect as he is by name—a dark Celt, with a quiet resolute face, and a wiry well-built frame.

Nothing could be better than his manner and bearing, at once respectful and self-respectful: that manner of a natural gentleman one so often sees in the Irish peasant. He is a devout Catholic, but no admirer of Father M'Fadden.

As to his evidence, he explains very clearly that he was not sent to report Father M'Fadden's speech at all, but to note and take down and report language used in the speech of a sort to excite the people against the law. He was selected for this duty for three reasons: he is a Donegal man who has lived at Gweedore for sixteen years; he is a fair stenographer; and he speaks Irish, in which language Father M'Fadden made his speech.

"I speak Irish quite as well as he does," said the Sergeant quietly, "and he knows I do. What I did was to put down in English words what I heard said in Irish. This I had to do because I have no stenographic signs for the Irish words." He tells me he taught himself stenography.

"As for Father M'Fadden," he said, "he told the people that 'he was the law in Gweedore, and they should heed no other.' He spoke the truth, too, for he makes himself the law in Gweedore. He dislikes me because I am a living proof that he is not the only law in Gweedore!" Of the business shrewdness and ability of Father M'Fadden, Sergeant Mahony expressed a very high opinion, though hardly in terms which would have gratified such an eccclesiastic as the late Cardinal Barnabo. Possibly Cardinal Cullen might have relished them no better. "Certainly he has the finest house in Gweedore, sir, and what's more he made it the finest himself."

"Do you mean that he built it?"

"He did, indeed; and did you not notice the beautiful stone fences he is putting up all about it, and the four farms he has?"

"Then he is certainly a man of substance?"

"And of good substance, sir! The Government, they gave him a hundred pounds towards the house. But it was the flood that was the blessed thing for him and made a great man of him!"

"The flood?" I asked, with some natural astonishment; "the flood? What flood?"

"And did you never hear of the great flood of Gweedore? It was in August 1880. You will mind the water that comes down behind the chapel? Well, there was a flood, and it swelled, and it swelled, and it burst the small pipe there behind the chapel: too small it was entirely for carrying off the great water, and nobody took notice of it, or that there was anything wrong, and so the water was piled up behind the chapel, and at Mass on the Sunday, while the chapel was full, the walls gave way, and the water rushed in, and was nine feet deep. There were five people that couldn't get out in time, and were drowned—two old people and three children, young people. It was a great flood. And Father M'Fadden wrote about it—oh, he is a clever priest with the pen—and they made a great subscription in London for the poor people and the chapel. I can't rightly say how much, but it was in the papers, a matter of seven hundred pounds, I have heard say. And it was all sent to Father M'Fadden."

"And it was spent, of course," I said, "on the repairs of the chapel, or given to the relatives of the poor people who were drowned."

"Oh, no doubt; very likely it was, sir! But the repairs of the chapel — there isn't a mason in Donegal but will tell you a hundred pounds would not be wanted to make the chapel as good as it ever was. And for the people that were drowned—two of them were old people, as I said to you, sir, that had no kith or kin to be relieved, and for the others they were of well-to-do people that would not wish to take anything from the parish."

"What was done with it, then?"

"Oh! that I can't tell ye. It was spent for the people some way. You must ask Father M'Fadden. He is the fund in Gweedore, just as he is the law in Gweedore. Oh! they came from all parts to see the great ruin of the flood at Gweedore. They did, indeed. And some of them, it was poor sight they had; they couldn't see the big rift in the walls, when Father M'Fadden pointed it out to them. 'Whisht! there it is!' he would say, pointing with his finger. Then they saw it!"

I asked him at what figure he put the income of Father M'Fadden from his parish. Without a moment's hesitation he answered, "It's over a thousand pounds a year, sir, and nearer twelve hundred than eleven." I expressed my surprise at this, the whole rental of Captain Hill, the landlord, falling, as I had understood, below rather than above £700 a year; and Gweedore, as Father Walker had told me, containing fewer houses than Burtonport.

"Fewer houses, mayhap," said the sergeant, "though I'm not sure of that; but if fewer they pay more. There's but one curate—poor man, he does all the parish work, barring the high masses, and a good man he is, but he gets £400 a year, and that is but a third of the income!"

I asked by what special stipends the priest's income at Gweedore could be thus enhanced. "Oh, it's mainly the funeral-money that helps it up," he replied. "You see, sir, since Father M'Fadden came to Gweedore it's come to be the fashion."

"The fashion?" I said.

"Yes, sir, the fashion. This is the way it is, you see. When a poor creature comes to be buried—no matter who it is, a pauper, or a tenant, or any one—the people all go to the chapel; and every man he walks up and lays his offering for the priest on the coffin; and the others, they watch him. And, you see, if a man that thinks a good deal of himself walks up and puts down five shillings, why, another man that thinks less of him, and more of himself, he'll go up and make it a gold ten-shilling piece, or perhaps even a sovereign! I've known Father

M'Fadden, sir, to take in as much as £15 in a week in that way."

Sergeant Mahony told us a curious tale, too, of the way in which Father M'Fadden dealt with the people of the neighbouring parish of Falcarragh. He would go down to the parish boundary, if he wanted to address the people of Falcarragh, and stand over the line, with one foot in each parish!

At our request Sergeant Mahony made some remarks in Irish; very wooing and winning they were in sound. Before he left Baron's Court he promised to make out and send me a schedule of the parochial income at Gweedore, under the separate heads of the sources whence it is derived.

Obviously Sergeant Mahony would make a good "devil's advocate" at the canonization of Father M'Fadden. But, all allowances made for this, one thing would seem to be tolerably clear. Of the three personages who take tribute of the people of Gweedore, the law intervenes in their behalf with only one —the landlord. The priest and the "Gombeen man" deal with them on the old principle of "freedom of contract." But it is by no means so clear which of the three exacts and receives the greatest tribute.

We leave Baron's Court in an hour for Dublin, whence I go on alone to-night into Queen's County.

CHAPTER IV.

ABBEYLEIX, *Sunday, Feb.* 12.—Newtown-Stewart, through which I drove yesterday afternoon with Lord Ernest to the train, is a prettily situated town, with the ruins of a castle in which James II. slept for a night on his flight to France. He was cordially received, and by way of showing his satisfaction left the little town in flames when he departed. Here appears to be a case, not of rack-renting, but of absenteeism. The town belongs to a landlord who lives in Paris, and rarely, if ever, comes here. There are no improvements — no sanitation—but the inhabitants make no complaint. "Absenteeism" has its compensations as well as its disadvantages. They pay low rents, and are little troubled; the landlord drawing, perhaps, £400 a year from the whole place. The houses are small, though neat enough in appearance, but the town has a sleepy, inert look. On the railway between Dundalk and Newry, we passed a spot known by the ominous name of "The Hill of the Seven Murders," seven agents having been murdered there since 1840! I suppose this must be set down to the force of habit. At Newry a cavalry officer whom Lord Ernest knew got into our carriage. He was full of hunting, and mentioned a place to which he was going as a " very fine country."

" From the point of view of the picturesque?" I asked.

" Oh no! from the point of view of falling off your horse!"

At Maple's Hotel I found a most hospitable telegram, insisting that I should give up my intention of spending the night at Maryborough, and come on to this lovely place in my host's carriage, which would be sent to meet me at that station. I left Kingsbridge Station in Dublin about 7 P.M. We had rather a long train, and I observed a number of people talking together about one of the carriages before we started; but there was no crowd at all, and nothing to attract special attention. As we moved out of the station, some lads at the end of the platform set up a cheer. We ran on quietly till we reached Kildare. There quite a gathering awaited our arrival on the platform, and as we slowed up, a cry went up from among them of, "Hurrah for Mooney! hurrah for Mooney!" The train stopped just as this cry swelled most loudly, when to my surprise a tall man in the gathering caught one or two of the people by the shoulder, shaking them, and called out loudly, "Hurrah for Gilhooly—you fools, hurrah for Gilhooly!"

This morning I learned that I had the honour, unwittingly, of travelling from Dublin to Maryborough with Mr. Gilhooly, M.P., who appears to have been arrested in London on Friday, brought over yesterday by the day train, and sent on at once from Dublin to his destined dungeon.

An hour's drive through a rolling country, showing white and weird under its blanket of snow in the night, brought us to this large, rambling, delightful house, the residence of Viscount de Vesci. Mr. Gladstone came here from Lord Meath's on his one visit to Ireland some years ago. I find the house full of agreeable and interesting people; and the chill of the drive soon vanished under the genial influences of a light supper, and of pleasant chat in the smoking-room. A good story was told there, by the way, of Archbishop Walsh, who being rather indiscreetly importuned to put his autograph on a fan of a certain Conservative lady well known in London, and not a little addicted to lion-hunting, peremptorily refused, saying, " no, nor any of the likes of her!" And another of Father Nolan, a well-known priest, who died at the age of ninety-seven. When some one remonstrated with him on his association with an avowed unbeliever in Christianity, like Mr. Morley, Father Nolan replied, " Oh, faith will come with time!" The same excellent priest, when he came to call on Mr. Gladstone, here at Abbeyleix, on his arrival from the Earl of Meath's, pathetically and patriarchally adjured him, on his next visit to Ireland, " not to go from one lord's house to another, but to stay with the people." This was better than the Irish journal which, finding itself obliged to chronicle the fact that Mr. Gladstone, with his wife and daughter, was visiting Abbeyleix, gracefully observed that he " had been entrapped into going there!" Some one lamenting the lack of Irish humour and spirit in the present Nationalist movement, as compared with the earlier movements, Lord de Vesci cited as a solitary but refreshing instance of it, the incident which occurred the other day at an eviction in

Kerry,[1] of a patriotic priest who chained himself to a door, and put it across the entrance of the cabin to keep out the bailiffs!

It is discouraging to know that this delightful act was bitterly denounced by some worthy and well-meaning Tory in Parliament as an "outrage"!

Despite the snow the air this morning, in this beautiful region, is soft and almost warm, and all the birds are singing again. The park borders upon and opens into the pretty town of Abbeyleix, the broad and picturesque main thoroughfare of which, rather a rural road than a street, is adorned with a fountain and cross, erected in memory of the late Lord de Vesci. There is a good Catholic chapel here (the ancient abbey which gave the place its name stood in the grounds of the present mansion), and a very handsome Protestant Church.

It is a curious fact that two of the men implicated in the Phœnix Park murders had been employed, one, I believe, as a mason, and one as a carver, in the construction of this church. Both the chapel and the church to-day were well attended. I am told there has been little real trouble here, nor has the Plan of Campaign been adopted here. Sometimes

---

[1] The incident occurred in Clare. See p. 45.

Lord de Vesci finds threatening images of coffins and guns scratched in the soil, with portraits indicating his agent or himself; but these mean little or nothing. Lady de Vesci, who loves her Irish home, and has done and is doing a good deal for the people here, tells me, as an amusing illustration of the sort of terrorism formerly established by the local organisations, that when she met two of the labourers on the place together, they used to pretend to be very busy and not to see her. But if she met one alone, he greeted her just as respectfully as ever.

The women here do a great deal of embroidery and lace work, in which she encourages them, but this industry has suffered what can only be a temporary check, from the change of fashion in regard to the wearing of laces. Why the loveliest of all fabrics made for the adornment of women should ever go "out of fashion" would be amazing if anything in the vagaries of that occult and omnipotent influence could be. The Irish ladies ought to circulate Madame de Flavigny's exquisite *Livre d'Heures*, with its incomparable illustrations by Carot and Méaulle, drawn from the lace work of all ages and countries, as a tonic against despair in respect to this industry. In one of the large rooms of her own house, Lady de Vesci has established and superintends a school of carving for the children of poor tenants. It has proved a school of civilisation also. The lads show a remarkable aptitude for the arts of design, and of their own accord make themselves neat and trim as soon as they begin to understand what it is they are doing. They are always busy at home with their drawings and their blocks, and some of them are already beginning to earn money by their work.

What I have seen at Adare Manor near Limerick, where the late Earl of Dunraven educated all the workmen employed on that mansion as stone-cutters and carvers, suffices to show that the people of this country have not lost the aptitudes of which we see so many proofs in the relics of early Irish art.

Among the guests in the house is a distinguished officer, Colonel Talbot, who saw hard service in Egypt, and in the advance on Khartoum, with camels across the desert—a marvellous piece of military work. I find that he was in America in 1864-65, with Meade and Hunt and Grant before Petersburg, being in fact the only foreign officer then present. He there formed what seem to me very sound and just views as to the ability of the Federal commanders in that closing campaign of the Civil War, and spoke of Hunt particularly with much admiration. Of General Grant he told me a story so illustrative of the simplicity and modesty which were a keynote in his character that I must note it. The day before the evacuation of Petersburg by the Confederates, Grant was urged to order an attack upon the Confederate positions. He refused to do so. The next day the Confederates were seen hastily abandoning them. Grant watched them quietly for a while, and then putting down his glass, said to one of the officers who had urged the assault, "You were right, and I was wrong. I ought to have attacked them."

It is provoking to know that the notes taken by this British officer at that time, being sent through the Post Office by him some years ago to Edinburgh for publication, were lost in the transmission, and have never been recovered. Curiously enough, however, he thinks he has now and then discerned indications in articles upon the American War, published in a newspaper which he named, going to show that his manuscripts are in existence somewhere.

ABBEYLEIX, *Monday, Feb.* 13.—To-day, in company with Lord de Vesci and a lady, I went over to Kilkenny. We left and arrived in a snowstorm, but the trip was most interesting. Kilkenny, chiefly known in America, I fear, as the city of the cats, is a very picturesque place, thanks to its turrets and towers. It has two cathedrals, a Round Tower (one of these in Dublin was demolished in the last century!), a Town Hall with a belfry, and looming square and high above the town, the Norman keep of its castle. The snow enlivened rather than diminished the scenic effect of the place. Bits of old architecture here and there give character to the otherwise commonplace streets. Notable on the way to the castle is a bit of mediæval wall with Gothic windows, and fretted with the scutcheon in stone of the O'Sheas. The connection of a gentleman of this family with the secret as well as the public story of the Parnellite movement may one day make what Horace Greeley used to call " mighty interestin' reading." A dealer in spirits now occupies what is left of the old Parliament House of Kilkenny, in which the rival partisans of Preston and O'Neill outfought the legendary cats, to the final ruin of the cause of the

Irish confederates, and the despair of the loyal legate of Pope Innocent.

Of Kilkenny Castle, founded by Strongbow, but two or three towers remain. The great quadrangle was rebuilt in 1825, and much of it again so late as in 1860. There is little, therefore, to recall the image of the great Marquis who, if Rinuccini read him aright, played so resolutely here two centuries and a half ago for the stakes which Edward Bruce won and lost at Dundalk. The castle of the Butlers is now really a great modern house.

The town crowds too closely upon it, but the position is superb. The castle windows look down upon the Nore, spanned by a narrow ancient bridge, and command, not only all that is worth seeing in the town, but a wide and glorious prospect over a region which is even now beautiful, and in summer must be charming.

Over the ancient bridge the enterprise of a modern brewer last week brought a huge iron vat, so menacingly ponderous that the authorities made him insure the bridge for a day.

Within the castle, near the main entrance, are displayed some tapestries, which are hardly shown to due advantage in that position. They were made here at Kilkenny in a factory established by Piers Butler, Earl of Ormonde, in the sixteenth century, and they ought to be sent to the Irish Exhibition of this year in London, as proving what Irish art and industry well directed could then achieve. They are equally bold in design and rich in colour. The blues are especially fine.

The grand gallery of the castle, the finest in the kingdom, though a trifle narrow for its length, is hung with pictures and family portraits. One of the most interesting of these is a portrait of the black Earl of Ormonde, a handsome swarthy man, evidently careful of his person, who was led by that political flirt, Queen Elizabeth, to believe that she meant to make him a visit in Ireland, and, perhaps, to honour him with her hand. He went to great expenses thereupon. At a parley with his kinsman, the Irish chieftain O'Moore of Abbeyleix, this black earl was traitorously captured, and an ancient drawing representing this event hangs beneath his portrait.

The muniment room, where, thanks to Lord Ormonde's courtesy, we found everything prepared to receive us, is a large, airy, and fire-proof chamber, with well-arranged shelves and tables for consulting the records. These go back to the early Norman days, long before Edward III. made James Butler Earl of Ormonde, upon his marriage with Alianore of England, granddaughter of Edward I. The Butlers came into Ireland with Henry II., and John gave them estates, the charters of some of which, with the seals annexed, are here preserved. There are fine specimens of the great seals also of Henry III., and of his sons Edward I. and Edmund Crouchback, and of the Tudor sovereigns, as well as many private seals of great interest. The wax of the early seals was obviously stronger and better than the wax since used. Of Elizabeth, who came of the Butler blood through her mother, one large seal in yellow wax, attached to a charter dated Oct. 24, 1565, is remarkable for the beauty of the die. The Queen sits on the obverse under a canopy; on the reverse she rides in state on a pacing steed as in her effigy at the Tower of London. The seals of James I. follow the design of this die. Two of these are particularly fine. At the Restoration something disappears of the old stateliness. A seal of Charles II., of 1660, very large and florid in style, shows the monarch sitting very much at his ease, with one knee thrown negligently over the other.

Many of the private letters and papers of the seventeenth and early eighteenth centuries, during which Kilkenny, as it had been often before, was a great centre of Irish politics and intrigues, have been bound up in volumes, and the collection has been freely drawn upon by historians. But it would obviously bear and reward a more thorough co-ordination and examination than it has ever yet received.

There is a curious Table Book here preserved of Charles I. while at Oxford in 1644, from which it appears that while the colleges were melting up their plate for the King, his Majesty fared better than might have been expected. His table was served with sixty pounds of mutton a day; and he wound up his dinner regularly with "sparaguss" so long as it lasted, and after it went out with artichokes.

An Expense Book, too, of the great Marquis, after he became the first Duke of Ormonde, Colonel Blood's Duke, kept at Kilkenny in 1668 throws some interesting light on the cost of living and the customs of great houses at that time. The Duke, who was in some respects the greatest personage in the realm, kept up his state here at a weekly cost of about £50, a good deal less—allowing for the fall in the power of the pound sterling—than it would now cost him to live at a fashionable London hotel. He paid £9, 10s. a week for the keep of nineteen horses, 18 shillings board wages for three laundry-maids, and £1, 17s. 4d. for seven dozen of tallow-candles. The wines served at the ducal table were Burgundy, Bordeaux, "Shampane," Canary, " Renish," and Port-aport, the last named at a shilling a bottle, while he paid no more than £3, 18s. for six dozen bottles of Bordeaux, and £1, 1s. for a dozen and a half of " Shampane." This of course was not the sparkling beverage which in our times is the only contribution of Champagne to the wine markets of the world, for the *Ay Mousseux* first appears in history at the beginning of the eighteenth century. It was the red wine of Champagne, which so long contested the palm with the vintages of Burgundy. St. Evremond, who with the Comte d'Olonne and the great *gourmets* of the seventeenth century thought Champagne the best, as the Faculty of Paris also pronounced it the most wholesome of wines, doubtless introduced his own religion on the subject into England—but the entry in the Duke's Expense Book of 1668 is an interesting proof that the duel of the vintages was even then going as it finally went in favour of Burgundy. While the Duke got his Champagne for 1s. 2d. a bottle, he had to pay twenty shillings a dozen, or 1s. 8d. a bottle, for five dozen of Burgundy. He got his wines from Dublin, which then, as long before, was the most noted wine mart of Britain. The English princes drew their best supplies thence in the time of Richard II.

From the castle we drove through the snow to the Cathedral of St. Canice, a grand and simple Norman edifice of the twelfth century, now the Church of the Protestant bishop. An ancient Round Tower of much earlier date stands beside it like a campanile, nearly a hundred feet in height.

There is a legend that Rinuccini wanted to buy and carry away one of the great windows of this Cathedral, in which mass was celebrated while he was here. The Cathedral contains some interesting monuments of the Butlers, and there are many curiously channelled burial slabs in the floor, like some still preserved in the ruins of Abbeyleix. Lord de Vesci pointed out to me several tombs of families of English origin once powerful here, but now sunk into the farmer class,

On one of these I think it was that we saw a remarkably well-preserved effigy of a lady, wearing a plaited cap under a "Waterford cloak"—one of the neatest varieties of the Irish women's cloak—a garment so picturesque at once, and so well adapted to the climate, that I am not surprised to learn from Lady de Vesci that it is very fast going out of fashion. This morning before we left Abbeyleix she showed us two such cloaks, types from two different provinces, each in its way admirable. Put on and worn about the room by two singularly stately and graceful ladies, they fell into lines and folds which recalled the most exquisitely beautiful statuettes of Tanagra; and all allowance made for the glamour lent them by these two "daughters of the gods, divinely tall," it was impossible not to see that no woman could possibly look commonplace and insignificant in such a garment. Yet Lady de Vesci says that more than once she has known peasant women, to whom such cloaks had been presented, cut off the characteristic and useful hood, and trim the mangled robe with tawdry lace. So it is all over the world! Women who are models for an artist when they wear some garment indigenous to their country and appropriate to its conditions, prefer to make guys of themselves in grotesque travesties of the latest "styles" from London and Paris and Dublin!

Kilkenny boasts that its streets are paved with marble. It is in fact limestone, but none the worse for that. The snow did not improve them. So without going on a pilgrimage to the Kilkenny College, at which Swift, Congreve, and Farquhar, —an odd concatenation of celebrities—were more or less educated, we made our way to the Imperial Hotel for luncheon. The waiter was a delightful Celt. Upon my asking him whether the house could furnish anything distantly resembling good Irish whisky, he produced a bottle of alleged Scotch whisky, which he put upon the table with a decisive air, exclaiming, "And this, yer honour, is the most excellent whisky in the whole world, or I'm not an Irishman!"

Urged by the cold we tempered it with hot water and tasted it. It shut us up at once to believe the waiter a Calmuck or a Portuguese—anything, in short, but an Irishman. It is an extraordinary fact that, so far, the whisky I have found at Irish hotels has been uniformly quite execrable. I am almost tempted to think that the priests sequestrate all the good whisky in order to discourage the public abuse of it, for the "wine of the country" which they offer one is as uniformly excellent.

Kilkenny ought to be and long was a prosperous town. In 1702, the second Duke of Ormonde made grants (at almost nominal ground-rents) of the ground upon which a large portion of the city of Kilkenny was then standing, or upon which houses have since been built.

These grants have passed from hand to hand, and form the "root of title" of very many owners of house property in Kilkenny. The city is the centre of an extensive agricultural region, famous, according to an ancient ditty, for "fire without smoke, air without fog, water without mud, and land without bog"; but of late it has been undeniably declining. For this there are many reasons. The railways and the parcel-post diminish its importance as a local emporium. The almost complete disappearance of the woollen manufacture, the agricultural depression which has made the banks and wholesale houses "come down" upon the small dealers, and the "agitation," bankrupting or exiling the local gentry, have all conspired to the same result.

From Abbeyleix station we walked back to the house through the park under trees beautifully silvered with the snow. At dinner the party was joined by several residents of the county. One of them gave me his views of the working of the "Plan of Campaign." It is a plan, he maintains, not of defence as against unjust and exacting landlords, but of offence against "landlordism," not really promoted, as it appears to be, in the interest of the tenants to whose cupidity it appeals, but worked from Dublin as a battering engine against law and order in Ireland. Every case in which it is applied needs, he thinks, to be looked into on its own merits. It will then be found precisely why this or that spot has been selected by the League for attack. At Luggacurren, for instance, the "Plan of Campaign" has been imposed upon the tenants because the property belongs to the Marquis of Lansdowne, who happens to be Governor-General of Canada, so that to attack him is to attack the Government. The rents of the Lansdowne property at Luggacurren, this gentleman offers to prove to me, are not and never have been excessive; and Lord Lansdowne has expended very large sums on improving the property, and for the benefit of the tenants. Two of the largest tenants having got into difficulties through reckless racing and other forms of extravagance found it convenient to invite the league into Luggacurren, and compel other tenants in less embarrassed circumstances to sacrifice their holdings by refusing to pay rents which they knew to be fair, and were abundantly able and eager to pay. At Mitchelstown the "Plan of Campaign" was aimed again, not at the Countess of Kingston, the owner, but at the Disestablished Protestant Church of Ireland, the trustees of which hold a mortgage of a quarter of a million sterling on the estates. On the Clanricarde property in Galway the "Plan of Campaign" has been introduced, my informant says, because Lord Clanricarde happens to be personally unpopular. "Go down to Portumna and Woodford," he said, "and look into the matter for yourself. You will find that the rents on the Clanricarde estates are in the main exceptionally fair, and even low. The present Marquis has almost never visited Ireland, I believe, and he is not much known even in London. People who dislike him for one reason or another readily believe anything that is said to his disadvantage as a landlord. Most people who don't like the cut of

Dr. Fell's whiskers, or the way in which he takes soup, are quite disposed to listen to you if you tell them he beats his wife or plays cards too well. The campaigners are shrewd fellows, and they know this, so they start the 'Plan of Campaign' on the Portumna properties, and get a lot of English windbags to come there and hobnob with some of the most mischievous and pestilent parish priests in all Ireland—and then you have the dreadful story of the 'evictions,' and all the rest of it. Lord Clanricarde, or his agent, or both of them, getting out of temper, will sit down and do some hasty or crabbed or injudicious thing, or write a provoking letter, and forthwith it is enough to say 'Clanricarde,' and all common sense goes out of the question, to the great damage, not so much of Lord Clanricarde—for he lives in London, and is a rich man, and, I suppose, don't mind the row—but of landlords all over Ireland, and therefore, in the long-run, of the tenants of Ireland as well."

At Luggacurren, this gentleman thinks, the League is beaten. There are eighty-two tenants there, evicted and living dismally in what is called the Land League village, a set of huts erected near the roadside, while their farms are carried on for the owner by the Land Corporation. As they were most of them unwilling to accept the Plan, and were intimidated into it for the benefit of the League, and of the two chief tenants, Mr. Dunn and Mr. Kilbride, men of substance who had squandered their resources, the majority of the evicted are sore and angry.

"At first each man was allowed £3 a month by the League for himself and his family. But they found that Mr. Kilbride, who has been put into Parliament by Mr. Parnell for Kerry, a county with which he has no more to do than I have with the Isle of Skye, was getting £5 a week, and so they revolted, and threatened to bolt if their subsidy was not raised to £4 a month."

"And this they get now? Out of what funds?"

"Out of the League funds, or, in other words, out of their own and other people's money, foolishly put by the tenants into the keeping of the League to 'protect' it! They give it the kind of 'protection' that Oliver gave the liberties of England: once they get hold of it, they never let go!"

I submitted that at Gweedore Father M'Fadden had paid over to Captain Hill the funds confided to him.

"No doubt; but there the landlord gave in, and the more fool he!"

With another guest I had an interesting conversation about the Ulster tenant-right, which got itself more or less enacted into British law only in 1870, and of which Mr. Froude tells me he sought in vain to discover the definite origin. "The best lawyers in Ireland" could give him no light on this point. He could only find that it did not exist apparently in 1770, but did exist apparently twenty years later. The gentleman with whom I talked to-night tells me that the custom of Ulster was really once general throughout Ireland, and is called the "Ulster" custom, only because it survived there after disappearing elsewhere. There is a tradition too, he says, in Ulster that the recognition of this tenant-right as a binding custom there is really due to Lord Castlereagh. It would be a curious thing, could this be verified, to find Lord Castlereagh, whose name has been execrated in Ireland for fourscore years, recommending and securing a century ago that recognition of the interest of the Irish tenant in his holding, which, in our time, Mr. Gladstone, just now the object of Irish adulation, was, with much difficulty and reluctance, brought to accord in the Compensation for Disturbances clause of his Act of 1870!

Of this clause, too, I am told to-night that the scale of compensation fixed for the awards of the Court in the third section of it was devised (though Mr. Gladstone did not know this) by an Irish member in the interest of the "strong farmers," who wish to root out the small farmers. There is an apparent confirmation of this story in the fact that under this section the small farmers, under £10, may be awarded against the landlord seven years' rent as compensation for disturbance, while the number of years to be accounted for in the award diminishes as the rental increases, a discrimination not unlikely to strengthen the preference of the landlords for the large farm system.

CHAPTER V.

DUBLIN, *Tuesday, Feb. 14th.*—I left Abbeyleix this morning for Dublin, in company with Mr. and Mrs. Henry Doyle. Mr. Doyle, C.B., a brother of that inimitable master of the pencil, and most delightful of men, Richard Doyle, is the Director of the Irish National Gallery. He was kind enough to come and lunch with me at Maple's, after which we went together to the Gallery. It occupies the upper floors of a stately and handsome building in Merrion Square, in front of which stands a statue of the founder, Mr. William Dargan, who defrayed all the expenses of the Dublin Exhibition in 1853, and declined all the honours offered to him in recognition of his public spirited liberality, save a visit paid to his wife by Queen Victoria. The collection now under Mr. Doyle's charge was begun only in 1864, and the Government makes it an annual grant of no more than £2500, or about one-half the current price, in these days, of a fine Gainsborough or Sir Joshua! "They manage these things better in France," was evidently the impression of a recent French tourist in Ireland, M. Daryl, whose book I picked up the other day in Paris, for after mentioning three or four of the pictures, and gravely affirming that the existence here of a gallery of Irish portraits proves the passionate devotion of Dublin to Home Rule, he dismisses the collection with the verdict that "*ce ne vaut pas le diable.*" Nevertheless it already contains more really good pictures than the Musée either of Lyons or of Marseilles, both of them much larger and wealthier cities than Dublin. Leaving out the Three Maries of Perugino at Marseilles, and at Lyons the Ascension, which was once the glory of San Pietro di Perugia, the Moses of Paul Veronese, and Palma Giovanni's Flagellation, these two galleries put together cannot match Dublin with its Jan Steen, most characteristic without being coarse, its Terburg, a life-size portrait of the painter's favourite model, a young Flemish gentleman, presented to him as a token of regard, its portrait of a Venetian personage by Giorgione, with a companion portrait by Gian Bellini, its beautiful Italian landscape by

Jan Both, its flower-wreathed head of a white bull by Paul Potter, its exquisitely finished "Vocalists" by Cornelis Begyn, its admirable portrait of a Dutch gentleman by Murillo, and its two excellent Jacob Ruysdaels. A good collection is making, too, of original drawings, and engravings, and a special room is devoted to modern Irish art. I wish the Corcoran Gallery (founded, too, by an Irishman!) were half as worthy of Washington, or the Metropolitan Museum one-tenth part as worthy of New York!

The National Gallery in London has loaned some pictures to Dublin, and Mr. Doyle is getting together, from private owners, a most interesting gallery of portraits of men and women famous in connection with Irish history. The beautiful Gunnings of the last century, the not less beautiful and much more brilliant Sheridans of our own, Burke, Grattan, Tom Moore, Wellington, Curran, Lord Edward Fitzgerald, O'Connell, Peg Woffington, Canning, and Castlereagh, Dean Swift, Laurence Sterne are all here—wits and statesmen, soldiers and belles, rebels and royalists, orators and poets. Two things strike one in this gallery of the "glories of Ireland." The great majority of the faces are of the

Anglo-Irish or Scoto-Irish type; and the collection owes its existence to an accomplished public officer, who bears an Irish name, who is a devout Catholic, and who is also an outspoken opponent of the Home Rule contention as now carried on.

The gallery is open on liberal conditions to students. Mr. Doyle tells me that a young sister of Mr. Parnell was at one time an assiduous student here. He used to stop and chat with her about her work as he passed through the gallery. One day he met her coming out. "Mr. Doyle," she said, "are you a Home Ruler?" "Certainly not," he replied good-naturedly. Whereupon, with an air of melancholy resignation, the young lady said, "Then we can never more be friends!" and therewith flitted forth.

A small room contains some admirable bits of the work of Richard Doyle, among other things a weird and grotesque, but charming cartoon of an elfish procession passing through a quaint and picturesque mediæval city. It is a *conte fantastique* in colour— a marvel of affluent fancy and masterly skill.

I found here this morning letters calling me over to Paris for a short time, and one also from Mr. Davitt, in London, explaining that my note to him through the National League had never reached him, and that he had gone to London on his woollen business. I have written asking him to meet me to-morrow in London, and I shall cross over to-night.

LONDON, *Wednesday, Feb.* 15*th.*—Mr. Davitt spent an hour with me to-day, and we had a most interesting conversation. His mind is just now full of the woollen enterprise he is managing, which promises, he thinks, in spite of our tariff, to open the American markets to the excellent woollen goods of Ireland. He has gone into it with all his usual earnestness and ability. This is not a matter of politics with him, but of patriotism and of business. He tells me he has already secured very large orders from the United States. I hope he is not surprised, as I certainly am not, to find that the Parliamentarian Irish party give but a half-hearted and lukewarm support to such enterprises as this. Perhaps he has forgotten, as I have not, the efforts which a certain member of that party made in 1886 to persuade an Irish gentleman from St. Louis, who had brought over a considerable sum of money for the relief of the distress in North-Western Ireland, into turning it over to the League, on the express ground that the more the people were made to feel the pinch of the existing order of things, the better it would be for the revolutionary movement.

The Irish Woollen Company will, nevertheless, be a success, I believe, and a success of considerably more value to Ireland than the election of Mr. Wilfrid Blunt as M.P. for Deptford would be.

As to this election, Mr. Davitt seems to feel no great confidence. He has spoken in support of Mr. Blunt's candidacy, and is hard at work now to promote it. But he is not sanguine as to the result, as on all questions, save Home Rule for Ireland, Mr. Blunt's views and ideas, he thinks, antagonise the record of Mr. Evelyn and the local feeling at Deptford. I was almost astonished to learn from Mr. Davitt that Mr. Blunt, by the way, had told him at Ballybrack, long before he was locked up, how Mr. Balfour meant to lock up and kill four men, the "pivots" of the Irish movement, to wit, Mr. O'Brien, Mr. Harrington, Mr. Dillon, and Mr. Davitt himself. But I was not at all astonished to learn that Mr. Blunt told him all this most seriously, and evidently believed it.

"How did you take it?" I asked.

"Oh, I only laughed," said Mr. Davitt, "and told him it would take more than Mr. Balfour to kill me, at any rate by putting me in prison. As for being locked up, I prefer Cuninghame Graham's way of taking it, that he meant 'to beat the record on oakum!'"

If all the Irish "leaders" were made of the same stuff with Mr. Davitt, the day of a great Democratic revolution, not in Ireland only, but in Great Britain, might be a good deal nearer than anything in the signs of the times now shows it to be. Mr. Parnell and the National League are really nothing but the mask of Mr. Davitt and the Land League. Mr. Forster knew what he was about when he proclaimed the Land League in October 1881, six months or more after he had arrested and locked up Mr. Davitt in Portland prison. This was shown by the foolish No-Rent manifesto which Mr. Parnell and his associates issued from Kilmainham shortly after their incarceration, and without the counsel or consent at that time of Mr. Davitt—a manifesto which the Archbishop of Cashel, despite his early sympathies and connection with the agrarian agitation of 1848, found it expedient promptly to disavow. It would have been still more clearly shown had not Mr. Gladstone and Mr. Forster parted company under the restiveness of Mr. Gladstone's Radical followers, and the pressure of the United States Government in the spring of 1882. But after the withdrawal of Mr. Forster, and the release of Mr. Davitt, the English lawyers and politicians who led Lord Spencer and Sir George Trevelyan into allowing the Land League to be revived under the transparent alias of the National League, gave Mr. Davitt an opportunity, of which he promptly availed himself, to regain the ground lost by the blundering of the men of Kilmainham. From that time forth I have always regarded him as the soul of the Irish agitation, of the war against "landlordism" (which is incidentally, of course, a war against the English influence in Ireland), and of the movement towards Irish independence. Whether the agitation, the war, and the movement have gone entirely in accordance with his views and wishes is quite another matter.

I have too good an opinion of his capacity to believe that they have ; and when the secret history of the Chicago Convention comes to be written, I expect to find such confirmation therein of my notions on this subject as I could neither ask nor, if I asked, could expect to get from him.

Meanwhile the manliness and courage of the man must always command for him the respect, not to say the admiration, even of those who most sternly condemn his course and oppose his policy.

Born the child of an evicted tenant, in the times when an eviction meant such misery and suffering as are seldom, if ever, now caused by the process—bred and maimed for life in an English factory—captured when hardly more than a lad in Captain M'Cafferty's daring attempt to seize Chester Castle, and sent for fifteen years by Lord Chief-Justice Cockburn into penal servitude of the most rigorous kind, Michael Davitt might have been expected to be an apostle of hate not against the English Government of Ireland alone, but against England and the English people. The truculent talk of too many of his countrymen presents Ireland to the minds of thoughtful men as a flagrant illustration of the truth so admirably put by Aubrey de Vere that "worse than wasted weal is wasted woe." But woe has not been wasted upon Michael Davitt, in this, that, so far as I know (and I have watched his course now with lively personal interest ever since I made his acquaintance on his first visit to America), he has never made revenge and retaliation upon England either the inspiration or the aim of his revolutionary policy. I have never heard him utter, and never heard of his uttering, in America, such malignant misrepresentations of the conduct of the English people and their sovereign during the great famine of 1847, for example, as those which earned for Mr. Parnell in 1880 the pretty unanimous condemnation of the American press. How far he went with Mr. Parnell on the lines of that speech at New Ross, in which murder was delicately mentioned as "an unnecessary and prejudicial measure of procedure" in certain circumstances, I do not know. But he can hardly have gone further than certain persons calling themselves English Liberals went when the assassins of Napoleon III. escaped to England. And he has a capacity of being just to opponents, which certainly all his associates do not possess. I was much struck to-day by the candour and respect with which he spoke of John Bright, whose name came incidentally into our conversation. He seemed to feel personally annoyed and hurt as an Irishman, that Irishmen should permit themselves to revile and abuse Mr. Bright because he will not go with them on the question of Home Rule, in utter oblivion of the great services rendered by him to the cause of the Irish people "years before many of those whose tongues now wag against him had tongues to wag." I was tempted to remind him that not with Irishmen only is gratitude a lively sense of favours to come.

I find Mr. Davitt quite awake to the great importance of the granite quarries of Donegal. He is bestirring himself in connection with some men of Manchester, in behalf of the quarries at Belmullet in Mayo, which, if I am not mistaken, is his native county. This bent of his mind towards the material improvement of the condition of the Irish people, and the development of the resources of Ireland, is not only a mark of his superiority to the rank and file of the Irish politicians—it goes far to explain the stronger hold which he undoubtedly has on the people in Ireland. "Home Rule," as now urged by the Irish politicians, certainly excites much more attention and emotion in America and England than it seems to do in Ireland. It seems so simple and elementary to John Bull and Brother Jonathan that people should be suffered to manage their own affairs! Yet the North would not suffer the South to do this—and what would become of India if England turned it over in fragments to the native races? The Land

Question, on the contrary, touches the "business and bosom" of every Irishman in Ireland, while it is so complicated with historical conditions and incidents as to be troublesome and therefore uninteresting to people not immediately affected by it. If I am right in my impressions the collapse of the National League will hardly weaken the hold of Mr. Davitt on the Irish people in Ireland, and it may even strengthen his hold on the agrarian movement in Wales, England, and Scotland, unless he identifies himself too completely in that collapse with his Parliamentary instruments. On the other hand, the triumph of the National League on its present lines of action would diminish the value for good or evil of any man's hold upon the Irish people, for the obvious reason that by driving out of Ireland, and ruining, the class of "landlords" and capitalists, it would leave the country reduced to a dead level of peasant-holdings, saddled with a system of poor-rates beyond the ability of the peasant-holders to carry, and at the mercy, therefore, of the first bad year. The "war against the landlords," as conducted by the National League, would end where the Irish difficulty began, in a general surrender of the people to "poverty and potatoes."

CHAPTER VI.

ENNIS, *Saturday, Feb.* 18.—I found it unnecessary to go on to Paris, and so returned to Ireland on Thursday night; we had a passage as over a lake. In the train I met a lively Nationalist friend, whose acquaintance I made in America. He is a man of substance, but not overburdened with respect for the public men, either of his own party or of the Unionist side. When I asked him whether he still thought it would be safe to turn over Ireland to a Parliament made up of the Westminster members, of whom he gave me such an amusing but by no means complimentary account, he looked at me with astonishment:—

"Do you suppose for a moment we would send these fellows to a Parliament in Dublin?"

He told me some very entertaining tales of the methods used by certain well-meaning occupants of the Castle in former days to capture Irish popularity, as, for example, one of a Vice-Queen who gave a fancy dress ball for the children of the local Dublin people of importance, and had a beautiful supper of tea and comfits, and cakes served to them, after which she made her appearance, followed by servants bearing huge bowls of steaming hot Irish potatoes, which she pressed upon the horrified and overstuffed infants as "the true food of the country," setting them herself the example of eating one with much apparent gusto, and a pinch of salt!

"Now, fancy that!" he exclaimed; "for the Dublin aristocracy who think the praties only fit for the peasants!"

Of a well-known and popular personage in politics, he told me that he once went with him on a canvassing tour. It was in a county the candidate had never before visited. "When we came to a place, and the people were all out crying and cheering, he would whisper to me, 'Now what is the name of this confounded hole?' And I would whisper back, 'Ballylahnich,' or whatever it was. Then he would draw himself up to the height of a round tower, and begin, 'Men of Ballylahnich, I rejoice to meet you! Often has the great Liberator said to me, with tears in his voice, 'Oh would I might find myself face to face with the noble men of Ballylahnich!"

"A great man he is, a great man!

"Did you ever hear how he courted the heiress? He walked up and down in front of her house, and threatened to fight every man that came to call, till he drove them all away!"

A good story of more recent date, I must also note, of a well-known priest in Dublin, who being asked by Mr. Balfour one day whether the people under his charge took for gospel all the rawhead and bloody-bones tales about himself, replied, "Indeed, I wish they only feared and hated the devil half as much as they do you!"

In a more serious vein my Nationalist friend explained to me that for him "Home Rule" really meant an opportunity of developing the resources of Ireland under "the American system of Protection." About this he was quite in earnest, and recalled to me the impassioned protests made by the then Mayor of Chicago, Mr. Carter Harrison, against the Revenue Reform doctrines which I had thought it right to set forth at the great meeting of the Iroquois Club in that city in 1883. "Of course," he said, "you know that Mr. Harrison was then speaking not only for himself, but for the whole Irish vote of Chicago which was solidly behind him? And not of Chicago only! All our people on your side of the water moved against your party in 1884, and will move against it again, only much more generally, this year, because they know that the real hope of Ireland lies in our shaking ourselves free of the British Free Trade that has been fastened upon us, and is taking our life." I could only say that this was a more respectable, if not a more reasonable, explanation of Mr. Alexander Sullivan's devotion to Mr. Blaine and the Republicans, and of the Irish defection from the Democratic party than had ever been given to me in America, but I firmly refused to spend the night between London and Dublin in debating the question whether Meath could be made as prosperous as Massachusetts by levying forty per cent. duties on Manchester goods imported into Ireland.

He had seen the reception of Mr. Sullivan, M.P., in London. "I believe, on my soul," he said, "the people were angry with him because he didn't come in a Lord Mayor's coach!"

When I told him I meant to visit Luggacurren, he said, a little to my surprise, "That is a bad job for us, and all because of William O'Brien's foolishness! He always thinks everybody takes note of whatever he says, and that ruins any man! He made a silly threat at Luggacurren, that he would go and take Lansdowne by the throat in Canada, and then he was weak enough to suppose that he was bound to carry it out. He couldn't be prevented! And what was the upshot of it? But for the Orangemen in Canada, that were bigger fools than he is, he would have been just ruined completely! It was the Orangemen saved him!"

I left Dublin this morning at 7.40 A.M. The day was fine, and the railway journey most interesting. Before reaching Limerick we passed through so much really beautiful country that I could not help expressing my admiration of it to my only fellow-traveller, a most courteous and lively gentleman, who, but for a very positive brogue, might have been taken for an English guardsman.

"Yes, it is a beautiful country," he said, "or would be if they would let it alone!"

I asked him what he specially objected to in the recent action of Parliament as respects Ireland?

"Object?" he responded; "I object to everything. The only thing that will do Ireland any good will be to shut up that talking-mill at Westminster for a good long while!"

This, I told him, was the remedy proposed by Earl Grey in his recent volume on Ireland.

"Is it indeed? I shall read the book. But what's the use? 'For judgment it is fled to brutish beasts, and men have lost their reason.'"

This he said most cheerily, as if it really didn't matter much; and, bidding me good-bye, disappeared at Limerick, where several friends met him. In his place came a good-natured optimistic squire, who thinks "things are settling down." There is a rise in the price of cattle. "Beasts I gave £8 for three months ago," he said, "I have just sold for £12. I call that a healthy state of things." And with this he also left me at Ardsollus, the station nearest the famous old monastery of Quin.

At Ennis I was met by Colonel Turner, to whom I had written, enclosing a note of introduction to him. With him were Mr. Roche, one of the local magistrates, and Mr. Richard Stacpoole, a gentleman of position and estate near Ennis, about whom, through no provocation of his, a great deal has been said and written of late years. Mr. Stacpoole at once insisted that I should let him take me out to stay at his house at Edenvale, which is, so to speak, at the gates of Ennis. Certainly the fame of Irish hospitality is well-founded! Meanwhile my traps were deposited at the County Club, and I went about the town. I walked up to the Court-house with Mr. Roche, in the hope of hearing a case set down for trial to-day, in which a publican named Harding, at Ennis—an Englishman, by the way— is prosecuted for boycotting. The parties were in Court; and the defendant's counsel, a keen-looking Irish lawyer, Mr. Leamy, once a Nationalist member, was ready for action; but for some technical reason the hearing was postponed. There were few people in Court, and little interest seemed to be felt in the matter. The Court-house is a good building, not unlike the White House at Washington in style. This is natural enough, the White House having been built, I believe, by an Irish architect, who must have had the Duke of Leinster's house of Carton, in Kildare, in his mind when he planned it. Carton was thought a model mansion at the beginning of this century; and Mr. Whetstone, a local architect of repute, built the Ennis Court-house some fifty years ago. It is of white limestone from quarries belonging to Mr. Stacpoole, and cost when built about £12,000. To build it now would cost nearly three times as much. In fact, a recent and smaller Court-house at Carlow has actually cost £36,000 within the last few years.

I was struck by the extraordinary number of public-houses in Ennis. A sergeant of police said to me, "It is so all over the country." Mr. Roche sent for the statistics, from which it appears that Ennis, with a population of 6307, rejoices in no fewer than 100 "publics"; Ennistymon, with a population of 1331, has 25; and Milltown Malbay, with a population of 1400, has 36. At Castle Island the proportion is still more astounding—51 public-houses in a population of 800. In Kiltimagh every second house is a public-house! These houses are perhaps a legacy of the old days of political jobbery.[1] No matter when or why granted, the licence appears to be regarded as a hereditary "right" not lightly to be tampered with; and of course the publicans are persons of consequence in their neighbourhood, no matter how

[1] Or they may date back to the Parliament of Grattan, who wrote to Mr. Guinness that he regarded the brewery of Ireland as "the actual nurse of the people, and entitled to every encouragement, favour, and exemption."

wretched it may be, or how trifling their legitimate business. Three police convictions are required to make the resident magistrates refuse the usual yearly renewal of a licence; and if an application is made against such a renewal, cause must be shown. The "publics" are naturally centres of local agitation, and the publicans are sharp enough to see the advantage to them of this. The sergeant told me of a publican here in Ennis, into whose public came three Nationalists, bent not upon drinking, but upon talking. The publican said nothing for a while, but finally, in a careless way, mentioned "a letter he had just received from Mr. Parnell on a very private matter." Instantly the politicians were eager to see it. The publican hesitated. The politicians immediately called for drinks, which were served, and after this operation had been three times repeated, the publican produced the letter, began with a line or two, and then said, "Ah, no! it can't be done. It would be a betrayal of confidence; and you know you wouldn't have that! But it's a very important letter you have seen!" So they went away tipsy and happy.

Only yesterday no fewer than twenty-three of these publicans from Milltown Malbay appeared at Ennis here to be tried for "boycotting" the police. One of them was acquitted; another, a woman, was discharged. Ten of them signed, in open court, a guarantee not further to conspire, and were thereupon discharged upon their own recognisances, after having been sentenced with their companions to a month's imprisonment with hard labour. The magistrate tells me that when the ten who signed (and who were the most prosperous of the publicans) were preparing to sign, the only representative of the press who was present, a reporter for *United Ireland*, approached them in a threatening manner, with such an obvious purpose of intimidation, that he was ordered out of the court-room by the police. The eleven who refused to sign the guarantee (and who were the poorest of the publicans, with least to lose) were sent to gaol.

An important feature of this case is the conduct of Father White, the parish priest of Milltown Malbay. In the open court, Colonel Turner tells me, Father White admitted that he was the moving spirit of all this local "boycott." While the court was sitting yesterday all the shops in Milltown Malbay were closed, Father White having publicly ordered the people to make the town "as a city of the dead." After the trial was over, and the eleven who elected to be locked up had left in the train, Father White visited all their houses to encourage the families, which, from his point of view, was no doubt proper enough; but one of the sergeants reports that the Father went by mistake into the house of one of the ten who had signed the guarantee, and immediately reappeared, using rather unclerical language. All this to an American resembles a tempest in a tea-pot. But it is a serious matter to see a priest of the Church assisting laymen to put their fellow-men under a social interdict, which is obviously a parody on one of the gravest steps the Church itself can take to maintain the doctrine and the discipline of the Faith. What Catholics, if honest, must think of this whole business, I saw curiously illustrated by some marginal notes pencilled in a copy of Sir Francis Head's *Fortnight in Ireland*, at the hotel in Gweedore. The author of the *Bubbles from the Brunnen* published this book in 1852. At page 152 he tells a story, apparently on hearsay, of "boycotting" long before Boycott. It is to the effect that, in order to check the proselyting of Catholics by a combination of Protestant missionary zeal with Protestant donations of "meal," certain priests and sisters in the south of Ireland personally instructed the people to avoid all intercourse of any sort with any Roman Catholic who "listened to a Protestant clergyman or a Scripture Reader"; and Sir Francis cites an instance—still apparently on hearsay—of a "shoemaker at Westport," who, having seceded from the Church, found that not a single "journeyman dared work for him"; that only "one person would sell him leather"; and, "in short, lost his custom, and rapidly came to a state of starvation."

On the margin of the pages which record these statements, certain indignant Catholics have pencilled comments, the mildest of which is to the effect that Sir Francis was "a most damnable liar." It is certainly most unlikely that Catholics should have arrogated to themselves the Church's function of combating heresy and schism in the fashion described by Sir Francis. But without mooting that question, these expressions are noteworthy as showing how just such proceedings, as are involved in the political "boycottings" of the present day, must be regarded by all honest and clear-headed people who call themselves Catholics; and it is a serious scandal that a parish priest should lay himself open to the imputation of acting in concert with any political body whatever, on any pretext whatever, to encourage such proceedings.

I asked one of the sergeants how the publicans who had signed the guarantee would probably be treated by their townspeople. He replied, there was some talk of their being "boycotted" in their turn by the butchers and bakers. "But it's all nonsense," he said, "they are the snuggest (the most prosperous) publicans in this part of the country, and nobody will want to vex them. They have many friends, and the best friend they have is that they can afford to give credit to the country people. There'll be no trouble with them at all at all!"

Walking about the town, I saw many placards calling for subscriptions in aid of a news-vendor who has been impounded for selling *United Ireland*. "It'll be a good thing for him," said a cynical citizen, to whom I spoke of it, "a good deal better than he'd be by selling the papers." And, in fact, it is noticeable all over Ireland how small the sales of the papers appear to be. The people about the streets in Ennis, however, seemed to me much more effervescent and hot in tone than the

Dublin people are—and this on both sides of the question. One very decent and substantial-looking man, when I told him I was an American, assured me that "if it was not for the soldiers, the people of Ennis would clear the police out of the place." He told me, too, that not long ago the soldiers of an Irish regiment here cheered for Home Rule in the Court-house, "but they were soon sent away for that same." On the other hand, a Protestant man of business, of whom I made some inquiries about the transmission of an important paper to the United States in time to catch to-morrow's steamer from Queenstown, spoke of the Home Rulers almost with ferocity, and thought the "Coercion" Government at Dublin ought to be called the "Concession" Government. He was quite indignant that the Morley and Ripon procession through the streets of Dublin should not have been "forbidden."

There are some considerable shops in Ennis, but the proprietor of one of the best of them says all this agitation has "killed the trade of the place." I am not surprised to learn that the farmers and their families are beginning seriously to demand that the "reduction screw" shall be applied to other things besides rent. "A very decent farmer," he says, " only last week stood up in the shop and said it was ' a shame the shopkeepers were not made to reduce the tenpence muslin goods to sixpence!'"

This shopkeeper finds some dreary consolation for the present state of things in standing at his deserted shop-door and watching the doors of his brethren. He finds them equally deserted. In his own he has had to dismiss a number of his attendants. "When a man finds he is taking in ten shillings a day, and laying out three pounds ten, what can he do but pull up pretty short?" As with the shopkeepers, so it is with the mechanics. "They are losing custom all the time. You see the tenants are expecting to come into the properties, so they spend nothing now on painting or improvements. The money goes into the bank. It don't go to the landlords, or to the shopkeepers, or the mechanics; and then we that have been selling on credit, and long credit too, where are we? Formerly, from one place, Dromoland, Lord Inchiquin's house, we used regularly to make a bill of a hundred pounds at Christmas, for blankets and other things given away. Now the house is shut up and we make nothing!"

It is a short but very pleasant drive from Ennis

to Edenvale—and Edenvale itself is not ill-named. The park is a true park, with fine wide spaces and views, and beautiful clumps of trees. A swift river flows beyond the lawn in front of the spacious goodly house—a river alive with wild fowl, and overhung by lofty trees, in which many pairs of herons build. A famous heronry has existed here for many years, and the birds are held now by Mr. and Mrs. Stacpoole as sacred as are the storks in Holland. Where the river widens to a lake, fine terraced gardens and espalier walls, on which nectarines, apricots, and peaches ripen in the sun, stretch along the shore. Deer come down to the further bank to drink, and in every direction the eye is charmed and the mind is soothed by the loveliest imaginable sylvan landscapes.

EDENVALE, *Sunday, Feb.* 19.—I was awakened at dawn by the clamour of countless wild ducks, to a day of sunshine as brilliant and almost as warm as one sees at this season in the south of France. Mrs. Stacpoole speaks of this place with a kind of passion, and I can quite understand it. Clearly this, again, is not a case of the absentee landlord draining the lifeblood of the land to lavish it upon an alien soil! The demesne is a sylvan sanctuary for the wild creatures of the air and the wood, and they congregate here almost as they did at Walton Hall in the days of that most delightful of naturalists and travellers, whose adventurous gallop on the back of a cayman was the delight of all English-reading children forty years ago, or as they do now at Gosford. Yet the crack of the gun, forbidden in the precincts of Walton Hall, is here by no means unknown—the whole family being noted as dead shots. I asked Mr. Stacpoole this morning whether the park had been invaded by trespassers since the local Nationalists declared war upon him. He said that his only experience of anything like an attack befell not very long ago, when his people came to the house on a Sunday afternoon and told him that a crowd of men from Ennis, with dogs, were coming towards the park with a loudly proclaimed intent to enter it, and go hunting upon the property.

Upon this Mr. Stacpoole left the house with his brother and another person, and walked down to the park entrance. Presently the men of Ennis made their appearance on the highway. A very brief parley followed. The men of Ennis announced their intention of marching across the park, and occupying it.

"I think not," the proprietor responded quietly. "I think you will go back the way you came. For you may be sure of one thing: the first man who crosses that park wall, or enters that gate, is a dead man."

There was no show of weapons, but the revolvers were there, and this the men of Ennis knew. They also knew that it rested with themselves to create the right and the occasion to use the revolvers, and that if the revolvers were used they would be used to some purpose. To their credit, be it said, as men of sense, they suddenly experienced an almost Caledonian respect for the "Sabbath-day," and after expressing their discontent with Mr. Stacpoole's inhospitable reception, turned about and went back whence they had come.

This morning an orderly from Ennis brought out news of the arrest yesterday, at the Clare Road, of Mr. Lloyd, a Labour delegate from London, on his return from an agitation meeting at Kildysart. Harding, the Englishman I saw awaiting his trial yesterday, became bail for Lloyd.

In the afternoon we took a delightful walk to

Killone Abbey, a pile of monastic ruins on a lovely site near a very picturesque lake. The ruins have been used as a quarry by all the country, and are now by no means extensive. But the precincts are used as a graveyard, not only by the people of Ennis, but by the farmers and villagers for many miles around. Nothing can be imagined more painful than the appearance of these precincts. The graves are, for the most part, shallow, and closely huddled together. The cemetery, in truth, is a ghastly slum, a "tenement-house" of the dead. The dead of to-day literally elbow the dead of yesterday out of their resting-places, to be in their turn displaced by the dead of to-morrow. Instead of the crosses and the fresh garlands, and the inscriptions full of loving thoughtfulness, which lend a pathetic charm to the German "courts of peace" —instead of the carefully tended hillocks and flower-studded turf which make the churchyard of a typical old English village beautiful,—all here is confusion, squalor, and neglect. Fragments of coffins and bones lie scattered among the sunken and shattered stones. We picked up a skull lying quite apart in a corner of the enclosure. A clean round bullet hole in the very centre of the frontal bone was dumbly and grimly eloquent. Was it the skull of a patriot or of a policeman? of a "Whiteboy" or of a "landlord"?

One thing only was apparent from the conformation of the grisly relic. It was the skull of a Celt. Probably, therefore, not of a land agent, shot to repress his fiduciary zeal, but perhaps of some peasant selfishly and recklessly bent on paying his rent.

While we wandered amid the ruins we came suddenly upon a woman wearing a long Irish cloak, and accompanied by two well-dressed men. One of the men started upon catching sight of Colonel Turner, who was of our party, grew quite red for a moment, and then very civilly exchanged salutations with him. The party walked quietly away on a lower road leading to Ennis. When they had gone Colonel Turner told us that the man who had spoken to him was a local Nationalist of repute and influence in Ennis. "He would never have ventured to be civil to me in the town," he said. A discussion arose as to the probable object of the party in visiting these ruins. A gentleman who was with us half-laughingly suggested that they might have been putting away dynamite bombs for an attack on Edenvale. Colonel Turner's more practical and probable theory was that they were looking about for a site for the grave of the Fenian veteran, Stephen J. Meany, who died in America not long ago. He was a native, I believe, of Ennis, and his remains are now on their way across the Atlantic for interment in his birth-place. "Would a processional funeral be allowed for him?" I asked. Colonel Turner could see no reason why it should not be.

One exception I noted to the general slovenliness of the graves. A new and handsome monument had just been set up by a man of Ennis, living in Australia, to the memory of his father and mother, buried here twenty years ago. But this touching symbol of a heart untravelled, fondly turning to its home, had been so placed, either by accident or by design, as to block the entrance way to the vault of a family living, or rather owning property, in this neighbourhood. Until within a year or two past this family had occupied a very handsome mansion in a park adjoining the park of Edenvale. But the heir, worn out with local hostilities, and reduced in fortune by the pressure of the times and of the League, has now thrown up the sponge. His ancestral acres have been turned over for cultivation to Mr. Stacpoole. His house, a large fine building, apparently of the time of James II., containing, I am told, some good pictures and old furniture, is shut up, as are the model stables, ample enough for a great stud; and so another centre of local industry and activity is made sterile.

Near the ruins of Killone is a curious ancient shrine of St. John, beside a spring known as the Holy Well. All about the rude little altar in the open air simple votive offerings were displayed, and Mrs. Stacpoole tells me pilgrims come here from Galway and Connemara to climb the hill upon their knees, and drink of the water. Last year for the first time within the memory of man the well went dry. Such was the distress caused in Ennis by this news, that on the eve of St. John certain pious persons came out from the town, drew water from the lake, and poured it into the well!

As we walked away one of the party pointed to a rabbit fleeing swiftly into a hole in one of the graves. "I was on this hill," he said, "one day not very long ago when a funeral train came out from Ennis. As it entered the precincts a rabbit ran rapidly across the grounds. Instantly the procession broke up; the coffin was literally dropped to the ground, and the bearers, the mourners, and the whole company united in a hot and general chase of bunny. Of course, I need not say," he added, " that there was no priest with them. The fixed charge of the priest for a burial is twenty shillings, but there is usually no service at the grave whatever."

This may possibly be a trace of the practices which grew up under the Penal Laws against Catholics. When Rinuccini came to Ireland in the time of the Civil War, he found the observances of the Church all fallen into degradation through these laws. The Holy Sacrifice was celebrated in the cabins, and not unfrequently on tables which had been covered half-an-hour before with the remains of the last night's supper, and would be cleared half-an-hour afterwards for the midday meal, and perhaps for a game of cards.

Several guests joined us at dinner. One gentleman, a magistrate familiar with Gweedore, told me he believed the statements of Sergeant Mahony as to the income of Father M'Fadden to fall within the truth. While he believes that many people in that region live, as he put it, " constantly within a hair's-breadth of famine," he thinks that the great body of the peasants there are in a position, "with industry and thrift, not only to make both ends meet, but to make them overlap."

Mr. Stacpoole told us some of his own experiences nearer home. Not long ago he was informed that the National League had ordered some decent people, who hold the demesne lands of his neighbour, Mr. Macdonald (already alluded to) at a very low rental, to make a demand for a reduction, which would have left Mr. Macdonald without a penny of income. To counter this Mr. Stacpoole offered to take the lands over for pasture at the existing rental, whereupon the tenants promptly made up their minds to keep their holdings in defiance of the League.

Last year a man, whom Mr. Stacpoole had regarded as a "good" tenant, came to him, bringing the money to pay his rent. "I have the rint, sorr," the man said, "but it is God's truth I dare not pay it to ye!" Other tenants were waiting outside. "Are you such a coward that you don't dare be honest?" said Mr. Stacpoole. The man turned rather red, went and looked out of all the windows, one after another, lifted up the heavy cloth of the large table in the room, and peeped under it nervously, and finally walked up to Mr. Stacpoole and paid the money. The receipt being handed to him, he put it back with his hand, eyed it askance as if it were a bomb, and finally took it, and carefully put it into the lining of his hat, after which, opening the door with a great noise, he exclaimed as he went out, "I'm very, very sorry, master, that I can't meet you about it!" This man is now as loud in protestation of his "inability" to pay his rent as any of the "Campaigners." Mr. Stacpoole thinks one great danger of the actual situation is that men who were originally "coerced" by intimidation into dishonestly refusing to pay just rents, which they were abundantly able to pay, are beginning now to think that they will be, and ought to be, relieved by the law of the land from any obligation to pay these rents.

It seems to be his impression that things look better, however, of late for law and order. On Monday of last week at Ennis an example was made of a local official, which, he thinks, will do good. This was a Poor-Law Guardian named Grogan. He was bound over on Monday last to keep the peace for twelve months towards one George Pilkington. Pilkington, it appears, in contempt of the League, took and occupied, in 1886, a certain farm in Tarmon

West. For this he was "boycotted" from that time forth. In December last he was summoned, with others, before the Board of Guardians at Kilrush, to fix the rents of certain labourers' cottages. While he sat in the room awaiting the action of the Board, Grogan, one of its members, rose up, and, looking at Pilkington, said in a loud voice, "There's an obnoxious person here present that should not be here, a land-grabber named Pilkington." There was a stir in the room, and Pilkington, standing up, said, "I am here because I have had notice from the Guardians. If I am asked to leave the place, I shall not come back." The Chairman of the Board upon this declared that "while the ordinary business of the Board was transacting, Mr. Pilkington would be there only by the courtesy of the Board;" and treating the allusions of Grogan to Pilkington as a part of the business of the Board, he said, ". A motion is before the Board, does any one second it?" Another guardian, Collins, got up, and said "I do." Thereupon the Chairman put it to the vote whether Pilkington should be requested to leave. The ayes had it, and the Chairman of the Board thereupon invited Pilkington to leave the meeting which the Board had invited him to attend!

Grogan has now been prosecuted for the offence of "wrongfully, and without legal authority, using violence and intimidation to and towards George Pilkington of Tarmon West, with a view to cause the said Pilkington to abstain from doing an act which he had a legal right to do, namely, to hold, occupy, and work on a certain farm of land at Tarmon West."

Plainly this case is one of a grapple between the two Governments which have been and are now contending for the control of Ireland: the Government of the Queen of Ireland, which authorises Pilkington to take and farm a piece of land, and the Government of the National League, which forbids him to do this. Is it possible to doubt which of the two is the government of Liberty, as well as the government of Law?

It illustrates the demoralising influence upon society in Ireland of the protracted toleration of such a contest as has been waging between the authority of the Law and the authority of the League, that, when this case came up for consideration ten days ago, an official here actually thought it ought to be put off. Colonel Turner insisted it should be dealt with at once; and so

Mr. Grogan was proceeded against, with the result I have stated.

The trees on this demesne are the finest I have so far seen in Ireland, beautiful and vigorous pencil-cedars, ilexes, Scotch firs, and Irish yews. There is one noble cedar of Lebanon here worth a special trip to see. In conversation about the country to-night, Mr. Stacpoole mentioned that tobacco was grown here, strong and of good quality, and he was much interested, as I remember were also the charming châtelaine of Newtown Anner and Mr. Le Poer of Gurteen four or five years ago, to learn how immensely successful has been the tobacco-culture introduced into Pennsylvania only a quarter of a century ago, as a consequence of the Civil War. The climatic conditions here are certainly not more unfavourable to such an experiment in agriculture than they were at first supposed to be in the Pennsylvanian counties of York and Lancaster. Of course the Imperial excise would deal with it as harshly as it is now dealing with a similar experiment in England. But the Irish tobacco-growers would not now have to fear such hostile legislation as ruined the Irish linen industries in the last century. The "Moonlighters" of 1888 lineally represent, if they do not simply reproduce, the "Whiteboys" of 1760; and the domination of the "uncrowned king" constantly reminds one of Froude's vivid and vigorous sketch of the sway wielded by "Captain Dwyer" and "Joanna Maskell" from Mallow to Westmeath, between the years 1762 and 1765. On that side of the quarrel there seems to be nothing very new under the sun in Ireland. But the spirit and the forms of the Imperial authority over the country have unquestionably undergone a great change for the better, not only since the last century, but since the accession of Queen Victoria.

Upon the question of land improvements, Mr. Stacpoole told me, to-night, that he borrowed £1000 of the Government for drainage improvements on his property here, the object of which was to better the holdings of tenants. Of this sum he had to leave £400 undrawn, as he could not get the men to work at the improvements, even for their own good. They all wanted to be gangers or chiefs. It reminded me of Berlioz's reply to the bourgeois who wanted his son to be made a "great composer." "Let him go into the army," said Berlioz, "and join the only regiment he is fit for." "What regiment is that?" "The regiment of colonels."

THE DIARY OF AN AMERICAN 229

In the course of the evening a report was brought out from Ennis to Colonel Turner. He read it, and then handed it to me, with an accompanying document. The latter, at my request, he allowed me to keep, and I must reproduce it here. It tells its own tale.

A peasant came to the authorities and complained that he was " tormented " to make a subscription to a " testimonial " for one Austen Mackay of Kilshanny, in the County Clare, producing at the same time a copy of the circular which had been sent about to the people. It is a cheaply-printed leaflet, not unlike a penny ballad in appearance, and thus it runs :—

" *Testimonial to* Mr. AUSTEN MACKAY,
Kilshanny, County Clare.

" We, the Nationalists and friends of Mr. Austen Mackay, at a meeting held in March 1887, agreed and resolved on presenting the long-tried and trusted friend—the persecuted widow's son—with a testimonial worthy of the fearless hero who on several occasions had to hide his head in the caves and caverns of the mountains, with a price set on his body. First, for firing at and wounding a spy in his neighbourhood, as was alleged in '65, for which he had to stand his trial at Clare Assizes. Again, for firing at and wounding his mother's agent and under-strapper while in the act of evicting his widowed mother in the broad daylight of Heaven, thus saved his mother's home from being wrecked by the robber agent, the shock of which saved other hearths from being quenched; but the noble widow's son was chased to the mountains, where he had to seek shelter from a thousand bloodhounds.

"The same true widow's son nobly guarded his mother's homestead and that of others from the foul hands of the exterminators. This is the same widow's son who bravely reinstated the evicted, and helped to rebuild the levelled houses of many; for this he was persecuted and convicted at Cork Assizes, and flung into prison to sleep on the cold plank beds of Cork and Limerick gaols. Many other manly and noble services did he which cannot be made known to the public. At that meeting you were appointed collector with other Nationalists of Clare at home and abroad. This is the widow's son, Austen Mackay, whom we, the Committee to this testimonial, hope and trust every Irishman in Clare will cheerfully subscribe, that he may be enabled in his present state of health to get into some business under the protection of the Stars and Stripes, where he is a citizen of."

"Subscriptions to be sent to Henry Higgins, Ennis.

"Treasurers: Daniel O'Loghlen, Lisdoonvarna; James Kennedy, Ennistymon."

Then follow, with the name of the Society, the names of the committee.

In behalf of the Stars and Stripes, "where he is a citizen of," I thanked Colonel Turner for this interesting contribution to the possible future history of my country, there being nothing to prevent the election of any heir of this illustrious "widow's son," born to him in America, to the Presidency of the Republic. The use of this phrase, the "widow's son," by the way, gives a semi-masonic character to this curious circular.

One officer says in his report upon this Committee: "All the persons named are well known to their respective local police, and, except one, have little or no following or influence in their respective localities. They are all members of the National League." The same officer subjoins this instructive observation: "I beg to add that I find no matter how popular a man may be in Clare, start a testimonial for him, and from that time forth his influence is gone."

Can it be possible that the "testimonial," which, as the papers tell me, is getting up all over Ireland for Mr. Wilfrid Blunt, can have been "started" with a sinister eye to this effect, by local patriots jealous of any alien intrusion into their bailiwick? I am almost tempted to suspect this, remembering that a Nationalist with whom I talked about Mr. Blunt in Dublin, after lavishing much praise upon his disinterested devotion to the cause of Ireland, moodily remarked, "For all that, I don't believe he will do us any good, for he comes of the blood of Mountjoy, I am told!"

EDENVALE, *Monday, Feb.* 20. — This morning Colonel Turner called my attention to the report in the papers of a colloquy between the Chief Secretary for Ireland and Mr. J. Redmond, M.P., in the House, on the subject of last week's trials at Ennis. In speaking of the boycotting at Milltown Malbay of a certain Mrs. Connell, Mr. Balfour described the case as one of barbarous inhumanity shown to a helpless old woman. Mr. Redmond denying this, asserted that he had seen the woman Connell a fortnight ago in Court, and that so far from her being a decrepit old woman, she was only fifty years of age, hale and hearty, but disreputable and given to drink; he also said she was drunk at the trial, so drunk that the Crown prosecutor, Mr. Otter, was obliged to order her down from the table.

"What are the facts?" I asked. "Mr. Balfour speaks from report and belief, Mr. Redmond asserts that he speaks from actual observation."

"The facts," said Colonel Turner quietly, "are that Mr. Balfour's statement is accurate, and that Mr. Redmond, speaking from actual observation, asserts the thing that is not."

"Where is this old woman?" I asked. "Would it be possible for me to see her?"

"Certainly; she is at no great distance, and I will with pleasure send a car with an officer to bring her here this afternoon!"

"Meanwhile, how came the old woman into Court? and what is her connection with the cases of boycotting last week tried?"

"Those cases arose out of her case," said Colonel Turner; "the publicans last week arraigned, 'boycotted' a fortnight ago the police and soldiers who were called in to keep the peace during the trial of the dealers who 'boycotted' her.

"Her case was first publicly made known by a letter which appeared in the Dublin *Express* on the 28th of January. That day a line was sent to me from Dublin ordering an inquiry into it. I endorsed upon the order, 'Please report. I imagine this is greatly exaggerated.' This was on January 30th. The next day, January 31st, I received a full report from Milltown Malbay. Here it is,"—taking a document from a portfolio and handing it to me—"and you may make what use you like of it."

It is worth giving at length :—

"James Connell, ex-soldier, and his mother, Hannah Connell, of Fintamore, in this sub-district are boycotted, and have been since July last. James Connell held a farm and a garden from one Michael Carroll, a farmer, who was evicted from his holding for non-payment of three years' rent, July 14, 1886. After the period of redemption, six months, had passed, the agent made Connell a tenant for his house and garden, giving him in addition about half an acre (Irish) of the evicted farm which adjoins his house. In consequence Connell was regarded by the National League here as a 'land-grabber.' About the same time the agent also appointed him a rent-warner.

"On the 22d June last Connell received a letter through the Post-Office threatening him if he did not give up his place as a rent-warner. I have no doubt the letter was written by (here a resident was named). On the 10th, and again on the 17th, of July, Connell was brought before indoor meetings of the

THE DIARY OF AN AMERICAN 235

National League here for having taken the half acre of land, when he through fear declared he had not done it.

"At the first meeting the Rev. J. S. White, P.P., suggested that in order to test whether Connell had taken the land, Carroll, the evicted tenant, should go and cut the meadowing on it, which he did, when Connell interfered and prevented him. At the next meeting Carroll brought this under notice, and Connell was thereupon boycotted. Immediately afterwards the men who had been engaged fishing for Connell refused to fish, saying that if they fished for him the sale of the fish would be boycotted, which was true.

"Since then Connell has been deprived of his means of livelihood, and no one dare employ him. He, however, through his mother, was able to procure the necessaries of life until about the 22d of November last, when his mother was refused goods by the tradesmen with whom she had dealt, owing to a resolution passed at a meeting of the 'suppressed' branch of the League here, to the effect that any person supplying her would be boycotted. December 23d she came into Milltown Malbay for goods, and was refused. The police accompanied her, but no person would supply her. On the 2d of January she came again, when one trader supplied her with some bread, but refused groceries. The police accompanied her to several traders, who all refused. Ultimately she was supplied by the post-mistress. On the 7th of January she came, and the police accompanied her to several traders, all of whom refused her even bread. Believing she wanted it badly, we, the police, supplied her with some. On these three occasions she was followed by large numbers of young people about the street, evidently to frighten and intimidate her, and their demeanour was so hostile that we were obliged to disperse them and protect her home. On a subsequent occasion she stated that stones were thrown at her. Since then she has not come here for goods, and, in my opinion, it would not be safe for her to do so without protection. She and her son are now getting goods from Mrs. Moroney's shop at Spanish Point, which she opened a few years ago to supply boycotted persons.

"The Connells find it hard to get turf, and are obliged to bring it a distance in bags so that it may not be observed. As for milk, the person who did supply them privately for a considerable time declined some weeks ago to do so any longer. They are now really destitute, as any little money Connell had saved is spent, and, although willing and anxious to work, no person will employ him. Summonses have been issued against the tradesmen for refusing to supply Hannah Connell on the occasions already referred to. I have only to add that I have from time to time reported fully the foregoing facts with regard to the persecution of this poor man and his aged mother; and I regret to say that boycotting and intimidation never prevailed to a greater extent here than at present. Connell's safety is being looked after by patrols from this and Spanish Point station."

Three things seem to me specially noteworthy in this tale of cowardly and malignant tyranny. The victims of this vulgar Vehmgericht are neither landlords nor agents. They are a poor Irish labourer and his aged mother. The "crime" for which these poor creatures are thus persecuted is simply that one of them—the man—chose to obey the law of the land in which he lives, and to work for his livelihood and that of his mother. And the priest of the parish, instead of sheltering and protecting these hunted creatures, is presented as joining in the hunt, and actually devising a trap to catch the poor frightened man in a falsehood.

Upon this third point, a correspondence which

passed between Father White and Colonel Turner, after the conviction of the boycotters of Mrs. Connell, and copies of which the latter has handed to me at my request, throws an instructive light.

When the report of January 31st reached him, Colonel Turner ordered the tradespeople implicated in the persecution to be proceeded against. Six of them were put on their trials on the 3d and 4th of February. All the shops in Milltown Malbay were closed, by order of the local League, during the trial, and the police and the soldiers called in were refused all supplies.

On the 4th, one of the persons arraigned was bound over for intimidation, and the five others were sentenced to three months' imprisonment with hard labour.

A week later, February 11th, Colonel Turner addressed the following letter to Father White, twenty-six publicans of Milltown Malbay having meanwhile been prosecuted for boycotting the police and the soldiers:—

"DEAR SIR,—I write to you as a clergyman who possesses great influence with the people in your part of the country, to put it to you whether it would not be better for the interests of all concerned if the contemptible system of petty persecution, called boycotting, were put an end to in and about

Milltown Malbay, which would enable me to drop prosecutions. If it is not put a stop to, I am determined to stamp it out, and restore to all the ordinary rights of citizenship.

"But I should very greatly prefer that the people should stop it themselves, and save me from taking strong measures, which I should deplore. The story of a number of men combining to persecute a poor old woman is one of the most pitiful I ever heard.—I am, sir, yours truly, ALFRED TURNER."

As the cost of the extra policemen sent to Milltown Malbay at this time falls upon the people there, this letter in effect offered the priest an opportunity to relieve his parish of a burden as well as to redeem its character.

The next day Father White replied:—

"DEAR SIR,—No one living is more anxious for peace in this district than I. During very exciting times I have done my best to keep it free from outrage, and with success, except in one mysterious instance.[1] There is but one obstacle to it now. If ever you can advise Mrs. Moroney to restore the evicted tenant, whose rent you admitted was as high as Colonel O'Callaghan's, I can guarantee on the part of the people the return of good feelings; or, failing that, if she and her employees are content with the goods which she has of all kinds in her own shop, there need be no further trouble.

"I have a promise from the people that the police will be supplied for the future. This being so, if you will kindly have

---

[1] This refers, I am told, to the murder, in open daylight, in 1881, of an old man, Linnane, who acted as a "caretaker" for Mrs. Moroney. It should gratify Father White to know that, as I am now informed (May 21, 1888), a clue has just been found to the assassins, who appear to have received the same price for doing their work that was paid the murderers of Fitzmaurice.

the prosecutions withdrawn, or even postponed for say a month, it will very much strengthen me in the effort I am making to calm down the feeling. Regarding Mrs. Connell, the head-constable was told by me that she was to get goods, and she did get bread, till the police went round with her. This upset my arrangements, as I had induced the people to give her what she might really want. In fact she was a convenience to Mrs. Moroney for obvious reasons, and her son is now in her employment in place of Kelly, who has been dismissed since his very inconvenient evidence. It is, and was, well known they were not starving as they said, they having a full supply of their accustomed food.—Thanking you for your great courtesy, I am, dear sir, truly yours,

"J. WHITE."

On the 14th Colonel Turner replied :—

"MY DEAR SIR,—We cannot adjourn the cases. But if those who are prosecuted are prepared to make reparation by promising future good conduct in Court, I can then see my way to interfere, and to prevent them from suffering imprisonment.

"These cases have nothing whatever to do with Mrs. Moroney.[1] They are simply between the defendants and the police and other officials, who were at Milltown Malbay that day. I am greatly pleased at your evident wish to co-operate with me in calming down the ill-feeling which unfortunately exists, and I am satisfied that success will attend our efforts."

On Thursday and Friday last, as I have recorded, the cases came on of the twenty-six publicans charged. Between February 4th, when the offences were committed, and the 17th of February, one of

[1] Mrs. Moroney, so often referred to here, is the widow of a gentleman formerly High Sheriff and Deputy-Lieutenant for the County Clare, who died in 1870. She lives at Milton House, and has fought the local League steadily and successfully.

these publicans had died, one had fled to America, and there proved to be an informality in the summons issued against a third. Twenty-three only were put upon their trial. As I have stated, one was acquitted and the others were found guilty, and sentenced to be imprisoned. In accordance with his promise made to Father White, Colonel Turner offered to relieve them all of the imprisonment if they would sign an undertaking in Court not to repeat the offence. Ten, the most prosperous and substantial of the accused, accepted this offer and signed, as has been already stated. One, a woman, was discharged without being required to sign the guarantee, the other eleven refused to sign, and were sent to prison. Father White, whose own evidence given at the trial, as his letter to Colonel Turner would lead one to expect, had gone far to prove the existence of the conspiracy, encouraged the eleven in their attitude.

This was his way of "co-operating" with Colonel Turner to "calm down the ill-feeling which exists"!

During the morning Mrs. Stacpoole sent for the clerk and manager of the estate, and asked him to show me the books. He is a native of these parts, by name Considine, and has lived at Edenvale for eighteen years. In his youth he went out to America, but there found out that he had a "liver," an unpleasant discovery, which led him to return to the land of his birth, and to the service of Mr. Stacpoole. He is perfectly familiar with the condition of the country here, and as the accounts of this estate are kept minutely and carefully from week to week, he was able this morning to show me the current prices of all kinds of farm produce and of supplies in and about Ennis—not estimated prices, but prices actually paid or received in actual transactions during the last ten years. I am surprised to see how narrow has been the range of local variations during that time; and I find Mr. Considine inclined to think that the farmers here have suffered very little, if at all, from these fluctuations, making up from time to time on their reduced expenses what they have lost through lessened receipts. The expenses of the landlord have however increased, while his receipts have fallen off. In 1881 Edenvale paid out for labour £466, 0s. 1½d., in 1887 £560, 6s. 3½d., though less labour was employed in 1887 than in 1881. The wages of servants, where any change appears, have risen. In 1881 a gardener received £14 a year, in 1888 he receives 15s. a week, or at the rate of £39 a year. A housemaid receiving £12 a year in 1881, receives now £17 a year. A butler receiving in 1881 £26 a year, now receives £40 a year. A kitchenmaid receiving in 1881 £6, now receives £10, 10s. a year. Meanwhile, the Sub-Commissioners are at this moment cutting down the Edenvale rents again by £190, 3s. 2d., after a walk over the property in the winter. Yet in July 1883 Mr. Reeves, for the Sub-Commission, "thought it right to say there was no estate in the County Clare so fairly rented, to their knowledge, or where the tenants had less cause for complaint." In but one case was a reduction of any magnitude made by the Commission of 1883, and in one case that Commission actually increased the rent from £11, 10s. to £16. In January 1883 the rental of this property was £4065, 5s. 1d. The net reduction made by the Commissioners in July 1883 was £296, 14s. 0½d.

After luncheon a car came up to the mansion, bringing a stalwart, good-natured-looking sergeant of police, and with him the boycotted old woman Mrs. Connell and her son. The sergeant helped the old woman down very tenderly, and supported her into the house. She came in with some trepidation and uneasiness, glancing furtively all about her, with the look of a hunted creature in her eyes. Her son, who followed her, was more at his ease, but he also had a worried and careworn look. Both were warmly but very poorly clad, and both worn and weatherbeaten of aspect. The old woman might have passed anywhere for a witch, so wizened and weird she was, of small stature, and bent nearly double by years and rheumatism. Her small hands were withered away into claws, and her head was covered with a thick and tangled mat of hair, half dark, half grey, which gave her the look almost of the Fuegian savages who come off from the shore in their flat rafts and clamour to you for "rum" in the Straits of Magellan. Her eyes were intensely bright, and shone like hot coals in her dusky, wrinkled face. It was a raw day, and she came in shivering with the cold. It was pathetic to see how she positively gloated with extended palms over the bright warm fire in the drawing-room, and clutched at the cup of hot tea which my kind hostess instantly ordered in for her.

This was the woman of whom Mr. Redmond wrote to Mr. Parnell that she was "an active strong dame of about fifty." When Mr. Balfour, in Parliament, described her truly as a "decrepit old woman of eighty," Mr. Redmond contradicted him, and accused her of being "the worse for liquor" in a public court.

"How old is your mother?" I asked her son.

"I am not rightly sure, sir," he replied, "but she is more than eighty."

"The man himself is about fifty," said the sergeant; "he volunteered to go to the Crimean War, and that was more than thirty years ago!"

"I did indeed, sir," broke in the man, "and it was from Cork I went. And I'd be a corpse now if it wasn't for the mercy of God and the protection. God bless the police, sir, that protected my old mother, sir, and me. That Mr. Redmond, sir, they read me what he said, and sure he should be ashamed of his shadow, to get up there in Parliament, and tell those lies, sir, about my old mother!"

I questioned Connell as to his relations with Carroll, the man who brought him before the League. He was a labourer holding a bit of ground under Carroll. Carroll refused to pay his own rent to the landlord. But he compelled Connell to pay rent to him. When Carroll was evicted, the landlord offered to let Connell have half an acre more of land. He took it to better himself, and "how did he injure Carroll by taking it?" How indeed, poor man! Was he a rent-warner? Yes; he earned something that way two or three times a year; and for that he had to ask the protection of the police—"they would kill him else." What with worry and fright, and the loss of his livelihood, this unfortunate labourer has evidently been broken down morally and physically. It is impossible to come into contact with such living proofs of the ineffable cowardice and brutality of this business of "boycotting" without indignation and disgust.

While Connell was telling his pitiful tale a happy thought occurred to the charming daughter of the house. Mrs. Stacpoole is a clever amateur in photography. "Why not photograph this 'hale and hearty woman of fifty,' with her son of fifty-three?" Mrs. Stacpoole clapped her hands at the idea, and went off at once to prepare her apparatus.

While she was gone the sergeant gave me an account of the trial, which Mr. Redmond, M.P., witnessed. He was painfully explicit. "Mr. Redmond knew the woman was sober," he said; "she was lifted up on the table at Mr. Redmond's express request, because she was so small and old, and spoke in such a low voice that he could not hear what she said. Connell had always been a decent, industrious fellow—a fisherman. But for the lady,

Mrs. Moroney, he and his mother would have starved, and would starve now. As for the priest, Father White, Connell went to him to ask his intercession and help, but he could get neither."

The sergeant had heard Father White preach yesterday. "It was a curious sermon. He counselled peace and forbearance to the people, because they might be sure the wicked Tory Government would very soon fall!"

Presently the sun came out with golden glow, and with the sun came out Mrs. Stacpoole. It was a job to "pose" the subjects, the old woman evidently suspecting some surgical or legal significance in the machinery displayed, and her son finding some trouble in making her understand what it meant. But finally we got the tall, personable sergeant, with his frank, shrewd, sensible face, to put himself between the two, in the attitude as of a guardian angel; the camera was nimbly adjusted, and lo! the thing was done.

Mrs. Stacpoole thinks the operation promises a success. I suppose it would hardly be civil to send a finished proof of the group to Mr. J. Redmond, M.P.

APPENDIX

APPENDIX.

Note A.
MR. GLADSTONE AND THE AMERICAN WAR.
(Prologue, p. xxix.)

THIS statement as to the action of Lord Palmerston in connection with Mr. Gladstone's Newcastle speech of October 7th, 1862, made upon the authority of a British public man whose years and position entitle him to speak with confidence on such a subject, appeared to me of so much interest, that after sending it to the printer I caused search to be made for the speech referred to as made by Sir George Cornewall Lewis. My informant's statement was that Lord Palmerston insisted that Sir George Lewis should find or make an immediate opportunity of covering what Mr. Gladstone had said at Newcastle. He was angry about it, and his anger was increased by an article which Mr. Delane printed in the *Times*, intimating that Mr. Gladstone's speech was considered by many people to be a betrayal of Cabinet secrets. Sir George Lewis was far from well (he died the next spring), and reluctant to do what his chief wished; but he did it on the 17th of October 1862 in a speech at Hereford. Mr. Milner-Gibson was also put forward to the same end, and after

Parliament met, in February 1863, Mr. Disraeli gave the Government a sharp lashing for sending one or two Ministers into the country in the recess to announce that the Southern States would be recognised, and then putting forward the President of the Board of Trade (Milner-Gibson) to attack the Southern States and the pestilent institution of slavery. Mr. Gladstone's speech at Newcastle, coming as it did from the Chancellor of the Exchequer, after the close of a session during which everybody knew that the Emperor of the French had been urging upon England the recognition of the Confederate States, and that Mr. Mason had been in active correspondence on that subject with Lord Russell, was taken at Newcastle, and throughout the country, to mean that the recognition was imminent. Mr. Gladstone even went so far as to say he rather rejoiced that the Confederates had not been able to hold Maryland, as that might have made them aggressive, and so made a settlement more difficult, it being, he said, as certain as anything in the future could be that the South must succeed in separating itself from the Union. This remark about Maryland distinctly indicated consultation as to what limits and boundaries between the South and the North should be recognised in the recognition, and on that account, it seems, was particularly resented by Earl Russell as well as by Lord Palmerston.

Sir George Cornewall Lewis's speech of October 17, 1862, was a most skilful and masterly attempt to protect the Cabinet against the consequences of what the *Times*, on the 9th of October, had treated as the "indiscretion or treason" of his colleague. But it did not save the Government from the scourge of Mr. Disraeli, or much mitigate the effect in America of Mr. Gladstone's performance at Newcastle, which was a much more serious matter from the American point of view than any of the speeches recently delivered about "Home Rule" in the American Senate can be fairly said to be from the British point of view.

NOTE B.

MR. PARNELL AND THE DYNAMITERS.

(Prologue, p. xxxiii.)

THE relation of Mr. Parnell and his Parliamentary associates to what is called the extreme and "criminal" section of the Irish American Revolutionary Party can only be understood by those who understand that it is the ultimate object of this party not to effect reforms in the administration of Ireland as an integral part of the British Empire, but to sever absolutely the political connection between Ireland and the British Empire. Loyal British subjects necessarily consider this object a "criminal" object, just as loyal Austrian subjects considered the object of the Italian Revolutionists of 1848 to be a "criminal" object. But the Italian Revolutionists of 1848 did not accept this view of their object. On the contrary, they held their end to be so high and holy that it more or less sanctified even assassination when planned as a means to that end. Why should the Italian Revolutionists of 1848 be judged by one standard and the Irish Revolutionists of 1888 by another?

If Mr. Parnell and his Parliamentary associates were to declare in unequivocal terms their absolute loyalty to the British Crown, and their determination to maintain in all circumstances the political connection between Great Britain and Ireland, they might or might not retain their hold upon Mr. Davitt and upon their constituents in Ireland, but they would certainly put themselves beyond the pale of support by the great Irish American organisations. Nor do I believe they could retain the confidence of those organisations if it were supposed that they really regarded the most extreme and violent of the Irish Revolutionists, the "Invincibles" and the "dynamiters" as "criminals," in the sense in which the "Invincibles" and the "dynamiters" are so regarded by the rest of the civilised world. Can it, for example, be doubted that any English or Scottish public man who co-operates with Mr. Parnell and his Parliamentary associates would instantly hand over to the police any "Invincible" or "dynamiter" who might come within his reach? And can it for a moment be believed that Mr. Parnell, or any one of his Parliamentary associates, would do this? There are thousands of Irish citizens in the United States who felt all the horror and indignation expressed by Mr. Parnell at the murders in the Phœnix Park, but I should be very much surprised to learn that any one of them all ever did, or ever would do, anything likely to bring any one of the authors of these murders to the bar of justice. Mr. Parnell and his Parliamentary associates are held and bound by the essential conditions of their political existence to treat with complaisance the most extreme and violent men of their party. Nor is this true of them alone.

There is no more respectable body of men in the United States than the Hibernian Society of Philadelphia. This society was instituted in 1771, five years before the declaration of American Independence. It is a charitable and social organisation only, with no political object or colour. It is made up of men of character and substance. Its custom has always been to celebrate St. Patrick's Day by a banquet, to which the most distinguished men of the country have repeatedly been bidden. Immediately after the inauguration of Mr. Cleveland as President, on the 4th of March 1885, Mr. Bayard, the new Secretary of State of the United States, was invited by this Society to attend its one hundred and fourteenth banquet. It will be remembered that, on the 30th of May 1884, London had been startled and shocked by an explosion of dynamite in St. James's Square, which shattered many houses and inflicted cruel injuries upon several innocent people. It was not so fatal to life as that explosion at the Salford Barracks, which Mr. Parnell treated as a "practical joke." But it excited lively indignation on both sides of the Atlantic, and Mr. Bayard, who at that time was a Senator of the United States, sternly denounced it and its authors on the floor of the American Senate. What he had said as a Senator he thought it right to repeat as the Foreign Secretary of the United States in his reply to the invitation of the Hibernian Society in March 1885. This reply ran as follows:—

"WASHINGTON, D.C., *March* 9, 1885.

" NICHOLAS J. GRIFFIN, Esq., *Secretary of the
Hibernian Society of Philadelphia.*

" DEAR Sir,—I have your personal note accompanying the card of invitation to dine with your ancient and honourable Society on their one hundred and fourteenth anniversary, St. Patrick's Day, and I sincerely regret that I cannot accept it. The obvious and many duties of my public office here speak for themselves, and to none with more force than to American citizens of Irish blood or birth who are honestly endeavouring to secure liberty by maintaining a government of laws, and who realise the constant attention that is needful.

"In the midst of anarchical demonstrations which we witness in other lands, and the echoes of which we can detect even here in our own free country, where base and silly individuals seek to stain the name of Ireland by associating the honest struggle for just government with senseless and wicked crimes, there are none of our citizens from whom honest reprobation can be more confidently expected than from such as compose your respected and benevolent Society. Those who worthily celebrate the birthday[1] of St. Patrick will not forget that he drove out of Ireland the reptiles that creep and sting.

"The Hibernian Society can contain no member who will not resent the implication that sympathy with assassins can dwell in a genuine Irish heart, which will ever be opposed to cruelty and cowardice, whatever form either may take.

"Present to your Society my thanks for the kind remembrance, and assure them of the good-will and respect with which I am—Your obedient servant, T. F. BAYARD."

What was the response of this Society, representing all the best elements of the Irish American population of the United States, to this letter of the Secretary of State, the highest executive officer of the American Government after the President, upon whom under an existing law the succession of the chief magistracy now devolves in the event of the death or disability of the President and the Vice-President?

The letter was not read at the banquet.

But it was given to the press by the officers of the Society, and the most influential Irish American newspaper in the United States did not hesitate to describe it as an "insulting letter," going to show that its author was "an Englishman in spirit who will not allow any opportunity to go by, however slight, without testifying his sympathy with the British Empire and his antipathy for its foes."

This was capped by an American political journal which used the following language: "Lord Granville himself would hardly strike a more violent attitude against the dynamite section of the Irish people. When Lord Wolseley, whom it is proposed to make Governor-General of the Soudan, is offering a reward for the head of Ollivier Pain, it is hardly in good taste

---

[1] As Secretary Bayard is not a Catholic, this misapprehension of the meaning of a Saint's Day may be pardoned.

for an American Secretary of State to condemn so bitterly a class of Irishmen which, while it includes bad men no doubt, also includes men who are moved by as worthy motives as Lord Wolseley."

In the face of this testimony to the "solidarity" of all branches of the Irish revolutionary movement in America, how can Mr. Parnell, or any other Parliamentary Irishman who depends upon Irish American support, be expected by men of sense to condemn in earnest "the dynamite section of the Irish people"?

NOTE C.

THE AMERICAN "SUSPECTS" OF 1881.

(Prologue, p. xlvii.)

IN his recently published and very interesting *Life of Mr. Forster*, Mr. Wemyss Reid alludes to some action taken by the United States Government in the spring of 1882 as one of the determining forces which brought about the abandonment at that time by Mr. Gladstone of Mr. Forster's policy in Ireland. Without pretending to concern myself here with what is an essentially British question as between Mr. Forster and Mr. Gladstone, it may be both proper and useful for me to throw some light, not, perhaps, in the possession of Mr. Reid, upon the part taken in this matter by the American Government. Sir William Harcourt's "Coercion Bill" was passed on the 2d of March 1881, two days before the inauguration of General Garfield as President of the United States. Mr. Blaine, who was appointed by the new President to take charge of the Foreign Relations of the American Government, received, on the 10th of March, at Washington, a despatch written by Mr. Lowell, the American Minister in London, on the 26th of February, being the day after the third reading in the Commons of the "Coercion Bill." In this despatch Mr. Lowell called the attention of the American State Department to a letter from Mr. Parnell to the Irish National Land League, dated at Paris, February 13, 1881, in which Mr. Parnell attempted to make what Mr. Lowell accurately enough described as an "extraordinary" distinction between "the American people" and "the Irish nation in America."

"This double nationality," said Mr. Lowell, "is likely to be of great practical inconvenience whenever the 'Coercion Bill' becomes law." By "this double nationality" in this passage, the American Minister, of course, meant "this claim of a double nationality;" for neither by Great Britain nor by the United States is any man permitted to consider himself at one and the same time a citizen of the American republic and a subject of the British monarchy. Nor was he quite right in anticipating "great practical inconvenience" from this "claim," upon which neither the British nor the American Government for a moment bestowed, or could bestow, the slightest attention.

The "great practical inconvenience" which, first to the American Legation in England, then to the United States Government at Washington, and finally to the Cabinet of Mr. Gladstone, did, however, arise from the application of Sir William Harcourt's Coercion Act of 1881 to American citizens in Ireland, had its origin not in Mr. Parnell's preposterous idea of an Irish nationality existing in the United States, but in the failure of the authorities of the United States to deal promptly and firmly with the situation created for American citizens in Ireland by the administration of Sir William Harcourt's Act.

As I have said, Sir William Harcourt's Act became

law on the 2d of March 1881, two days before the inauguration of President Garfield at Washington. Without touching the question of the relations between Great Britain and Ireland, and between the British Parliament and the Irish National Land League, it was clearly incumbent upon the Secretary of State of the United States, who entered upon his duties three days after Sir William Harcourt's Bill went into force in Ireland, to inform himself minutely and exactly as to the possible effects of that Bill upon the rights and interests of American citizens travelling or sojourning in that country. This was due not only to his own Government and to its citizens, but to the relations which ought to exist between his own Government and the Government of Great Britain. It was no affair of an American Secretary of State either to impede or to further the execution of "Coercion Acts" in Ireland against British subjects. But it was his affair to ascertain without delay the nature and the measure of any new and unusual perils, or "inconveniences," to which American citizens in Ireland might be exposed in the execution there by the British authorities of such Acts.

And it is on record, under his own hand, in a despatch to the American Minister in London, dated May 26, 1881, that Mr. Blaine had not so much as seen a copy of Sir William Harcourt's Coercion Act at that date, three months after it had gone into effect; three months after many persons claiming American citizenship had been arrested and imprisoned under it; and two months after his own official attention had been called by the American Minister in London, in an elaborate despatch, to the arrest under it of one such person, a man of Irish birth, who based his claim of American citizenship upon allegations of military service during the Civil War, of residence and citizenship in New York, and of the granting to him, by an American Secretary of State, of a citizen's passport. And when he did finally take the trouble to look at this Act, Mr. Blaine seems to have examined it so cursorily, and with such slight attention, that he overlooked a provision made in it, under which, had its true force and meaning been perceived by him, the State Department of the United States might, in the early summer of 1881, have secured for American citizens in Ireland the consideration due to them as the citizens of a friendly State. A curious despatch from Mr. Sackville West, the British Minister at Washington, to Earl Granville, published in a British Blue-book now in my possession, plainly intimates that in the summer of 1881 the American Secretary of State had given the British Minister to understand that no representations made to him or to his Government by the Government of the United States touching American-Irish "suspects" need be taken at all seriously. The whole diplomatic correspondence on this subject which went on between the two Governments while Mr. Blaine was Secretary of State, from the 4th of March 1881 to the 20th of December 1881, was of a sort to lull the British Government into the belief that "suspects" might be freely and safely arrested and locked up all over Ireland, with no more question of their nationality than of any evidence to establish their guilt or their innocence. During the whole of that time the State Department at Washington seems to have substantially remained content with the declaration of Earl Granville, in a letter sent to the American Legation on the 8th of July 1881, four months after the Coercion Act went into effect, that "no distinction could be made in the circumstances between foreigners and British subjects, and that in the case of British subjects the only information given was that contained in the warrant."

No fault can be found with the British Government for standing by this declaration so long as it thus seemed to command the assent of the Government of the United States.

But when Mr. Frelinghuysen was called into the State Department by President Arthur in December 1881, to overhaul the condition into which our foreign relations had been brought by his predecessor, he found that in no single instance had Mr. Blaine succeeded in inducing the British Government, either to release any American citizen arrested under a general warrant without specific charges of criminal conduct, and on "suspicion" in Ireland, or to order the examination of any such citizen. The one case in which an American citizen arrested under the Coercion Act in Ireland during Mr. Blaine's tenure of office had been liberated when Mr. Frelinghuysen took charge of the State Department, was that of Mr. Joseph B. Walsh, arrested at Castlebar, in Mayo, March 8, 1881, and discharged by order of the Lord-Lieutenant, October 21, 1881, not because he was an American citizen, nor after any examination, but expressly and solely on the ground of ill-health.

When Mr. Frelinghuysen became Secretary of State in December 1881 the Congress of the United States was in session. So numerous were the American "suspects" then lying in prison in Ireland, some of whom had been so confined for many months, that the doors of Congress were soon besieged by angry demands for an inquiry into the subject. A resolution in this sense was adopted by the House of Representatives, and forwarded, through the American Legation in London, to the British Foreign Office. Memorials touching particular cases were laid before both Houses of the American Congress. On the 10th of February 1882, Mr. Bancroft Davis, the Assistant-

Secretary of State, instructed the American Minister at London to take action concerning one such case, and to report upon it. The Minister not moving more rapidly than he had been accustomed to do under Mr. Blaine, Mr. Davis grew impatient, and on the 2d of March 1882 (being the anniversary of the adoption of the Coercion Act in England) the American Secretary of State cabled to the Minister in London significantly enough, "Use all diligence in regard to the late cases, especially of Hart and M'Sweeney, and report by cable."

Mr. Lowell replied the next day, giving the views in regard to Hart of the American Vice-Consul, and of the British Inspector of Police at Queenstown, and adding an expression of his own opinion that neither Hart nor M'Sweeney was "more innocent than the majority of those under arrest."

This was an unfortunate despatch. It roused the American Secretary of State into responding instantly by cable in the following explicit and emphatic terms: "Referring to the cases of O'Connor, Hart, M'Sweeney, M'Enery, and D'Alton, American citizens imprisoned in Ireland, say to Lord Granville that, without discussing whether the provisions of the Force Act can be applied to American citizens, the President hopes that the Lord-Lieutenant will be instructed to exercise the powers intrusted to him by the first section to order early trials in these and all other cases in which Americans may be arrested."

There was no mistaking the tone of this despatch. It was instantly transmitted to the British Foreign Secretary, who replied the same day that "the matter would receive the immediate attention of Her Majesty's Government."

The reference made to the Coercion Act by Mr. Frelinghuysen touched a plain and precise provision,

NOTE C   261

that persons detained under the Act "should not be discharged or tried by any court without the direction of the Lord-Lieutenant." Had the Coercion Act received from Mr. Blaine in March 1881 the attention bestowed upon it in March 1882 by Mr. Frelinghuysen, this provision might have been used to obviate the dangerous accumulation of injustice to individuals, and of international irritation, resulting from the application to possibly innocent foreign citizens in Ireland of the despotic powers conferred by that Act upon Mr. Gladstone's Government, powers as nearly as possible analogous with those which Mr. Gladstone himself, years before, had denounced in unmeasured terms when they were claimed and exercised by the Government of Naples in dealing with its own subjects.

After the consideration by Her Majesty's Government of this despatch of the United States Government, it is understood in America that Mr. Forster, as Chief Secretary for Ireland, was invited to communicate with the Lord-Lieutenant, and request him to exercise his discretion in the sense desired, and that Mr. Forster positively refused to do this.

How this may be I do not pretend to say. But as no satisfactory reply was made to the American despatch, and as public feeling in the United States grew daily more and more determined that a stop should be put to the unexplained arrest and the indefinite detention of American citizens in Ireland, the American Secretary of State made up his mind towards the end of the month of March to repeat his despatch of March 3d in a more terse and peremptory form. As a final preliminary to this step, however, Mr. Frelinghuysen was induced to avail himself of the unusual and officious intervention of his most distinguished living predecessor in the State Department, Mr. Hamilton Fish. After measuring the gravity of the situation, Mr. Fish at the end of March sent a despatch to an eminent public man, well known on both sides of the Atlantic, and now resident in London, with authority to show it personally to Mr. Gladstone, to the effect that if any further delay occurred in complying with the moderate and reasonable demand of the American Government for the immediate release or the immediate trial of the American "suspects," the relations between Great Britain and the United States would be very seriously "strained."

This despatch was at once communicated to Mr. Gladstone. Within the week, the liberation was announced of six American "suspects." Within a fortnight, Mr. Parnell, Mr. O'Kelly, and Mr. Dillon, it is understood, imprisoned members of Parliament, were offered their liberty if they would consent to a sham exile on the Continent for a few weeks, or even days; and within a month Mr. Forster, in his place in Parliament, was imputing to his late chief and Premier the negotiation of that celebrated "Treaty of Kilmainham," which was repudiated with equal warmth by the three Irish members already named, and by Mr. Gladstone.

NOTE D.

THE PARNELLITES AND THE ENGLISH PARTIES.

(Prologue, p. 1.)

As I am not writing a history of English parties, I need not discuss here the truth or falsehood of this contention. But I cannot let it pass without a word as to two cases which came under my own observation, and which aggravate the inherent improbability of the tale. In November 1885 I went to America, and on my way passed through Stockport, where my friend,

NOTE D 263

Mr. Jennings, long my correspondent in England, was then standing as a Conservative candidate. I attended one of his meetings and heard him make an effective speech, much applauded, which turned exclusively upon imperial and financial issues. That he had no understanding whatever with the "managers" of the Irish vote in Stockport, I have the best reason to believe. But he was assured by them that the Irish intended to vote for him; and at a subsequent time he was rashly assailed in the House of Commons by an Irish member with the charge that he had broken faith with the Irish who elected him. It was an unlucky assault for the assailant, as it gave Mr. Jennings an opportunity, which he promptly improved, to show that he owed nothing to the Irish voters of Stockport. Whether they voted for him in any number in 1885 was more than doubtful; while in 1886 they voted solidly against him, with the result of swelling his majority from 369 to 518 votes.

In January 1886 I returned to Europe, and going on a visit into Yorkshire, there met a prominent Irish Nationalist, who told me that he had come into the north of England expressly to regiment the Irish voters, and throw their votes for the Conservative candidates, on the ground that it was necessary to make the Liberals fully understand their power. He had fully expected in this way to elect a Conservative member for the city of York. Great was his chagrin, therefore, when he found the Liberal candidate returned. Upon investigation he discovered, as he told me, that the catastrophe was due to the activity of a local Irish priest, *who was a devoted Fenian*, utterly opposed to the Parliamentary programme, and who had exerted his authority over the local Irish to bring them to the polls for the Liberal candidate.

Sir Frederick Milner, Bart., the defeated Conservative candidate for York, afterwards told me that the local priest referred to here was a most excellent man, and that so far from playing the part thus ascribed to him, he took the trouble, as a matter of fair dealing, to see his parishioners on the morning of the election and warn them against believing a pamphlet which was sedulously circulated among the Irish voters on the night before the polling, with a message to the effect that Sir Frederick despised the Irish, and wanted nothing to do with them or their votes. Sir Frederick has no doubt, from his knowledge of what occurred during the canvass, that direct instructions were sent by Mr. Parnell or his agents to the Irish voters in York to throw their votes against the Radical candidates. These latter brought down a Home Rule lecturer to counteract the effect of these instructions, and the pamphlet above referred to was an eleventh-hour blow in the same interest. It was successful; the Irish votes, some 500 in number, being polled early in the morning under the impression produced by it. The moral of this incident would seem to be, not that there was any real understanding in 1885 between the Parnellites and the English Conservatives at all, but simply that the English Radical wirepullers are more alert and active than either the Irish Parnellites or the English Conservatives. It is interesting, too, as it illustrates the deep dread and distrust of the "Fenians" in which the Parnellites habitually go.

NOTE E.

THE "BOYCOTT" AT MILTOWN-MALBAY.

(Vol. i. p. 209.)

FATHER WHITE of Miltown-Malbay, taking exception to the statement made by me, upon the authority of

NOTE E   265

Colonel Turner, that he was "the moving spirit" of
the local "boycott" of policemen and soldiers at that
place, addressed a note to Colonel Turner on the 5th
of September, in which he desired to know whether
Colonel Turner, had given me grounds for making this
statement. To this note Colonel Turner tells me he
returned at once the following reply, which he kindly
forwards to me for publication :—

"ENNIS, 6*th September* 1888.

"REV. SIR,—I am in receipt of your letter of yesterday, and
in reply thereto beg to state that I informed Mr. Hurlbert that
you said 'in open court' that you had directed (I believe from
the altar) that the town was to be 'made as a city of the
dead' during the trials of 23 publicans who were charged for
conspiracy in boycotting the forces of the Crown who had been
employed in preserving the peace on the occasion of a former
trial—this you said you did in the interests of peace. The
magistrates, however, took a different view, viz., that it was
done with the object of preventing the military and police from
obtaining any supplies, which they were unable to do ; and that
their view was the correct one was proved by the fact that
half of the accused pleaded guilty to the offence, and on promise
of future good behaviour were allowed out on their own
recognisances. That the people followed your instructions on
that day, coupled with the fact that in your letter to the *Freeman's Journal*, dated 17th March of this year, you stated that
you offered me peace all round on certain conditions, thereby
showing that at least you consider yourself possessed of
authority to bring about a state of peace or otherwise, probably
led Mr. Hurlbert, to whom I showed a copy of this letter, to
infer that you admitted that you were the moving spirit of all
this 'local boycott,' while you only did so in the particular
case above mentioned. Whether Mr. Hurlbert is correct in
drawing the inference he does as to your being the moving
spirit, and as to your conduct, may perhaps be gathered from
the numerous numbers of *United Ireland* and other papers
which he saw giving reports of illegal meetings of the suppressed branch of the Miltown-Malbay National League, at
which you were stated to have presided, and at some of which
condemnatory resolutions were passed, and also from the
fact that you are reported to have presided at a meeting

on Sunday, April 8, which was held at Miltown-Malbay in defiance of Government proclamation.—I am, dear Sir, yours faithfully, ALFRED E. TURNER.
"Rev. P. White, P.P.,
Miltown-Malbay."

On further investigation of his records, Colonel Turner found it necessary to follow up this letter with another, a copy of which, through his courtesy, I subjoin :—

"ENNIS, 10*th September* 1888.

"REV. SIR,—A slight inaccuracy has been pointed out to me in my letter to you of the 6th inst., which I hasten to correct. It occurred in transcribing my letter from the original draft. I should have said that I told Mr. Hurlbert that you stated in open court, at the trial of 23 publicans charged with boycotting the forces of the Crown on the occasion of a former trial, that you had told the people (I believe from the altar) that the town was to be made as a city of the dead during the former trial; and that in consequence the soldiers and police could get nothing to eat or drink in Miltown that day.

"I also told him that this boycotting of the police was by no means new, since on the 13th March 1887, at a meeting of the Miltown-Malbay branch of the League at which you are reported to have presided, in *United Ireland* of 19/3/87, the following resolution was unanimously adopted :—

"'That from this day any person who supplies the police while engaged in work which is opposed to the wishes of the people with drink, food, or cars, be censured by this branch, and that no further intercourse be held with them.'

"I regret that through inadvertence I have had to trouble you with a second letter.—I am, Rev. Sir, yours faithfully,

"ALFRED E. TURNER.

"Rev. P. White, P.P."

15A CASTLE STREET,
EDINBURGH, *October* 1888.

LIST OF BOOKS PUBLISHED BY
DAVID DOUGLAS.

View of the Political State of Scotland in the last
Century. A Confidential Report on the Political Opinions, Family Connections, or Personal Circumstances, of the 2662 County Voters in 1788. Edited, with an introductory account of the Law relating to County Elections, by Sir CHARLES ELPHINSTONE ADAM of Blair-Adam, Bart., Barrister-at-Law. Crown 8vo, 5s.

On the Philosophy of Kant.
By ROBERT ADAMSON, M.A., Professor of Logic and Mental Philosophy, Owens College; formerly Examiner in Philosophy in the University of Edinburgh. Ex. fcap. 8vo, 6s.

The New Amphion; Being the Book of the Edinburgh
University Union Fancy Fair, in which are contained sundry Artistick, Instructive, and Diverting Matters, *all now made publick for the first time*. 12mo, Illustrated, 5s.; Large-Paper Edition, 21s. (only 100 Copies printed).

"An especially dainty little morsel for the lovers of choice books."—*Academy*.
"There is no need to say that the book is valuable. It will be eagerly and widely sought for.... The external appointments are such as would charm the most fastidious bibliomaniac."—*Scotsman*.

Stories by Thomas Bailey Aldrich.
THE QUEEN OF SHEBA. 1s., or in cloth, gilt top, 2s.
MARJORIE DAW, and other Stories. 1s., or in cloth, gilt top, 2s.
PRUDENCE PALFREY. 1s., or in cloth, gilt top, 2s.
THE STILLWATER TRAGEDY. 2 vols. 2s., or in cloth, gilt top, 4s.

"Mr. Aldrich is, perhaps, entitled to stand at the head of American humourists."
—*Athenæum*.
"*Marjorie Daw* is a clever piece of literary work."—*Saturday Review*.

Johnny Gibb of Gushetneuk in the Parish of Pyketillim,
with Glimpses of Parish Politics about A.D. 1843. By WILLIAM ALEXANDER, LL.D. Ninth Edition, with Glossary, Ex. fcap. 8vo, 2s.
Seventh Edition, with Twenty Lithographic Illustrations—Portraits and Landscapes—by GEORGE REID, R.S.A. Demy 8vo, 12s. 6d.

"A most vigorous and truthful delineation of local character, drawn from a portion of the country where that character is peculiarly worthy of careful study and record."—*The Right Hon. W. E. Gladstone.*

Life among my Ain Folk.
By WILLIAM ALEXANDER, LL.D., Author of "Johnny Gibb of Gushetneuk."
Ex. fcap. 8vo. Second Edition. Cloth, 2s. 6d. Paper, 2s.

Notes and Sketches of Northern Rural Life in the
Eighteenth Century, by WILLIAM ALEXANDER, LL.D., the Author of "Johnny Gibb of Gushetneuk." Ex. fcap. 8vo, 1s. Cloth, 2s. 6d.

American Authors.

Latest Editions. Revised by the Authors. In 1s. volumes. By Post, 1s. 2d. Printed by Constable, and published with the sanction of the Authors.

By W. D. HOWELLS.
A FOREGONE CONCLUSION.
A CHANCE ACQUAINTANCE.
THEIR WEDDING JOURNEY.
A COUNTERFEIT PRESENTMENT.
THE LADY OF THE AROOSTOOK. 2 vols.
OUT OF THE QUESTION.
THE UNDISCOVERED COUNTRY. 2 vols.
A FEARFUL RESPONSIBILITY.
VENETIAN LIFE. 2 vols.
ITALIAN JOURNEYS. 2 vols.
THE RISE OF SILAS LAPHAM. 2 vols.
INDIAN SUMMER. 2 vols.

By FRANK R. STOCKTON.
RUDDER GRANGE.
THE LADY OR THE TIGER?
A BORROWED MONTH.

By GEO. W. CURTIS.
PRUE AND I.

By J. C. HARRIS (*Uncle Remus*).
MINGO, AND OTHER SKETCHES.

By GEO. W. CABLE.
OLD CREOLE DAYS.
MADAME DELPHINE.

By B. W. HOWARD.
ONE SUMMER.

By JOHN BURROUGHS.
WINTER SUNSHINE.
PEPACTON.
LOCUSTS AND WILD HONEY.
WAKE-ROBIN.
BIRDS AND POETS.
FRESH FIELDS.

By OLIVER WENDELL HOLMES.
THE AUTOCRAT OF THE BREAKFAST TABLE. 2 vols.
THE POET. 2 vols.
THE PROFESSOR. 2 vols.

By G. P. LATHROP.
AN ECHO OF PASSION.

By R. G. WHITE.
MR. WASHINGTON ADAMS.

By T. B. ALDRICH.
THE QUEEN OF SHEBA.
MARJORIE DAW.
PRUDENCE PALFREY.
THE STILLWATER TRAGEDY. 2 vols.

By B. MATTHEWS and H. C. BUNNER.
IN PARTNERSHIP.

By WILLIAM WINTER.
SHAKESPEARE'S ENGLAND.

*** *Other Volumes of this attractive Series in preparation.*
Any of the above may be had bound in Cloth extra, at 2s. each vol.

"A set of charming little books."—*Blackwood's Magazine.*

"A remarkably pretty series."—*Saturday Review.*

"These neat and minute volumes are creditable alike to printer and publisher."—*Pall Mall Gazette.*

"The most graceful and delicious little volumes with which we are acquainted."—*Freeman.*

"Soundly and tastefully bound . . . a little model of typography, . . . and the contents are worthy of the dress."—*St. James's Gazette.*

"The delightful shilling series of 'American Authors' introduced by Mr. David Douglas has afforded pleasure to thousands of persons."—*Figaro.*

"The type is delightfully legible, and the page is pleasant for the eye to rest upon; even in these days of cheap editions we have seen nothing that has pleased us so well."—*Literary World.*

American Statesmen.

A Series of Biographies of men conspicuous in the Political History of the United States. Edited by JOHN T. MORSE, Jun.

Small crown 8vo, price 6s. each vol.

1. THOMAS JEFFERSON. By JOHN T. MORSE, Jun.
2. SAMUEL ADAMS. By JAMES K. HOSMER.
   "A man who, in the history of the American Revolution, is second only to Washington."
3. ALEXANDER HAMILTON. By HENRY CABOT LODGE.
   With a Preface containing the "Declaration of Independence," "Articles of Confederation," and the Constitution of the United States.
4. HENRY CLAY. By CARL SCHURZ. 2 vols., 12s.

Alma Mater's Mirror.

Edited by THOMAS SPENCER BAYNES and LEWIS CAMPBELL, Professors in the University, St. Andrews. Printed in red and black, on antique paper. Bound in white, richly tooled in gold in the ancient manner, with ribbon fastening. In box, Price 5s.

Modern Horsemanship. A New Method of Teaching
Riding and Training by means of pictures from the life. By E. L. ANDERSON. Third Edition, with fresh Illustrations of the "Gallop-Change" of unique and peculiar interest. Illustrated by 32 Instantaneous Photographs. Demy 8vo. 21s.

Vice in the Horse and other Papers on Horses and
Riding. By E. L. ANDERSON, Author of "Modern Horsemanship." Illustrated. Demy 8vo, 5s.

The Gallop.
By E. L. ANDERSON. Illustrated by Instantaneous Photography. Fcap. 4to, 2s. 6d.

Scotland in Early Christian Times.
By JOSEPH ANDERSON, LL.D., Keeper of the National Museum of the Antiquaries of Scotland. (Being the Rhind Lectures in Archæology for 1879 and 1880.) 2 vols. Demy 8vo, profusely Illustrated. 12s. each volume.
 Contents of Vol. I.—Celtic Churches—Monasteries—Hermitages—Round Towers—Illuminated Manuscripts—Bells—Crosiers—Reliquaries, etc.
 Contents of Vol. II.—Celtic Medal-Work and Sculptured Monuments, their Art and Symbolism—Inscribed Monuments in Runics and Oghams—Bilingual inscriptions, etc.

Scotland in Pagan Times.
By JOSEPH ANDERSON, LL.D. (Being the Rhind Lectures in Archæology for 1881 and 1882.) In 2 vols. Demy 8vo, profusely Illustrated. 12s. each volume.
 Contents of Vol. I.—THE IRON AGE.—Viking Burials and Hoards of Silver and Ornaments—Arms, Dress, etc., of the Viking Time—Celtic Art of the Pagan Period—Decorated Mirrors—Enamelled Armlets—Architecture and Contents of the Brochs—Lake-Dwellings—Earth Houses, etc.
 Contents of Vol. II.—THE BRONZE AND STONE AGES.—Cairn Burial of the Bronze Age and Cremation Cemeteries—Urns of Bronze-Age Types—Stone Circles—Stone Settings—Gold Ornaments—Implements and Weapons of Bronze—Cairn Burial of the Stone Age—Chambered Cairns—Urns of Stone-Age Types—Implements and Weapons of Stone.

Scotland as it was and as it is.
By the DUKE OF ARGYLL. 1 vol. Demy 8vo. Illustrated. New Edition. Carefully Revised. 7s. 6d.
 Contents.—Celtic Feudalism—The Age of Charters—The Age of Covenants—The Epoch of the Clans—The Appeal from Chiefs to Owners—The Response to the Appeal—Before the Dawn—The Burst of Industry—The Fruits of Mind.
 "Infinitely superior as regards the Highland land question to any statement yet made by the other side."—*Scotsman.*
 "It presents a series of strikingly picturesque sketches of the wild society and rude manners of the olden time."—*Times.*

The New British Constitution and its Master-Builders.
By the DUKE OF ARGYLL. 1 vol. crown 8vo, 3s. 6d.

Crofts and Farms in the Hebrides:
Being an account of the Management of an Island Estate for 130 Years. By the DUKE OF ARGYLL. Demy 8vo, 83 pages, 1s.

Continuity and Catastrophes in Geology.
An Address to the Edinburgh Geological Society on its Fiftieth Anniversary, 1st November 1883. By the DUKE OF ARGYLL. Demy 8vo, 1s.

The History of Liddesdale, Eskdale, Ewesdale, Wauch-
opedale, and the Debateable Land. Part I. from the Twelfth Century to 1530. By ROBERT BRUCE ARMSTRONG. The edition is limited to 275 copies demy quarto, and 105 copies on large paper (10 inches by 13). 42s. and 84s.

Reminiscences of Golf on St. Andrews Links.
By JAMES BALFOUR. Price 1s.

On Both Sides. By FRANCES C. BAYLOR. 1 vol. 6s.

Pugin Studentship Drawings. Being a selection from Sketches, Measured Drawings, and details of Domestic and Ecclesiastic Buildings in England and Scotland. By G. WASHINGTON-BROWNE, F.S.A. Scot., Architect. 1 vol. Folio, Illustrated, 45s.

"The Red Book of Menteith." Reviewed.
By GEORGE BURNETT, Advocate, Lyon King of Arms. Small 4to, 6s.

Next Door. A Novel. By CLARE LOUISE BURNHAM. Crown 8vo, 7s. 6d.
"A strangely interesting story."—*St. James's Gazette.*

John Burroughs's Essays.
Six Books of Nature, Animal Life, and Literature. Choice Edition. Revised by the Author. 6 vols., cloth, 12s.; or in smooth ornamental wrappers, 6s.; or separately at 1s. each vol., or 2s. in cloth.

WINTER SUNSHINE.	FRESH FIELDS.
LOCUSTS AND WILD HONEY.	BIRDS AND POETS.
WAKE-ROBIN.	PEPACTON.

"Whichever essay I read, I am glad I read it, for pleasanter reading, to those who love the country, with all its enchanting sights and sounds, cannot be imagined."—*Spectator.*

"Mr. Burroughs is one of the most delightful of American Essayists, steeped in culture to the finger-ends."—*Pall Mall Gazette.*

FRESH FIELDS. By JOHN BURROUGHS. Library Edition. Crown 8vo, 6s.
SIGNS AND SEASONS. Library Edition. Crown 8vo, 6s.

Dr. Sevier: A Novel.
By GEO. W. CABLE, Author of "Old Creole Days," etc. In 2 vols., crown 8vo, price 12s.

Old Creole Days. By GEO. W. CABLE. 1s.; and in Cloth, 2s.
"We cannot recall any contemporary American writer of fiction who possesses some of the best gifts of the novelist in a higher degree."—*St. James's Gazette.*

Madame Delphine.
By GEO. W. CABLE, Author of "Old Creole Days." 1s.; and in cloth, 2s.
Contents.—Madame Delphine—Carancro—Grande Pointe.

Memoir of John Brown, D.D.
By JOHN CAIRNS, D.D., Berwick-on-Tweed. Crown 8vo, 7s. 6d.

My Indian Journal.
Containing Descriptions of the principal Field Sports of India, with Notes on the Natural History and Habits of the Wild Animals of the Country. By Colonel WALTER CAMPBELL, Author of "The Old Forest Ranger." Small demy 8vo, with Illustrations by Wolf, 16s.

Life and Works of Rev. Thomas Chalmers, D.D., LL.D.
MEMOIRS OF THE REV. THOMAS CHALMERS. By Rev. W. HANNA, D.D., LL.D. New Edition. 2 vols. crown 8vo, cloth, 12s.
DAILY SCRIPTURE READINGS. Cheap Edition. 2 vols. crown 8vo, 10s.
ASTRONOMICAL DISCOURSES, 1s.
COMMERCIAL DISCOURSES, 1s.
SELECT WORKS, in 12 vols., crown 8vo, cloth, per vol. 6s.
   Lectures on the ROMANS. 2 vols.
   Sermons. 2 vols.
   Natural Theology, Lectures on Butler's Analogy, etc. 1 vol.
   Christian Evidences, Lectures on Paley's Evidences, etc. 1 vol.
   Institutes of Theology. 2 vols.
   Political Economy, with Cognate Essays. 1 vol.
   Polity of a Nation. 1 vol.
   Church and College Establishments. 1 vol.
   Moral Philosophy, Introductory Essays, Index, etc. 1 vol.

Lectures on Surgical Anatomy.
By JOHN CHIENE, M.D., Professor of Surgery in the University of Edinburgh.
In demy 8vo. With numerous Illustrations drawn on Stone by BERJEAU. 12s. 6d.
"The book will be a great help to both teachers and taught, and students can depend upon the teaching as being sound."—*Medical Times and Gazette.*

Lectures on the Elements or First Principles of Surgery.
By JOHN CHIENE, M.D., Professor of Surgery in the University of Edinburgh.
Demy 8vo, 2s. 6d.

The Odes of Horace.
Translated by T. RUTHERFURD CLARK, Advocate. 16mo, 6s.

Scala Naturæ, and other Poems.
By JOHN CLELAND. Fcap. 8vo, 5s.

An Examination of the Trials for Sedition which have hitherto occurred in Scotland. By the late LORD COCKBURN. 2 vols. demy 8vo, 28s.

Circuit Journeys from 1837 to 1854.
By the late LORD COCKBURN. 1 vol. crown 8vo, 7s. 6d.

Archibald Constable and his Literary Correspondents:
a Memorial. By his Son, THOMAS CONSTABLE. 3 vols. demy 8vo, 36s., with Portrait.
"He (Mr. Constable) was a genius in the publishing world. . . . The creator of the Scottish publishing trade."—*Times.*

The Earldom of Mar, in Sunshine and in Shade, during Five Hundred Years. With incidental Notices of the leading Cases of Scottish Dignities from the reign of King Charles I. till now. By ALEXANDER, EARL OF CRAWFORD AND BALCARRES, LORD LINDSAY, etc. etc. 2 vols. demy 8vo, 32s.

The Crime of Henry Vane: a Study with a Moral.
By J. S. of Dale, Author of "Guerndale." Crown 8vo, 6s.

A Clinical and Experimental Study of the Bladder during Parturition. By J. H. CROOM, M.B., F.R.C.P.E. Small 4to, with Illustrations, 6s.

Wild Men and Wild Beasts.
Adventures in Camp and Jungle. By Lieut.-Colonel GORDON CUMMING. With Illustrations by Lieut.-Colonel BAIGRIE and others. Small 4to, 24s.
Also a cheaper edition, with *Lithographic* Illustrations. 8vo, 12s.

Prue and I.
By GEORGE WILLIAM CURTIS. 1s. paper; or 2s. cloth extra
Contents.—Dinner Time—My Chateaux—Sea from Shore—Titbottom's Spectacles—A Cruise in the Flying Dutchman—Family Portraits—Our Cousin the Curate.
"This is a dainty piece of work, and well deserved reprinting."—*Athenæum.*
"These charming sketches will be enjoyed by all cultured readers."—*Daily Chronicle.*

The Story of Burnt Njal; or, Life in Iceland at the end of the Tenth Century. From the Icelandic of the Njals Saga. By Sir GEORGE WEBBE DASENT, D.C.L. 2 vols. demy 8vo, with Maps and Plans, 28s.

Gisli the Outlaw.
From the Icelandic. By Sir GEORGE WEBBE DASENT, D.C.L. Small 4to, with Illustrations, 7s. 6d.

Popular Tales from the Norse.
By Sir GEORGE WEBBE DASENT, D.C.L. With an Introductory Essay on the Origin and Diffusion of Popular Tales. Third Edition. Crown 8vo, 10s. 6d.

A Daughter of the Philistines: A Novel.
Crown 8vo, 6s. Also a cheaper edition in paper binding, 2s.
"The story is very powerfully told, possesses a piquantly satirical flavour, and possesses the very real attraction of freshness."—*Scotsman.*
"It is cleverly and brightly written."—*Academy.*

A Manual of Chemical Analysis.
By Professor WILLIAM DITTMAR. Ex. fcap. 8vo, 5s.
TABLES FORMING AN APPENDIX TO DITTO. Demy 8vo, 3s. 6d.

A Chat in the Saddle; or Patroclus and Penelope.
By THEO. A. DODGE, Lieut.-Colonel, United States Army. Illustrated by 14 Instantaneous Photographs. Demy 8vo, half-leather binding, 21s.

The Fireside Tragedy, etc.
By Sir GEORGE DOUGLAS, Bart. Fcap. 8vo, 5s.

Veterinary Medicines; their Actions and Uses.
By FINLAY DUN. Seventh Edition, revised and enlarged. Demy 8vo.
[*In the Press.*

Social Life in Former Days;
Chiefly in the Province of Moray. Illustrated by Letters and Family Papers. By E. DUNBAR DUNBAR, late Captain 21st Fusiliers. 2 vols. Demy 8vo, 19s. 6d.

The Graysons: A Story of Illinois.
By EDWARD EGGLESTON. [*Nearly Ready.*

Letters of Thomas Erskine of Linlathen.
Edited by WILLIAM HANNA, D.D., Author of the "Memoirs of Dr. Chalmers," etc. Fourth Edition. Crown 8vo, 7s. 6d.

The Unconditional Freeness of the Gospel.
By THOMAS ERSKINE of Linlathen. New Edition, revised. Crown 8vo, 3s. 6d.

By the same Author.

The Brazen Serpent:
Or, Life coming through Death. Third Edition. Crown 8vo, 5s.

The Internal Evidence of Revealed Religion.
Crown 8vo, 5s.

The Spiritual Order,
And other Papers selected from the MSS. of the late THOMAS ERSKINE of Linlathen. Third Edition. Crown 8vo, 5s.

The Doctrine of Election,
And its Connection with the General Tenor of Christianity, illustrated especially from the Epistle to the Romans. Second Edition. Crown 8vo, 6s.

The Fatherhood of God Revealed in Christ, the Comfort
and Hope of Man. A Lesson from "The Letters" of THOMAS ERSKINE, of Linlathen. Fcap. 8vo, 1s.

Three Visits to America.
By EMILY FAITHFULL. Demy 8vo, 9s.

Ogham Inscriptions in Ireland, Wales, and Scotland.
By the late SIR SAMUEL FERGUSON, President of the Royal Irish Academy, Deputy Keeper of the Public Records of Ireland, LL.D., Queen's Counsel, etc. (Being the Rhind Lectures in Archæology for 1884.) 1 vol. demy 8vo, 12s.

Twelve Sketches of Scenery and Antiquities on the
Line of the Great North of Scotland Railway. By GEORGE REID, R.S.A. With Illustrative Letterpress by W. FERGUSON of Kinmundy. 4to, 15s.

Guide to the Great North of Scotland Railway.
By W. FERGUSON of Kinmundy. Crown 8vo; in paper cover, 1s.; cloth cover, 1s. 6d.

Robert Ferguson "The Plotter," or, The Secret of the
Rye House Conspiracy and the Story of a Strange Career. By JAMES FERGUSON, Advocate. A Biography of one of the strangest figures of English Politics in the period between the Restoration and the Accession of the House of Hanover. Demy 8vo, 15s.

The Laird of Lag; A Life-Sketch of Sir Robert Grierson.
By ALEX. FERGUSSON, Lieut.-Colonel, Author of "Mrs. Calderwood's Journey."
Demy 8vo, with Illustrations, 12s.

Autobiography of Mrs. Fletcher
(of Edinburgh), with Letters and other Family Memorials. Edited by her Daughter. Third Edition. Crown 8vo, 7s. 6d.

L'Histoire de France.
Par M. LAME FLEURY. New Edition, corrected to 1883. 18mo, cloth, 2s. 6d.

The Deepening of the Spiritual Life.
By A. P. FORBES, D.C.L., Bishop of Brechin. Seventh Edition. Paper, 1s.; cloth, 1s. 6d. Calf, red edges, 3s. 6d.

Kalendars of Scottish Saints,
With Personal Notices of those of Alba, etc. By ALEXANDER PENROSE FORBES, D.C.L., Bishop of Brechin. 4to, price £3, 3s. A few copies for sale on large paper, £5, 15s. 6d.

"A truly valuable contribution to the archæology of Scotland."—*Guardian.*

"We must not forget to thank the author for the great amount of information he has put together, and for the labour he has bestowed on a work which can never be remunerative."—*Saturday Review.*

Missale Drummondiense. The Ancient Irish Missal in
the possession of the Baroness Willoughby d'Eresby. Edited by the Rev. G. H. FORBES. Half-Morocco, Demy 8vo, 12s.

Forestry and Forest Products.
Prize Essays of the Edinburgh International Forestry Exhibition 1884. Edited by JOHN RATTRAY M.A., B.Sc., and HUGH ROBERT MILL, D.Sc. Demy 8vo, Illustrated, 9s.

Fragments of Truth:
Being the Exposition of several Passages of Scripture. Third Edition. Ex. fcap. 8vo, 5s.

Studies in English History.
By JAMES GAIRDNER and JAMES SPEDDING. Demy 8vo, 12s.
Contents.—The Lollards—Sir John Falstaff—Katherine of Arragon's First and Second Marriages—Case of Sir Thomas Overbury—Divine Right of Kings—Sunday, Ancient and Modern.

Industrial Exhibitions and Modern Progress.
By PATRICK GEDDES. Fcap. 8vo, 1s.

Gifts for Men.
By X. H. Crown 8vo, 6s.
"There is hardly a living theologian who might not be proud to claim many of her thoughts as his own."—*Glasgow Herald.*

Sketches, Literary and Theological:
Being Selections from the unpublished MSS. of the Rev. GEORGE GILFILLAN. Edited by FRANK HENDERSON, Esq., M.P. Demy 8vo, 7s. 6d.

The Roof of the World:
Being the Narrative of a Journey over the High Plateau of Tibet to the Russian Frontier, and the Oxus Sources on Pamir. By Brigadier-General T. E. GORDON, C.S.I. With numerous Illustrations. Royal 8vo, 31s. 6d.

Ladies' Old-Fashioned Shoes.
By T. WATSON GREIG, of Glencarse. Folio, illustrated by 11 Chromolithographs. 31s. 6d.

Mingo, and other Sketches in Black and White.
By JOEL CHANDLER HARRIS (*Uncle Remus*). 1s.; and in cloth, 2s.

Works by Margaret Maria Gordon (née Brewster).

THE HOME LIFE OF SIR DAVID BREWSTER. By his Daughter. Second Edition. Crown 8vo, 6s. Also a cheaper Edition. Crown 8vo, 2s. 6d.

WORK; Or, Plenty to do and How to do it. Thirty-Sixth Thousand. Fcap. 8vo, cloth, 2s. 6d.

WORKERS. Fourth Thousand. Fcap. 8vo, limp cloth, 1s.

LITTLE MILLIE AND HER FOUR PLACES. Cheap Edition. Fifty-ninth Thousand. Limp cloth, 1s.

SUNBEAMS IN THE COTTAGE; Or, What Women may Do. A Narrative chiefly addressed to the Working Classes. Cheap Edition. Forty-fifth Thousand. Limp cloth, 1s.

PREVENTION; or, An Appeal to Economy and Common Sense. 8vo, 6d.

THE WORD AND THE WORLD. Twelfth Edition. 2d.

LEAVES OF HEALING FOR THE SICK AND SORROWFUL. Cheap Edition, limp cloth, 2s.

THE MOTHERLESS BOY. With an Illustration by Sir NOEL PATON, R.S.A. Cheap Edition, limp cloth, 1s.

OUR DAUGHTERS; An Account of the Young Women's Christian Association and Institute Union. 2d.

HAY MACDOWALL GRANT OF ARNDILLY; His Life, Labours, and Teaching. New and Cheaper Edition. 1 vol. crown 8vo, limp cloth, 2s. 6d.

The Life of our Lord.

By the Rev. WILLIAM HANNA, D.D., LL.D. 6 vols., handsomely bound in cloth extra, gilt edges, 30s.

Separate vols., cloth extra, gilt edges, 5s. each.

1. THE EARLIER YEARS OF OUR LORD. Fifth Edition.
2. THE MINISTRY IN GALILEE. Fourth Edition.
3. THE CLOSE OF THE MINISTRY. Sixth Thousand.
4. THE PASSION WEEK. Sixth Thousand.
5. THE LAST DAY OF OUR LORD'S PASSION. Twenty-third Edition.
6. THE FORTY DAYS AFTER THE RESURRECTION. Eighth Edition.

The Resurrection of the Dead.

By WILLIAM HANNA, D.D., LL.D. Second Edition. Fcap. 8vo, 5s.

Notes of Caithness Family History.

By the late JOHN HENDERSON, W.S. 4to, in cloth, 21s.

The High Estate of Service.

Fcap. 8vo, 1s.

Errors in the Use of English.

Illustrated from the Writings of English Authors, from the Fourteenth Century to our own Time. By the late W. B. HODGSON, LL.D., Professor of Political Economy in the University of Edinburgh. Fifth Edition. Crown 8vo, 3s. 6d.

"Those who most need such a book as Dr. Hodgson's will probably be the last to look into it. It will certainly amuse its readers, and will probably teach them a good deal which they did not know, or at least never thought about, before."—*Saturday Review.*

"His conversation, as every one who had the pleasure of his acquaintance knows, sparkled with anecdote and epigram, and not a little of the lustre and charm of his talk shines out of those pages."—*The Scotsman.*

Life and Letters of W. B. Hodgson, LL.D., late Professor of Political Economy in the University of Edinburgh. Edited by Professor J. M. D. MEIKLEJOHN, M.A. Crown 8vo, 7s. 6d.

Sketches: Personal and Pensive.

By WILLIAM HODGSON. Fcap. 8vo, 2s. 6d.

"Quasi Cursores." Portraits of the High Officers and

Professors of the University of Edinburgh. Drawn and Etched by WILLIAM HOLE, A.R.S.A. The book is printed on beautiful hand-made paper by Messrs. T. & A. Constable. It contains 45 Plates (64 Portraits), with Biographical Notices of all the present Incumbents. The impression is strictly limited. Quarto Edition (750 Copies only for sale), £2, 10s. Folio Edition, Japan Proofs (100 Copies only for sale), £5, 10s.

Memorial Catalogue of the French and Dutch Loan
Collection, Edinburgh International Exhibition. Letterpress by W. E. HENLEY. Etchings and Sketches by WILLIAM HOLE, A.R.S.A., and PHILIP ZILCKEN. The book is printed by CONSTABLE on wove handmade paper, in dark-green ink. It gives an account of the rise of Romanticism, a biography of the principal Masters of that School, and a description of each of the Pictures. It is illustrated by fifteen original Etchings and fifty-four outline Sketches. Pott folio. Edition limited to 520 Copies. £3, 3s.

The Breakfast Table Series.
In 6 vols. By OLIVER WENDELL HOLMES. New and Revised Editions, containing Prefaces and additional Bibliographical Notes by the Author.
THE AUTOCRAT OF THE BREAKFAST TABLE. 2 vols., 2s.
THE POET AT THE BREAKFAST TABLE. 2 vols., 2s.
THE PROFESSOR AT THE BREAKFAST TABLE. 2 vols., 2s.
Also bound in dark blue cloth, at 2s. a vol., or in a neat cloth box, 15s.
"Small enough to be carried in any sensibly constructed pocket, clear enough in type to accommodate any fastidious eyesight, pleasant and instructive enough for its perusal to be undertaken with the certainty of present enjoyment and the prospect of future profit."—*Whitehall Review.*
Also a LIBRARY EDITION, in 3 vols. crown 8vo, printed at the Riverside Press, Cambridge, with a Steel Portrait of the Author, 10s. 6d. each volume.
A COMPLETE EDITION of the Poems of OLIVER WENDELL HOLMES, revised by the Author, in 3 vols. [*In the Press.*

Traces in Scotland of Ancient Water Lines, Marine,
Lacustrine, and Fluviatile. By DAVID MILNE-HOME, LL.D., F.R.S.E. Demy 8vo, 3s. 6d.

A Sketch of the Life of George Hope of Fenton Barns.
Compiled by his DAUGHTER. Crown 8vo, 6s.

One Summer.
By BLANCHE WILLIS HOWARD. Paper, 1s.; cloth, 1s. 6d. and 2s.

W. D. Howells's Writings:—
In "American Author" Series.
INDIAN SUMMER. 2 vols., 2s.
THE RISE OF SILAS LAPHAM. 2 vols., 2s.
A FOREGONE CONCLUSION. 1 vol., 1s.
A CHANCE ACQUAINTANCE. 1 vol., 1s.
THEIR WEDDING JOURNEY. 1 vol., 1s.
A COUNTERFEIT PRESENTMENT, and THE PARLOUR CAR. 1 vol., 1s.
THE LADY OF THE AROOSTOOK. 2 vols., 2s.
OUT OF THE QUESTION, and AT THE SIGN OF THE SAVAGE. 1 vol. 1s.
THE UNDISCOVERED COUNTRY. 2 vols., 2s.
A FEARFUL RESPONSIBILITY, and TONELLI'S MARRIAGE. 1 vol., 1s.
VENETIAN LIFE. 2 vols., 2s.
ITALIAN JOURNEYS. 2 vols., 2s.
All the above may be had in cloth at 2s. each vol.
Copyright Library Edition.
A MODERN INSTANCE. 2 vols., 12s.
A WOMAN'S REASON. 2 vols., 12s.
DR. BREEN'S PRACTICE. 1 vol., 3s. 6d.
INDIAN SUMMER. 1 vol., 6s.
APRIL HOPES. 1 vol., 6s.
THE MINISTER'S CHARGE; OR, THE APPRENTICESHIP OF LEMUEL BARKER. 1 vol., 6s.
ANNIE KILBURN. [*In the Press.*
TUSCAN CITIES: WITH ILLUSTRATIONS FROM DRAWINGS AND ETCHINGS OF JOSEPH PENNELL and others. 4to, 16s.
MODERN ITALIAN POETS. 1 vol. 7s. 6d.

How to Catch Trout.
By Three Anglers. Third Edition. Fcap. 8vo, Illustrated. Price 1s.
"The advice given by the 'Three Anglers,' whose combined wisdom is bound within the covers of this book, is always sound."—*Field.*
"The work is sound in the essential doctrines of the craft."—*Scotsman.*

Ireland under Coercion. The Diary of an American.
By WILLIAM HENRY HURLBERT. 2 vols., crown 8vo, 15s.

"Mr. Hurlbert's conclusions and criticisms are worthy of all attention; but we attach still greater value to the book as a collection of evidence on the present phase of the Irish difficulty, the genuineness of which it would be idle to impeach."—*Times*.

"Mr. Hurlbert is a most acute observer and far-seeing thinker, and his style is as clear and lucid as his thought. His pages are full of important facts, interspersed with characteristic and humorous anecdotes. Mr. Hurlbert goes to the core of the Irish question in a manner which, perhaps, no other living writer could rival. His vast acquaintance with men, laws, and customs in America and Europe entitles him to speak with authority."—*Scotsman*.

A Memorial Sketch, and a Selection from the Letters
of the late Lieut. JOHN IRVING, R.N., of H.M.S. "Terror," in Sir John Franklin's Expedition to the Arctic Regions. Edited by BENJAMIN BELL, F.R.C.S.E. With Facsimiles of the Record and Irving's Medal and Map. Post 8vo, 5s.

Jack and Mrs. Brown, and other Stories.
By the Author of "Blindpits." Crown 8vo, paper, 2s. 6d.; cloth, 3s. 6d.

Epitaphs and Inscriptions from Burial-Grounds and
Old Buildings in the North-East of Scotland. By the late ANDREW JERVISE, F.S.A. Scot. With a Memoir of the Author. Vol. II. Cloth, small 4to, 32s.
Do.   do.   Roxburghe Edition, 42s.

The History and Traditions of the Land of the Lindsays
in Angus and Mearns. By the late ANDREW JERVISE, F.S.A. Scot. New Edition, Edited and Revised by the Rev. JAMES GAMMACK, M.A. Demy 8vo, 14s.
Large Paper, demy 4to, 42s.

Memorials of Angus and the Mearns: an Account,
Historical, Antiquarian, and Traditionary, of the Castles and Towns visited by Edward I., and of the Barons, Clergy, and others who swore Fealty to England in 1291-6. By the late ANDREW JERVISE, F.S.A. Scot. Rewritten and corrected by the Rev. JAMES GAMMACK, M.A. Illustrated with Etchings by W. HOLE, A.R.S.A. 2 vols. Demy 8vo, 28s.; Large Paper, 2 vols. Demy 4to, 63s.

Sermons by the Rev. John Ker, D.D., Glasgow.
Fourteenth Edition. Crown 8vo, 6s.

Sermons: Second Series: by the Rev. John Ker, D.D.
Fifth Thousand. Crown 8vo, 6s.

Thoughts for Heart and Life.
By the Rev. JOHN KER, D.D. Edited by the Rev. A. L. SIMPSON, D.D., Derby. With Portrait by JAMES FAED. Ex. fcap. 8vo, 4s. 6d.

Memories of Coleorton: Being Letters from Coleridge,
Wordsworth and his Sister, Southey and Sir Walter Scott, to Sir George and Lady Beaumont of Coleorton, Leicestershire. 1803 to 1833. Edited, with Notes and Introduction, by WILLIAM KNIGHT, St. Andrews. 2 vols. crown 8vo, 15s.

The English Lake District as interpreted in the Poems
of Wordsworth. By WILLIAM KNIGHT, Professor of Moral Philosophy in the University of St. Andrews. Ex. fcap. 8vo, 5s.

Colloquia Peripatetica (Deep Sea Soundings):
Being Notes of Conversations with the late John Duncan, LL.D., Professor of Hebrew in the New College, Edinburgh. By WILLIAM KNIGHT, Professor of Moral Philosophy in the University of St. Andrews. Fifth Edition, enlarged, 5s.

Lindores Abbey, and the Burgh of Newburgh;
Their History and Annals. By ALEXANDER LAING, LL.D., F.S.A. Scot. Small 4to. With Index, and thirteen Full-page and ten Woodcut Illustrations, 21s.

"This is a charming volume in every respect."—*Notes and Queries*.
"The prominent characteristics of the work are its exhaustiveness and the thoroughly philosophic spirit in which it is written."—*Scotsman*.

Recollections of Curious Characters and Pleasant
Places. By CHARLES LANMAN, Washington; Author of "Adventures in the Wilds of America," "A Canoe Voyage up the Mississippi," "A Tour to the River Saguenay," etc. etc. Small Demy 8vo, 12s.

Essays and Reviews.
By the late HENRY H. LANCASTER, Advocate; with a Prefatory Notice by the Rev. B. JOWETT, Master of Balliol College, Oxford. Demy 8vo, with Portrait, 14s.

An Echo of Passion.
By GEO. PARSONS LATHROP. 1s.; and in cloth, 2s.

On the Philosophy of Ethics. An Analytical Essay.
By S. S. LAURIE, A.M., F.R.S.E., Professor of the Theory, History, and Practice of Education in the University of Edinburgh. Demy 8vo, 6s.

Notes on British Theories of Morals.
By Prof. S. S. LAURIE. Demy 8vo, 6s.

Sermons by the Rev. Adam Lind, M.A., Elgin.
Ex. fcap. 8vo, 5s.

Only an Incident.
A Novel. By Miss G. D. LITCHFIELD. Crown 8vo, 6s.

Leaves from the Buik of the West Kirke.
By GEO. LORIMER. With a Preface by the Rev. JAS. MACGREGOR, D.D. 4to.

A Lost Battle. A Novel. 2 vols. Crown 8vo, 17s.
"This in every way remarkable novel."—*Morning Post.*
"We are all the more ready to do justice to the excellence of the author's drawing of characters."—*Athenæum.*

John Calvin, a Fragment by the late Thomas M'Crie,
Author of "The Life of John Knox." Demy 8vo, 6s.

Among the Old Scotch Minstrels. Studying their Ballads
of War, Folk-lore, and Fairyland. By WILLIAM MACDOWALL, F.S.A. Scot. Fcap. 8vo, 3s. 6d.

The Parish of Taxwood, and some of its Older Memories.
By Rev. J. R. MACDUFF, D.D. Extra fcap. 8vo, illustrated, 3s. 6d.

Principles of the Algebra of Logic, with Examples.
By ALEX. MACFARLANE, M.A., D.Sc. (Edin.), F.R.S.E. 5s.

The Castellated and Domestic Architecture of Scotland, from the Twelfth to the Eighteenth Century. By DAVID M'GIBBON and THOMAS ROSS, Architects. 2 vols., with about 1000 Illustrations of Ground Plans, Sections, Views, Elevations, and Details. Royal 8vo. 42s. each vol. Net.
"No one acquainted with the history of Great Britain can take up this neatly-bound volume . . . without being at once struck by its careful completeness and extreme archæological interest, while all students of architectural style will welcome the work specially for its technical thoroughness."—*Building News.*
"A learned, painstaking, and highly important work."—*Scottish Review.*
"One of the most important and complete books on Scottish architecture that has ever been compiled."—*Scotsman.*
"The authors merit the thanks of all architectural readers."—*Builder.*

Memoir of Sir James Dalrymple, First Viscount Stair.
A Study in the History of Scotland and Scotch Law during the Seventeenth Century. By Æ. J. G. MACKAY, Advocate. 8vo, 12s.

Storms and Sunshine of a Soldier's Life.
Lt.-General COLIN MACKENZIE, C.B., 1825-1881. With a Portrait. 2 vols. Crown 8vo, 15s.
"A very readable biography . . . of one of the bravest and ablest officers of the East India Company's army."—*Saturday Review.*

Nugæ Canoræ Medicæ.
Lays of the Poet Laureate of the New Town Dispensary. Edited by Professor DOUGLAS MACLAGAN. 4to, with Illustrations, 7s. 6d.

The Hill Forts, Stone Circles, and other Structural Remains of Ancient Scotland. By C. MACLAGAN, Lady Associate of the Society of Antiquaries of Scotland. With Plans and Illustrations. Folio, 31s. 6d.

"We need not enlarge on the few inconsequential speculations which rigid archæologists may find in the present volume. We desire rather to commend it to their careful study, fully assured that not only they, but also the general reader, will be edified by its perusal."—*Scotsman.*

The Light of the World.
By DAVID M'LAREN, Minister of Humbie. Crown 8vo, 6s.

The Book of Psalms in Metre.
According to the version approved of by the Church of Scotland. Revised by Rev. DAVID M'LAREN. Crown 8vo, 7s. 6d.

Omnipotence belongs only to the Beloved.
By Mrs. BREWSTER MACPHERSON. Extra fcap., 3s. 6d.

Humorous Masterpieces from American Literature, from 1810 to 1886. Edited by EDWARD T. MASON. Selections are made from the Works of: ALCOTT, ALDEN, ALDRICH, BALDWIN, BEECHER, BELLAMY, BROUNE, BUNNER, BUTLER, CABLE, CAVAZZA, CLEMENS, CONE, COZZENS, CRANE, CURTIS, DODGE, DUNNING, HALE, HARTE, HARRIS, HAWTHORNE, HOLMES, HOWE, HOWELLS, IRVING, JOHNSON, LANIGAN, LELAND, LOWELL, LUDLOW, M'DOWELL, MATTHEWS, OGDEN, PHELPS, QUINCEY, ROCHE, SAXE, SEBA, SMITH, STOFFORD, STOCKTON, STOWE, THORPE, THROWBRIDGE, WARNER, Etc. 3 vols. square 16mo, 3s. 6d. each vol.

In Partnership. Studies in Story-Telling.
By BRANDER MATTHEWS and H. C. BUNNER. 1s. in paper, and 2s. in cloth.

Antwerp Delivered in MDLXXVII.:
A Passage from the History of the Netherlands, illustrated with Facsimiles of a rare series of Designs by Martin de Vos, and of Prints by Hogenberg, the Wiericxes, etc. By Sir WILLIAM STIRLING-MAXWELL, Bart., K.T. and M.P. In 1 vol. Folio, 5 guineas.

"A splendid folio in richly ornamented binding, protected by an almost equally ornamental slip-cover. . . . Remarkable illustrations of the manner in which the artists of the time 'pursued their labours in a country ravaged by war, and in cities ever menaced by siege and sack.'"—*Scotsman.*

Studies in the Topography of Galloway, being a List of nearly 4000 Names of Places, with Remarks on their Origin and Meaning. By SIR HERBERT MAXWELL, Bart., M.P. 1 vol. demy 8vo, 14s.

The History of Old Dundee, narrated out of the Town Council Register, with Additions from Contemporary Annals. By ALEXANDER MAXWELL, F.S.A. Scot. 4to. Cloth, 21s.; Roxburghe, 24s.

Researches and Excavations at Carnac (Morbihan), The Bossenno, and Mont St. Michel. By JAMES MILN. Royal 8vo, with Maps, Plans, and numerous Illustrations in Wood-Engraving and Chromolithography.

Excavations at Carnac (Brittany), a Record of Archæological Researches in the Alignments of Kermario. By JAMES MILN. Royal 8vo, with Maps, Plans, and numerous Illustrations in Wood-Engraving. 15s.

The Past in the Present—What is Civilisation?
Being the Rhind Lectures in Archæology, delivered in 1876 and 1878. By Sir ARTHUR MITCHELL, K.C.B., M.D., LL.D. In 1 vol. demy 8vo, with 148 Woodcuts, 15s.

"Whatever differences of opinion, however, may be held on minor points, there can be no question that Dr. Mitchell's work is one of the ablest and most original pieces of archæological literature which has appeared of late years."—*St. James's Gazette.*

In War Time. A Novel. By S. WEIR MITCHELL, M.D. Crown 8vo, 6s.

Roland Blake. A Novel. By S. WEIR MITCHELL, M.D. Crown 8vo, 6s.

Our Scotch Banks:
Their Position and their Policy. By WM. MITCHELL, S.S.C. Third Edition. 8vo, 5s.

On Horse-Breaking.
By ROBERT MORETON. Second Edition. Fcap. 8vo, 1s.

Ecclesiological Notes on some of the Islands of Scotland, with other Papers relating to Ecclesiological Remains on the Scottish Mainland and Islands. By THOMAS S. MUIR, Author of "Characteristics of Church Architecture," etc. Demy 8vo, with numerous Illustrations, 21s.

The Birds of Berwickshire.
By GEO. MUIRHEAD. 2 vols. demy 8vo, Illustrated. To Subscribers only.
[*In the Press.*

Ancient Scottish Lake-Dwellings or Crannogs, with a Supplementary Chapter on Remains of Lake-Dwellings in England. By ROBERT MUNRO, M.D., F.S.A. Scot. 1 vol. demy 8vo, profusely illustrated, 21s.
"A standard authority on the subject of which it treats."—*Times.*
". . . Our readers may be assured that they will find very much to interest and instruct them in the perusal of the work."—*Athenæum.*

"The Lanox of Auld:" An Epistolary Review of "The Lennox, by William Fraser." By MARK NAPIER. With Woodcuts and Plates. 4to, 15s.

Tenants' Gain not Landlords' Loss, and some other Economic Aspects of the Land Question. By JOSEPH SHIELD NICHOLSON, M.A., Professor of Political Economy in the University of Edinburgh. Crown 8vo. 5s.

Camps in the Caribbees: Adventures of a Naturalist in the Lesser Antilles. By FREDERICK OBER. Illustrations, demy 8vo, 12s.
"Well-written and well-illustrated narrative of camping out among the Caribbees."—*Westminster Review.*
"Varied were his experiences, hairbreadth his escapes, and wonderful his gleanings in the way of securing rare birds."—*The Literary World.*

Cookery for the Sick and a Guide for the Sick-Room.
By C. H. OGG, an Edinburgh Nurse. Fcap. 1s.

The Lord Advocates of Scotland from the close of the Fifteenth Century to the passing of the Reform Bill. By G. W. T. OMOND, Advocate. 2 vols. demy 8vo, 28s.

The Arniston Memoirs—Three Centuries of a Scottish House, 1571-1838. Edited from Family Papers by GEO. W. T. OMOND, Advocate. 1 vol. 8vo, 21s., with Etchings, Lithographs, and Woodcuts.

An Irish Garland.
By Mrs. S. M. B. PIATT. Crown 8vo, 3s. 6d.

The Children Out of Doors. A Book of Verses.
By Two IN ONE HOUSE. Crown 8vo, 3s. 6d.

Phœbe.
By the Author of "Rutledge." Reprinted from the Fifth Thousand of the American Edition. Crown 8vo, 6s.
"'Phœbe' is a woman's novel."—*Saturday Review.*

Popular Genealogists;
Or, The Art of Pedigree-making. Crown 8vo, 4s.

The Gamekeeper's Manual: being Epitome of the Game Laws for the use of Gamekeepers and others interested in the Preservation of Game. By ALEXANDER PORTER, Deputy Chief Constable of Roxburghshire. Fcap. 8vo, 1s.

Scotland under her Early Kings.
A History of the Kingdom to the close of the 13th century. By E. WILLIAM ROBERTSON. In 2 vols. 8vo, cloth, 36s.

Historical Essays,
In connection with the Land and the Church, etc. By E. WILLIAM ROBERTSON, Author of "Scotland under her Early Kings." 8vo, 10s. 6d.

LIST OF BOOKS

A Rectorial Address delivered before the Students of
Aberdeen University, in the Music Hall at Aberdeen, on Nov. 5, 1880. By THE EARL OF ROSEBERY. 6d.

A Rectorial Address delivered before the Students of
the University of Edinburgh, Nov. 4, 1882. By THE EARL OF ROSEBERY. 6d.

Aberdour and Inchcolme. Being Historical Notices of
the Parish and Monastery, in Twelve Lectures. By the Rev. WILLIAM ROSS, LL.D., Author of "Burgh Life in Dunfermline in the Olden Time." Crown 8vo, 6s.

"If any one would know what Aberdour has been, or, indeed, what to some extent has been the history of many another parish in Scotland, he cannot do better than read these Lectures. He will find the task a pleasant one."—*Saturday Review.*

"We know no book which within so small a compass contains so varied, so accurate, and so vivid a description of the past life of the Scottish people, whether ecclesiastical or social, as Dr. Ross's 'Aberdour and Inchcolme.'"—*Scottish Review.*

"It seems a pity that so good a thing should have been so long withheld from a wider audience; but better late than never."—*Scotsman.*

Notes and Sketches from the Wild Coasts of Nipon.
With Chapters on Cruising after Pirates in Chinese Waters. By HENRY C. ST. JOHN, Captain R.N. Small demy 8vo, with Maps and Illustrations, 12s.

"One of the most charming books of travel that has been published for some time."—*Scotsman.*

"There is a great deal more in the book than Natural History. . . . His pictures of life and manners are quaint and effective, and the more so from the writing being natural and free from effort."—*Athenæum.*

"He writes with a simplicity and directness, and not seldom with a degree of graphic power, which, even apart from the freshness of the matter, renders his book delightful reading. Nothing could be better of its kind than the description of the Inland Sea."—*Daily News.*

Notes on the Natural History of the Province of Moray.
By the late CHARLES ST. JOHN, Author of "Wild Sports in the Highlands." Second Edition. In 1 vol. royal 8vo, with 40 page Illustrations of Scenery and Animal Life, engraved by A. DURAND after sketches made by GEORGE REID, R.S.A., and J. WYCLIFFE TAYLOR; also, 30 Pen-and-Ink Drawings by the Author in facsimile. 50s.

"This is a new edition of the work brought out by the friends of the late Mr. St. John in 1863; but it is so handsomely and nobly printed, and enriched with such charming illustrations, that we may consider it a new book."—*St. James's Gazette.*

"Charles St. John was not an artist, but he had the habit of roughly sketching animals in positions which interested him, and the present reprint is adorned by a great number of these, facsimiled from the author's original pen and ink. Some of these, as for instance the studies of the golden eagle swooping on its prey, and that of the otter swimming with a salmon in its mouth, are very interesting, and full of that charm that comes from the exact transcription of unusual observation."—*Pall Mall Gazette.*

A Tour in Sutherlandshire, with Extracts from the
Field-Books of a Sportsman and Naturalist. By the late CHARLES ST. JOHN, Author of "Wild Sports and Natural History in the Highlands." Second Edition, with an Appendix on the Fauna of Sutherland, by J. A. HARVIE-BROWN and T. E. BUCKLEY. Illustrated with the original Wood Engravings, and additional Vignettes from the Author's sketch-books. In 2 vols. small demy 8vo, 21s.

"Every page is full of interest."—*The Field.*

"There is not a wild creature in the Highlands, from the great stag to the tiny fire-crested wren, of which he has not something pleasant to say."—*Pall Mall Gazette.*

Life of James Hepburn, Earl of Bothwell.
By Professor SCHIERN, Copenhagen. Translated from the Danish by the Rev. DAVID BERRY, F.S.A. Scot. Demy 8vo, 16s.

Scotch Folk.

Illustrated. Fourth Edition enlarged. Ex. fcap. 8vo, 1s.

"They are stories of the best type, quite equal in the main to the average of Dean Ramsay's well-known collection."—*Aberdeen Free Press.*

Studies in Poetry and Philosophy.

By the late J. C. SHAIRP, LL.D., Principal of the United College of St. Salvator and St. Leonard, St. Andrews. Fourth Edition, with Portraits of the Author and Thomas Erskine, by WILLIAM HOLE, A.R.S.A. Crown 8vo, 7s. 6d.

"In the 'Moral Dynamic,' Mr. Shairp seeks for something which shall persuade us of the vital and close bearing on each other of moral thought and spiritual energy. It is this conviction which has animated Mr. Shairp in every page of the volume before us. It is because he appreciates so justly and forcibly the powers of philosophic doctrine over all the field of human life, that he leans with such strenuous trust upon those ideas which Wordsworth unsystematically, and Coleridge more systematically, made popular and fertile among us."—*Saturday Review.*

"The finest essay in the volume, partly because it is upon the greatest and most definite subject, is the first, on *Wordsworth*. . . . We have said so much upon this essay that we can only say of the other three that they are fully worthy to stand beside it."—*Spectator.*

Culture and Religion.

By the late PRINCIPAL SHAIRP. Seventh Edition. Fcap. 8vo, 3s. 6d.

"A wise book, and, unlike a great many other wise books, has that carefully shaded thought and expression which fits Professor Shairp to speak for Culture no less than for Religion."—*Spectator.*

"Those who remember a former work of Principal Shairp's, 'Studies in Poetry and Philosophy,' will feel secure that all which comes from his pen will bear the marks of thought, at once careful, liberal, and accurate. Nor will they be disappointed in the present work. . . . We can recommend this book to our readers."—*Athenæum.*

"We cannot close without earnestly recommending the book to thoughtful young men. It combines the loftiest intellectual power with a simple and childlike faith in Christ, and exerts an influence which must be stimulating and healthful."—*Freeman.*

Sketches in History and Poetry.

By the late PRINCIPAL SHAIRP. Edited by JOHN VEITCH, Professor of Logic and Rhetoric in the University of Glasgow. Crown 8vo. 7s. 6d.

Kilmahoe, a Highland Pastoral,

And other Poems. By PRINCIPAL SHAIRP. Fcap. 8vo, 6s.

Shakespeare on Golf. With special Reference to St. Andrews Links. 3d.

The Divine Comedy of Dante Alighieri, The Inferno.

A Translation in Terza Rima, with Notes and Introductory Essay. By JAMES ROMANES SIBBALD. With an Engraving after Giotto's Portrait. Small demy 8vo, 12s.

"Mr. Sibbald is certainly to be congratulated on having produced a translation which would probably give an English reader a better conception of the nature of the original poem, having regard both to its matter and its form in combination, than any other English translation yet published."—*Academy.*

The Use of what is called Evil.

A Discourse by SIMPLICIUS. Extracted from his Commentary on the Enchiridion of Epictetus. Crown 8vo, 1s.

The Near and the Far View,

And other Sermons. By Rev. A. L. SIMPSON, D.D., Derby. Ex. fcap. 8vo, 5s.

"Very fresh and thoughtful are these sermons."—*Literary World.*

"Dr. Simpson's sermons may fairly claim distinctive power. He looks at things with his own eyes, and often shows us what with ordinary vision we had failed to perceive. . . . The sermons are distinctively good."—*British Quarterly Review.*

Archæological Essays.
By the late Sir JAMES SIMPSON, Bart. Edited by the late JOHN STUART, LL.D. 2 vols. 4to, 21s.

1. Archæology.
2. Inchcolm.
3. The Cat Stane.
4. Magical Charm-Stones.
5. Pyramid of Gizeh.
6. Leprosy and Leper Hospitals.
7. Greek Medical Vases.
8. Was the Roman Army provided with Medical Officers?
9. Roman Medicine Stamps, etc. etc.

The Art of Golf.
By SIR W. G. SIMPSON, Bart., Captain of the Honourable Company of Edinburgh Golfers. With Twenty Plates from instantaneous photographs of Professional Players, chiefly by A. F. Macfie, Esq. Demy 8vo, Morocco back, price 15s.

Celtic Scotland: A History of Ancient Alban.
By WILLIAM F. SKENE, D.C.L., Historiographer-Royal for Scotland. In 3 vols. Demy 8vo, 45s. Illustrated with Maps.

I.—HISTORY and ETHNOLOGY. II.—CHURCH and CULTURE.
III.—LAND and PEOPLE.

"Forty years ago Mr. Skene published a small historical work on the Scottish Highlands which has ever since been appealed to as au authority, but which has long been out of print. The promise of this youthful effort is amply fulfilled in the three weighty volumes of his maturer years. As a work of historical research it ought in our opinion to take a very high rank."—*Times.*

The Four Ancient Books of Wales,
Containing the Cymric Poems attributed to the Bards of the sixth century. By WILLIAM F. SKENE, D.C.L. With Maps and Facsimiles. 2 vols. 8vo, 36s.

The Gospel History for the Young:
Being lessons on the Life of Christ, Adapted for use in Families and Sunday Schools. By WILLIAM F. SKENE, D.C.L. Small crown 8vo, 3 vols., with Maps, 2s. 6d. each vol., or in cloth box, 7s. 6d. net.

"In a spirit altogether unsectarian provides for the young a simple, interesting, and thoroughly charming history of our Lord."—*Literary World.*

"This 'Gospel History for the Young' is one of the most valuable books of the kind."—*The Churchman.*

Tommie Brown and the Queen of the Fairies; a new
Child's Book, by WILLIAM F. SKENE, D.C.L., in fcap. 8vo. With Illustrations, 4s. 6d.

Let pain be pleasure, and pleasure be pain.

LETTER from the late Dr. JOHN BROWN.

"DEAR MR. SKENE,—I have to thank you for making me a child, and a happy child, for an hour and forty minutes to-night. That is a delightful story, at once strange and yet sort of believable, and I was, like the other children, at the end, and like Oliver Twist, 'asking for more.' It is something to have written 'Little Tommie' and another book just published. With much regard and envy, yours sincerely, "J. BROWN."

"There is no wonder that children liked the story. It is told neatly and well, and is full of great cleverness, while it has that peculiar character the absence of which from many like stories deprives them of any real interest for children."—*Scotsman.*

Shelley: a Critical Biography.
By GEORGE BARNETT SMITH. Ex. fcap. 8vo, 6s.

The Sermon on the Mount.
By the Rev. WALTER C. SMITH, D.D. Crown 8vo, 6s.

Life and Work at the Great Pyramid.
With a Discussion of the Facts ascertained. By C. PIAZZI SMYTH, F.R.SS.L. and E., Astronomer-Royal for Scotland. 3 vols. Demy 8vo, 56s.

Madeira Meteorologic:
Being a Paper on the above subject read before the Royal Society, Edinburgh, on the 1st of May 1882. By C. PIAZZI SMYTH, Astronomer-Royal for Scotland. Small 4to, 6s.

Saskatchewan and the Rocky Mountains.
Diary and Narrative of Travel, Sport, and Adventure, during a Journey through part of the Hudson's Bay Company's Territories in 1859 and 1860. By the EARL OF SOUTHESK, K.T., F.R.G.S. 1 vol. demy 8vo, with Illustrations on Wood by WHYMPER, 18s.

By the same Author.

Herminius: A Romance. Fcap. 8vo, 6s.
Jonas Fisher: A Poem in Brown and White. Cheap Edition. 1s.
The Burial of Isis and other Poems.
Fcap. 8vo, 6s.

Darroll, and other Poems.
By WALTER COOK SPENS, Advocate. Crown 8vo, 5s.

Rudder Grange.
By FRANK R. STOCKTON. 1s.; and cloth, 2s.

"'Rudder Grange' is a book that few could produce, and that most would be proud to sign."—*Saturday Review.*

"It may be safely recommended as a very amusing little book."—*Athenæum.*

"Altogether 'Rudder Grange' is as cheery, as humorous, and as wholesome a little story as we have read for many a day."—*St. James's Gazette.*

"The minutest incidents are narrated with such genuine humour and gaiety, that at the close of the volume the reader is sorry to take leave of the merry innocent party."—*Westminster Review.*

The Lady or the Tiger? and other Stories.
By FRANK R. STOCKTON. 1s.; and cloth, 2s.

Contents.—The Lady or the Tiger?—The Transferred Ghost—The Spectral Mortgage—That same old 'Coon—His Wife's Deceased Sister—Mr. Tolman—Plain Fishing—My Bull Calf—Every Man his own Letter Writer—The Remarkable Wreck of the "Thomas Hyke."

"Stands by itself both for originality of plot and freshness of humour."—*Century Magazine.*

A Borrowed Month, and other Stories.
By FRANK R. STOCKTON, Author of "Rudder Grange." 1s.; and cloth, 2s.

Contents.—A Borrowed Month—A Tale of Negative Gravity—The Christmas Wreck—Our Archery Club—A Story of Assisted Fate—The Discourager of Hesitancy—Our Story.

Christianity Confirmed by Jewish and Heathen Testimony, and the Deductions from Physical Science, etc. By THOMAS STEVENSON, F.R.S.E., F.G.S., Member of the Institution of Civil Engineers. Second Edition. Fcap. 8vo, 3s. 6d.

What is Play?
A Physiological Inquiry. Its bearing upon Education and Training. By JOHN STRACHAN, M.D. Fcap., 1s.

Sketch of Thermodynamics.
By P. G. TAIT, Professor of Natural Philosophy in the University of Edinburgh. Second Edition, revised and extended. Crown 8vo, 5s.

Talks with our Farm-Servants.
By An Old Farm-Servant. Crown 8vo; paper, 6d.; cloth, 1s.

Walden; or, Life in the Woods.
By H. D. THOREAU. Crown 8vo, 6s.

Our Mission to the Court of Marocco in 1880, under
Sir JOHN DRUMMOND HAY, K.C.B., Minister Plenipotentiary at Tangier, and Envoy Extraordinary to His Majesty the Sultan of Marocco. By Captain PHILIP DURHAM TROTTER, 93d Highlanders. Illustrated from Photographs by the Hon. D. LAWLESS, Rifle Brigade. Square Demy 8vo, 24s.

The Upland Tarn: A Village Idyll.
Small Crown, 5s.

A Year in the Fields. By JOHN WATSON. Fcap. 8vo, 1s.

Mr. Washington Adams in England.
By RICHARD GRANT WHITE. 1s.; or in cloth, 2s.

"An impudent book."—*Vanity Fair.*
"This short, tiresome book."—*Saturday Review.*
"Brimful of genuine humour."—*Montrose Standard.*
"Mr. White is a capital caricaturist, but in portraying the ludicrous eccentri cities of the patrician Britisher he hardly succeeds so well as in delineating th peculiar charms of the representative Yankee."—*Whitehall Review.*

Rosetty Ends, or the Chronicles of a Country Cobbler
By Job Bradawl (A. DEWAR WILLOCK), Author of "She Noddit to me." Fcap 8vo, Illustrated. 2s. and 1s.

"The sketches are amusing productions, narrating comical incidents, con nected by a thread of common character running through them all—a threa waxed into occasional strength by the 'roset' of a homely, entertaining wit."—*Scotsman.*

The Botany of Three Historical Records:
Pharaoh's Dream, the Sower, and the King's Measure. By A. STEPHEN WILSON Crown 8vo, with 5 Plates, 3s. 6d.

"A Bushel of Corn."
By A. STEPHEN WILSON. An investigation by Experiments into all the mor important questions which range themselves round a Bushel of Wheat, a Bushe of Barley, and a Bushel of Oats. Crown 8vo, with Illustrations, 9s.

"It is full of originality and force."—*Nature.*
"A monument of painstaking research."—*Liverpool Mercury.*
"Mr. Wilson's book is interesting not only for agriculturists and millers, bu for all who desire information on the subject of corn, in which every one is s intimately concerned."—*Morning Post.*

Songs and Poems.
By A. STEPHEN WILSON. Crown 8vo, 6s.

Reminiscences of Old Edinburgh.
By DANIEL WILSON, LL.D., F.R.S.E., Professor of History and English Literatur in University College, Toronto, Author of "Prehistoric Annals of Scotland," et etc. 2 vols. post 8vo, 15s.

The India Civil Service as a Career for Scotsmen.
By J. WILSON, M.A. 1s.

Christianity and Reason:
Their necessary connection. By R. S. WYLD, LL.D. Extra fcap. 8vo, 3s. 6d.

Shakespeare's England.
By WILLIAM WINTER. 1s., paper, or 2s., cloth extra.
Contents.—The Voyage—The Beauty of England—Great Historic Places— Rambles in London—A Visit to Windsor—The Palace of Westminster—Warwic and Kenilworth—First View of Stratford-on-Avon—London Nooks and Corners— Relics of Lord Byron—Westminster Abbey—The Home of Shakespeare—Up t London—Old Churches of London—Literary Shrines of London—A Haunt Edmund Kean—Stoke-Pogis and Thomas Gray—At the Grave of Coleridge—O Barnet Battlefield—A Glimpse of Canterbury—The Shrines of Warwickshire—, Borrower of the Night.

Wanderers: being a Collection of the Poems of Willian
WINTER. [*In the Pres*

The East Neuk of Fife: its History and Antiquities.
Second Edition, Re-arranged and Enlarged. By the Rev. WALTER WOOD, M.A Elie. Edited, with Preface and Index, by the Rev. J. WOOD BROWN, M.A Gordon. Crown 8vo. 6s.

EDINBURGH: DAVID DOUGLAS, CASTLE STREET

www.ingramcontent.com/pod-product-compliance
Lightning Source LLC
Chambersburg PA
CBHW030304240426
43673CB00040B/1053